Basic Bible INTERPRETATION

BOOKS BY ROY B. ZUCK

A Biblical Theology of the Old Testament (editor)
Adult Education in the Church (coeditor)
Barb, Please Wake Up!
Basic Bible Interpretation
The Bib Sac Reader (coeditor)
The Bible Knowledge Commentary (coeditor)
Biblical Archaeology Leader's Guide
Childhood Education in the Church (coeditor)
Christian Youth: An In-Depth Survey (coauthor)
Church History Leader's Guide
Creation: Evidence from Scripture and Science
Communism and Christianity Leader's Guide
Devotions for Kindred Spirits (editor)
The Holy Spirit in Your Teaching
How to Be a Youth Sponsor
Job
Sitting with Job: Selected Studies in the Book of Job (editor)
The Life of Christ Commentary (coeditor)
Youth and the Church (coeditor)
Youth Education in the Church (coeditor)

Basic Bible
INTERPRETATION

A Practical Guide to Discovering Biblical Truth

Roy B. Zuck

David C Cook®
transforming lives together

BASIC BIBLE INTERPRETATION
Published by David C Cook
4050 Lee Vance View
Colorado Springs, CO 80918 U.S.A.

David C Cook Distribution Canada
55 Woodslee Avenue, Paris, Ontario, Canada N3L 3E5

David C Cook U.K., Kingsway Communications
Eastbourne, East Sussex BN23 6NT, England

The graphic circle C logo is a registered trademark of David C Cook.

Unless otherwise noted, Scripture quotations are taken from the *Holy Bible: New International Version*®. NIV®. Copyright © 1973, 1978, 1984 by International Bible Society. Used by permission of Zondervan Publishing House. All rights reserved. Other quotations are taken from the *New American Standard Bible*®. Copyright © The Lockman Foundation 1960, 1962, 1963, 1968, 1971, 1972, 1973, 1975, 1977, 1995. Used by permission; and the *Authorized (King James) Version*.

Library of Congress Cataloging-in-Publication Data
Zuck, Roy B.
Basic Bible Interpretation/Roy B. Zuck
p. cm.
Includes bibliographical references and indexes.
ISBN 978-0-7814-3877-3
1. Bible — Hermeneutics. I. Title
BS476.Z83   1991
220.6'01-dc20   90-45827
CIP

© 1991 Roy B. Zuck

Editor: Craig Bubeck, Sr. Editor over updating
Cover Design: RJS Design

Printed in the United States of America
First Edition 1991

24 25 26 27 28 29 30

052912

Began 11/8/13 reading

CONTENTS

FOREWORD

The scholarly and devout B.B. Warfield once said, "The Bible is the Word of God in such a way that when the Bible speaks, God speaks."

Christians in every century have held the Bible in high esteem and have accepted it as the Word of God written. But few have made the rash claim that it is easy to understand. Yet, since the Bible was given to reveal truth and not obscure it, God surely intends that we understand it. Further, understanding the Bible is vital because our doctrines of God, of man, of salvation, and of future things rest on a correct interpretation of the Scriptures.

It sometimes seems almost anything can be proved by the Bible, for there is scarcely a religion, sect, or cult in Christendom that does not use Scripture texts to "prove" its doctrine. In that respect the Bible may well be the most abused book in the world. The solution to this problem is not to be found alone in a correct view of inspiration, important as that is. Origen (A.D. 185–254), for example, held a high view of the inspiration of Scripture and yet was guilty of mishandling the Bible by minimizing its literal meaning and treating it as "one vast allegory" with many hidden meanings. The solution to this problem of widely differing interpretations is to employ the correct method of biblical interpretation. We believe that to be the literal method which approaches the Scripture in the normal, customary way in which we talk, write, and think. It means taking the Scriptures at face value in an attempt to know what God meant by what He said. And this is the method well defended and expounded in this book.

Along with a sound doctrine of inspiration, and a commitment to literal interpretation, Bible scholars have found it is important to have certain criteria of interpretation. Are there not principles to help the serious student of the Bible understand and apply Scripture, principles based on the Bible itself? What helps can be found for interpreting special features such as figures of speech, types, parables, and prophetic literature?

Dr. Zuck has accomplished the difficult task of providing us with a text that covers the entire field of hermeneutics. As a teacher and continuing student of this field, Dr. Zuck is acquainted with the literature bearing on his subject. The work he has produced is up to date; it deals with various current issues in hermeneutics.

Dr. Zuck has provided special help in the long neglected area of the application of Scripture. To minister to peoples' spiritual needs, the Bible must not only be rightly interpreted; it must also be properly applied. Important and much needed guidance is also provided in the important matter of interpreting prophecy. Too often other works on hermeneutics give an "uncertain sound" in this area, leaving readers confused about how to approach prophetic Scripture.

All in all, Dr. Zuck has produced a text that is thorough, biblical, readable, and enlightening. May it prove of great help to all students who love God's Word and seek to interpret and apply it correctly.

Donald K. Campbell, President
Dallas Theological Seminary

CHAPTER ONE

The What and Why of Bible Interpretation

A businessman was on a trip quite a distance from his hometown. A bachelor, he served as a top executive in a leading governmental agency. In fact he was the finance officer in charge of all the funds in that department.

Returning home from Palestine, he was on a desert road southwest of Jerusalem. Another person was driving, which gave him opportunity to read. As he was reading aloud, he looked up and saw a man who had come up beside him and had heard him reading. The man asked the vacationer if he understood what was being read.

The reader was an Ethiopian, a court official of Candace, Queen of Ethiopia (Acts 8:27). On his way back to Ethiopia, he was joined by Philip, whom God told to meet the official (vv. 26-29). Philip struck up a conversation with the man by asking him a question — a question of Bible interpretation. "Do you understand what you are reading?" (v. 30) The finance officer responded, "How can I . . . unless someone explains it to me?" (v. 31) Inviting Philip to join him in the chariot, the African asked if the Prophet Isaiah in Isaiah 53:7-8 was speaking about himself or someone else. His question revealed his need for help in interpreting the passage. Philip explained that the passage refers to Jesus. As a result of the conversation the African accepted the Lord as his Saviour.

This desert dialogue points up two things. First, seeing the words on a page of the Bible does not necessarily mean that the reader catches their meaning. Observing what the Bible says is the first of several steps in Bible study. It is important to know what the text actually states. But this may sometimes lead to questions on the meaning of what is read. Many people, on reading portions of the

Bible, come away confused about their meaning or come away with a false understanding.

Second, the evangelist-eunuch incident reveals that proper guidance can help others interpret what they read in the Bible. Philip's question, "Do you understand what you are reading?" implied that the reader probably did not understand but that it was possible to understand. In fact the treasurer's request for someone to explain the passage to him was an admission on his part that he could not properly understand the passage by himself and that he felt the need for help in interpretation.

Several months after Nehemiah completed the rebuilding of the Jerusalem walls and the Israelites had settled in their towns, Ezra the scribe read to them from "the Book of the Law of Moses" (the first five books of the Bible) as the people were assembled before the Water Gate at Jerusalem (Neh. 8:1). Ezra read from the Law from daybreak till noon (v. 3). The Levites also read aloud from the Law, "making it clear and giving the meaning so that people could understand what was being read" (vv. 7-8). As a result the people were joyful "because they now understood the words" (v. 12).

Why Is Bible Interpretation Important?

It Is Essential for Understanding and Teaching the Bible Properly

We must know the meaning of the Bible before we can know its message for today. We must understand its sense for then before we can see its significance for now. Without hermeneutics (the science and art of interpreting the Bible) we are jumping over and missing out on an indispensable step in Bible study. The first step, observation, asks, What does it say? The second step, interpretation, asks the question, What does it mean? The third step, application, raises the question, How does it apply to me?

Interpretation is perhaps the most difficult and time-consuming of these three steps. And yet cutting Bible study short in this area can lead to serious errors and faulty results. Some people knowingly "distort the Word of God" (2 Cor. 4:2). Some even "distort" the Scriptures "to their own destruction" (2 Peter 3:16). Others unknowingly come away from the Bible with faulty interpretations. Why? Because of inadequate attention to the principles involved in understanding the Scriptures. In recent years we have seen a great surge of interest in informal Bible study. Many small groups meet weekly in homes or in churches to discuss the Bible—what it means and how it applies. Do people in those groups always come away with the same understanding of the passage studied? Not necessarily. Some may say, "To me this verse means this," and another person in the group may respond, "To me the verse doesn't mean that; it means this." Studying the Bible in this way, without proper hermeneutical guidelines, can lead to confusion and interpretations that are even in direct conflict.

Did God intend for the Bible to be treated in this way? If it can be made to mean anything we want, how can it be a reliable guide?

Conflicting interpretations of many passages abound. For example, one person reads John 10:28, "I give them eternal life, and they shall never perish; no one can snatch them out of My hand," and understands that verse to be teaching eternal security. Others read the same verse and explain that though no one can snatch a Christian out of God's hand, the believer may remove himself from God's hand by persistent sin. Some people suggest that Paul's statement in Colossians 1:15 that Christ is "the Firstborn over all creation" means He was created. Others understand the verse to be saying that like a firstborn son in a family He is the Heir. Some Christians practice so-called speaking in tongues, based on 1 Corinthians 12–14. Others read the same chapters and understand that this practice was only for the Apostolic Age and not for today. Some have read Nahum 2:4, "The chariots storm through the streets, rushing back and forth through the squares," and have concluded that this verse was prophesying heavy automobile traffic in our cities today. In the Parable of the Good Samaritan (Luke 10:25-37), some have sought to give a "spiritual" meaning to the passage by explaining that the inn to which the Samaritan took the injured man represents the church and that the two silver coins given to the innkeeper represent the two ordinances of the Lord's Supper and water baptism.

The Mormon leader Brigham Young justified his having more than 30 wives by pointing to the fact that Abraham had more than 1 wife, namely, Sarah and Hagar. The Mormon practice of being baptized for dead relatives and others is based, they argue, on 1 Corinthians 15:29. Some people handle poisonous snakes, based on their reading of Mark 16:18. Whether women should teach men is based on how one interprets 1 Corinthians 11:5; 14:34-35; and 1 Timothy 2:12. Some teach that Christ's present reign in heaven means He will not establish a 1,000-year reign on the earth after His return. Others, however, say the Bible teaches that Christ, though reigning over the universe now, will manifest His kingdom in a physical way when He rules as the Messiah over the nation Israel on the earth in the Millennium.

All these—and many others—are matters of interpretation. Obviously these various conflicting views point up that not all readers are following the same principles for understanding the Bible.

The lack of proper hermeneutics has also led to the Bible being highly abused and maligned. Even some atheists seek to support their position by referring to Psalm 14:1, "There is no God." Obviously they are overlooking how those words are introduced: "The fool says in his heart, 'There is no God.'" "You can make the Bible say anything you want," some argue. And yet how many of the same people say, "You can make Shakespeare say anything you want"? Of course it is true that people can make the Bible say anything they wish so long as they disregard normal approaches for understanding written documents.

Bible Interpretation Is Essential as a Step beyond Observation

When many people approach the Bible, they jump from observation to application, skipping the essential step of interpretation. This is wrong because interpretation logically follows after observation. In observing what the Bible says, you probe; in interpretation, you mull. Observation is discovery; interpreting is digesting. Observation means depicting what is there, and interpretation is deciding what it means. The one is to explore, the other is to explain.

Observation is like a surgeon cutting into a problem area. He sees a growth, or perhaps loose blood, or discolored tissue, or a blockage. Then the question is, What does it mean? How is it to be explained? What kind of growth is it? What caused the diffused blood? Why the discolored tissue? Why is this blockage here?

Observing what we see in the biblical text, we then should correctly handle it (2 Tim. 2:15). The participle "correctly handling" (incorrectly translated in the *King James Version* "rightly dividing") translates the Greek word *orthotomounta*. This combines two words that mean "straight" (*ortho*) and "cut" (*tomeō*). One writer explains the meaning of this as follows:

> Because Paul is a tentmaker, he may have been using an expression that tied in with his trade. When Paul made tents, he used certain patterns. In those days tents were made from the skins

of animals in a patchwork sort of design. Every piece would have to be cut and fit together properly. Paul was simply saying, "If one doesn't cut the pieces right, the whole won't fit together properly." It's the same thing with Scripture. If one doesn't interpret correctly the different parts, the whole message won't come through correctly. In Bible study and interpretation the Christian should cut it straight. He should be precise . . . and accurate.[1]

Bible Interpretation Is Essential for Applying the Bible Properly
Interpretation should build on observation and then lead into interpretation. It is a means to an end, not an end in itself. The goal of Bible study is not simply to determine what it says and what it means, but rather to apply it to one's life. If we fail to apply the Scriptures, we cut short the entire process and have not finished what God wants us to do.

True, the Bible gives us many facts we need to know about God, ourselves, sin, salvation, and the future. We go to the Bible for information and insight, and this is proper. But the question is, What will we do with that information and insight? Interpretation is the step that moves us from reading and observing the text on to applying and living it out. Bible study is an intellectual pursuit in which we seek understanding of what God says. But Bible study must go beyond that to include spiritual discipline, in which we seek to put into practice what we read and understand.

Heart appropriation, not merely head apprehension, is the true goal of Bible study. Only in this way can believers grow spiritually. Spiritual maturity, in which we become more like Christ, comes not just from knowing more about the Bible. It comes from knowing more about the Bible and applying it to our spiritual needs. This was Paul's goal, that he might encourage and teach others so that they would become mature in Christ (Col. 1:28). And Peter wrote that we should "crave pure spiritual milk, so that by it [we] may grow up in [our] salvation" (1 Peter 2:2). Paul wrote that "knowledge puffs up" (1 Cor. 8:1). Jesus told the Jewish leaders of His day, "You diligently study the Scriptures" (John 5:39). But then He added that their study was of no value because they refused to come to Him to have life (v. 40).

One of the classic passages on the inspiration of the Scriptures is 2 Timothy 3:16. And yet most of that verse, along with the following verse, speaks of the *usefulness* of Scripture. It is to be used for "teaching, rebuking, correcting and training in righteousness, so that the man of God may be thoroughly equipped for every good work."

It is one thing to read 2 Timothy 1:9, noting that God has "called us to a holy life," and to understand that holiness is a life of purity and godliness, made possible by the sanctifying work of the Holy Spirit. But it is another thing to deal with sin in our lives so that we are in fact leading holy lives. It is one thing to study what the Scriptures say about the return of Christ in passages such as 1 Thessalonians 4:13-18 and 1 Corinthians 15:51-56. But it is another thing to build on and move beyond those facts to the point of loving His appearing (2 Tim. 4:8), that is, longing for and anticipating His coming, and continuing steadfast in serving the Lord (1 Cor. 15:58).

Bible interpretation, then, as the second step in Bible study is absolutely essential. Interpretation is foundational to application. If we do not interpret properly, we may end up applying the Bible wrongly. How you interpret many passages has a direct effect on your conduct and the conduct of other people as well. For example, if a pastor interprets certain passages as saying that remarriage is acceptable after divorce, then that influences how he counsels divorcees about remarriage. If a pastor understands 1 Corinthians 11:3-15 to teach that women should wear hats in church, then his interpretation affects what he teaches his congregation.

Whether abortion is right or wrong, how to find God's will, how to lead a meaningful life, how to be an effective husband or wife or parent, how to react to suffering—all these depend on and relate to hermeneutics and how you interpret various passages. As one writer put it, "Interpreting the Bible is one of the most important issues facing Christians today. It lies behind what we believe, how we live, how we get on together, and what we have to offer to the world."[2]

The Challenge of Bible Interpretation

We are responsible then to seek to know the truth as presented in God's Word. This is essential for our own spiritual lives and for effectiveness in ministering to others. In sharing the Word of God, whether in personal counseling, teaching a Sunday School class or Bible study group, or preaching, the knowledge we impart, based on our understanding of the Scriptures, will definitely affect others. Their lives are in our hands.

Without proper biblical interpretation, the theology of an individual or of an entire church may be misdirected or superficial and its ministry unbalanced.

Understanding the Bible is a lifelong process. As you study the Word, you will be asking yourself, What does this mean? Is this view correct? Why or why not? What about this interpretation? Is it valid? As you hear sermons and listen to teachers, you are continually confronted with the question, Is what he is saying about the Bible correct? As you discuss the Bible with others, you will be faced with the question of which of several possible views is more likely the meaning of the passage being considered. Seeking to determine what a passage really means is an intriguing intellectual and spiritual challenge. And as you share the Word of God, people will be asking you, "What does this verse mean?" "How are we to understand this passage?" Because of the extent of content in the Bible, and the diversity of the kinds of literature in the Bible, hermeneutics is an area of study with numerous problems and issues.

For example how do we know if a passage was intended only for the people to whom it was initially addressed or if it is intended for ensuing generations? Can a passage have more than one meaning, and if so, how are they to be determined? Did some of the Bible authors write more than they understood? Is the Bible more than a human book? If it is also a divine book, how does this affect our interpretation of various passages? How are we to interpret various proverbs in the Bible? Are they universally applicable? If we believe in literal interpretation, how does that affect our understanding of figures of speech? If the Bible includes figures of speech, then is all the Bible to be interpreted in a "spiritual" or mystical sense? How do we understand prophecy? Since there are varying views on how to interpret Bible prophecy, how can we know which view is more likely the accurate one? Why does the New Testament quote the Old Testament in ways that seemingly alter the way the verses read in the Old Testament? How can we move from interpretation to application?

Problems in Bible Interpretation

One of the major reasons the Bible is difficult to understand is that it is an ancient book. The first five Old Testament books were written by Moses around 1400 B.C. The last book of the Bible, Revelation, was written by the Apostle John around A.D. 90. So some of the books were written about 3,400 years ago and the latest one was written about 1,900 years ago. This suggests that in hermeneutics we must seek to bridge several gaps posed by our having such an ancient book in our hands.

A Time Gap (Chronological)

Because of the extensive time gap between ourselves and the writers and initial readers of the Bible, a huge chasm exists. Since we were not there, we cannot talk with the authors and with the initial hearers and readers to discover firsthand the meaning of what they wrote.

A Space Gap (Geographical)

Most readers of the Bible today live thousands of miles from the countries where Bible events took place. The Middle East, Egypt, and the southern Mediterranean nations of present-day Europe were the places where Bible people lived and traveled. These extend from Babylon in present-day Iraq to Rome (and possibly Spain, if Paul traveled there). This geographical distance puts us at a disadvantage.

The Customs Gap (Cultural)

Great differences exist between the way people in the Western world do things and think and the way people in Bible lands lived and thought. Therefore it is important to know the cultures and customs of peoples in Bible times. Often faulty interpretations stem from an ignorance of those customs. For this reason an entire chapter in this book is being given to that subject.

A Language Gap (Linguistic)

Besides gaps in time, space, and customs, there is also a chasm between our way of speaking and writing and the way people in Bible times spoke and wrote. The languages in which the Bible is written—Hebrew, Aramaic, and Greek—have peculiarities unknown in the English language. For example the Hebrew and Aramaic of the original Old Testament manuscripts included only consonants. Vowels were understood and therefore not written (though they were filled in hundreds of years later around A.D. 900 by the Masoretes). Also Hebrew and Aramaic are read from right to left rather than from left to right. In addition no spaces were inserted between words. The words in all three biblical languages ran together. An example of this in English would be the following:

DNRTCHTGNRB. Reading these words from right to left the Hebrew reader would automatically sense that it included four words, which in English would be as follows: BRNG TH CT RND. It is not too difficult to sense that the sentence is saying "Bring the cot around." On the other hand the two letters CT could be understood as cat or coat as well as cot. How then would a reader know which word was intended? Usually the context would give the reader a clue to the intended meaning. If earlier or later sentences referred to a cot, then it is most likely that this sentence would also refer to a cot. In some cases, however, the context may give no clue and therefore it becomes a problem in interpretation to know which word was actually intended.

Another reason the language gap is a problem is that the original Bible languages have unusual or obscure expressions, difficult to comprehend in English. Also some words occur only once in the entire Bible, thus making it impossible to compare them with how they are used in some other context to help us understand their meaning.

Another problem contributing to the linguistic gap is the transmission of the original manuscripts down to us today. As manuscripts were copied, scribal errors occasionally crept in. Sometimes one scribe read a manuscript to another scribe. The copyist wrote what sounded like the word pronounced by the reader. The words, "This is led" might be written, "This is lead." Sometimes a copier would mistake one letter for another letter that was very similar to it in shape. The Hebrew letters for *d* and *r* are similar (though not identical), as are the letters *w* and *y*. Sometimes a word was repeated and other times a word was skipped. If a manuscript included some of these accidental scribal mistakes, they might then be copied by the next copyist, thus transmitting the readings for probably several "generations" of manuscripts. Other times, however, a scribe would correct what he thought was an incorrect word or letter. The process of seeking to determine which readings are the original ones is called textual criticism. These variations, however, do not affect major doctrines of Scripture, nor do they affect the doctrine of the inerrancy of Scripture, which relates to the original manuscripts, not the copies.

A Writing Gap (Literary)

Differences exist between the styles and forms of writing in Bible times and the styles and forms of writing in the Western world today. We seldom speak in proverbs or parables, and yet a good portion of the Bible is proverbial or parabolic. In addition the fact that there are approximately 40 human authors of the Bible books sometimes poses problems for Bible interpreters. One Gospel writer stated, for example, that one angel was present at Jesus' empty tomb and another referred to two angels. Figurative language, frequently used, sometimes poses problems for our understanding. For instance Jesus said, "I am the door" and "I am the Shepherd." Obviously He did not mean He is literally made of wood with hinges nor that He actually owns sheep which He cares for in a field. It is the business of the interpreter to seek to ascertain what Jesus did mean by those statements.

A Spiritual Gap (Supernatural)

It is also important to note that a gap exists between God's way of doing things and our way. The fact that the Bible was written about God puts the Bible in a unique category. God, being infinite, is not fully comprehensible by the finite. The Bible speaks of God's performing miracles and making predictions about the future. The Bible also speaks of difficult-to-comprehend truths such as the Trinity, the two natures of Christ, God's sovereignty and man's will. All these and others contribute to our difficulty in understanding fully all that is in the Bible.

Since God is the divine Author of the Book, it is totally unique. It is one of a kind. The Bible is not simply a book with man's thoughts about God, though it includes them. It is also God's thoughts about God and man. The Bible reports what God did and communicates what He is and what He desires. The Bible is also unique in that it was written by God and man. Human authors wrote as they were guided by the Holy Spirit (2 Peter 1:21). This fact of dual authorship poses problems. How could God use people of differing personalities to record the Scriptures and yet have the final product be the work of the Holy Spirit? How does this affect the individual authors' own personalities and writing styles?

These six gaps pose serious problems when a person seeks to understand the Bible. Even the Ethiopian in Acts 8 faced several of these gaps, including the chronological, geographical, linguistic, and supernatural. While much of the Bible is plain and easy to understand, admittedly other parts are more difficult. Even Peter wrote, "Our dear brother Paul also wrote . . . some things that are hard to understand" (2 Peter 3:15-16). Some Bible verses remain a mystery even to the most skilled interpreters.

Definitions in Hermeneutics

Exactly what is hermeneutics? And how does it differ from exegesis and exposition? The English word "hermeneutics" comes from the Greek verb *hermēneuō* and the noun *hermēneia*. These words point back to the wing-footed messenger-god Hermes in Grecian mythology. He was responsible for transmuting what is beyond human understanding into a form that human intelligence can grasp. He is said to have discovered language and writing and was the god of literature and eloquence, among other things. He was the messenger or interpreter of the gods, and particularly of his father Zeus. Thus the verb *hermēneuō* came to refer to bringing someone to an understanding of something in his language (thus explanation) or in another language (thus translation). The English word *interpret* is used at times to mean "explain" and at other times "translate." Of the 19 times *hermēneuō* and *hermēneia* occur in the New Testament, they are more frequently used in the sense of translating. In Luke 24:27 the verb *diermēneuō* is used: "And beginning with Moses and all the Prophets, He explained to them what was said in all the Scriptures concerning Himself." When Jesus spoke to Simon He said, "'You will be called Cephas' (which, when translated, is Peter)" (John 1:42). The word "translated" renders the Greek *hermēneuō*. In a sense a translation is an explanation, explaining in one language what is conveyed in another language. Thus interpretation involves making clear and intelligible something that was unclear or unknown.

Hermeneutics, as mentioned earlier, is the science and art of interpreting the Bible. Another way to define hermeneutics is this: It is the science (principles) and art (task) by which the meaning of the biblical text is determined. As Terry wrote:

> Hermeneutics, therefore, is both a science and an art. As a science, it enunciates principles, investigates the laws of thought and language, and classifies its facts and results. As an art, it teaches what application these principles should have, and establishes their soundness by showing their practical value in the elucidation of the more difficult Scriptures. The hermeneutical art thus cultivates and establishes a valid exegetical procedure.[3]

What then is exegesis and exposition? Exegesis may be defined as the determination of the meaning of the biblical text in its historical and literary contexts. Exposition is the communication of the meaning of the text along with its relevance to present-day hearers. Exegesis is the actual interpretation of the Bible, and hermeneutics consists of the principles by which the meaning is determined.

Homiletics is the science (principles) and art (task) by which the meaning and relevance of the biblical text are communicated in a preaching situation, and pedagogy is the science (principles) and art (task) by which the meaning and relevance of the biblical text are communicated in a teaching situation.

Exegesis is the study in private, and exposition is the presentation in public. Exegesis is done in the study; exposition is done in the pulpit or at the teacher's desk or podium. The primary concern in exegesis is an *understanding* of a biblical text, whereas the primary concern of exposition is the *communication* of the meaning of the text.

Definitions of Hermeneutics and Related Terms

HERMENEUTICS
The science (principles) and art (task) by which
the meaning of the biblical text is determined.

EXEGESIS
The determination of the meaning of the biblical
text in its historical and literary contexts.

EXPOSITION
The communication of the meaning of the text along
with its relevance to present-day hearers.

HOMILETICS
The science (principles) and art (task) by which
the meaning and relevance of the biblical text
are communicated in a preaching situation.

PEDAGOGY
The science (principles) and art (task) by which
the meaning and relevance of the biblical text
are communicated in a teaching situation.

An effective expositor is first an effective exegete. Exegesis precedes exposition, just as baking a cake comes before serving it. The exegetical process takes place in the workshop, the warehouse. It is a process in private, a perspiring task in which the Bible student examines the backgrounds, meanings, and forms of words; studies the structure and parts of sentences; seeks to ascertain the original textual reading (textual criticism); etc. But not all those details are shared when he preaches or teaches the Bible. An artist, in the process of creating his work, agonizes over the minutia of his painting, but in the end he wants others to see not the fine details but the whole and how the parts are related.

Exegesis is thus a means to an end, a step toward exposition. Exegesis is more technical and is basic to exposition, which is more

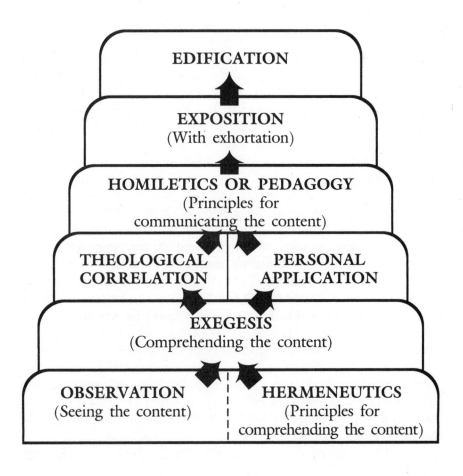

practical. In the privacy of his study the exegete seeks to comprehend the exact meaning of the Bible passage being studied. But in the pulpit or classroom the expositor, having built his material on an exegetical base, seeks to communicate that content. One is to the other as the foundation is to the building. "To be valid, exposition must be firmly based on exegesis: the meaning of the text for hearers today must be related to its meaning for the hearers to whom it was first addressed."[4]

Hermeneutics is like a cookbook. Exegesis is the preparing and baking of the cake, and exposition is serving the cake. The chart on page 21 illustrates the relationship of these and other elements, all of which lead to the final step of edification, that is, spiritual growth in the life of the interpreter/communicator and the hearers or readers.

In playing a game such as football or the table word game Boggle, rules are to be known and followed. If football players are on the field and have a football, but do not know the rules of the game, they can make no progress. If a person is playing Boggle, he may have all the parts but not know what to do with them. The rules enable the players to proceed. Similarly hermeneutics provides the rules or guidelines, the principles and theory governing a proper approach to understanding the Bible. Biblical interpretation, however, is not like a computer program. We cannot plug in certain principles and expect to receive automatically a printout with the proper interpretation.

Qualifications for Interpreting the Bible

No one can fully comprehend the meaning of the Bible unless he is regenerate. The unsaved person is spiritually blind (2 Cor. 4:4) and dead (Eph. 2:2). Paul wrote, "The man without the Spirit does not accept the things that come from the Spirit of God, for they are foolishness to him, and he cannot understand them, because they are spiritually discerned" (1 Cor. 2:14). Does this mean an unsaved person cannot understand the words of Scripture? No. Instead it means he has no spiritual capacity for welcoming and appropriating spiritual truths. As Martin Luther once said, the unregenerate can understand the grammar of John 3:16, but they do not act on those facts. It is in this sense that they are unable to know the things of the Spirit of God.

The unsaved do not welcome the truth of the Scriptures

because it strikes at the very core of their sinfulness. The Greek word rendered "accept" in 1 Corinthians 2:14 is the word *dechomai,* which means "to welcome." An unsaved person, devoid of the indwelling Holy Spirit may understand mentally what the Bible is saying, but he rejects its message, refusing to appropriate it and act on it. By contrast people in Berea "received [*dechomai*] the Word with great eagerness" (Acts 17:11, NASB) and the Thessalonians "welcomed [*dechomai*] the message with the joy given by the Holy Spirit" (1 Thes. 1:6).

First Corinthians 2:14 also states that the unsaved do not "understand spiritual things." The Greek word *ginōskō* ("to understand") does not mean comprehend intellectually; it means know by experience. The unsaved obviously do not experience God's Word because they do not welcome it. Only the regenerate have the capacity to welcome and experience the Scriptures, by means of the Holy Spirit.[5]

More than regeneration is necessary. Also reverence for and interest in God and His Word are essential to interpreting the Bible properly. A lackadaisical or cavalier attitude toward the Bible does not contribute to proper understanding of God's truth. The Scriptures are called holy and should be treated as such (2 Tim. 3:15).

Other spiritual qualifications are a prayerful attitude and humility. An interpreter must recognize that other readers of the Bible over the centuries have struggled to determine the meaning of many of the same biblical passages, and as a result, they may have some insights into those portions of Scripture. No interpreter is infallible. Therefore he should acknowledge the possibility that his interpretation of a given passage may not be correct.

The Scriptures should also be approached with a willingness to obey them, a willingness to put into practice what has been learned in the Word. When one sees how the Lord has worked in the lives of people in the Bible who obeyed or disobeyed Him, and when he comprehends the precepts and instructions given in the Bible for one's life, he should willingly follow those examples and instructions. Absence of a reverence for the Word, lack of prayer, pride, or an unwillingness to obey the truths of the Scriptures will hinder one's skill in comprehending what the Bible says.

The interpreter must also depend on the Holy Spirit. As Moule wrote, "The blessed Spirit is not only the true Author of the written Word but also its supreme and true Expositor."[6] The role of the Holy Spirit in biblical interpretation suggests several things.

First, His role does not mean that one's interpretations are infallible. Inerrancy and infallibility are characteristics of the Bible's original manuscripts, but not of the Bible's interpreters. Individuals have the right to interpret the Bible but this right does not mean that all the results of private interpretation will be accurate.

Second, the work of the Spirit in interpretation does not mean that He gives some interpreters a "hidden" meaning divergent from the normal, literal meaning of the passage.

Third, as already suggested, a Christian who is living in sin is susceptible to making inaccurate Bible interpretations because his heart and mind are not in harmony with the Holy Spirit.

Fourth, the Holy Spirit guides into all truth (John 16:13). The word *guide* means "to lead the way or guide along the way or road." Jesus' promise to the disciples was that the Holy Spirit would clarify and amplify what Christ had given them. After Christ ascended, the Holy Spirit came on the Day of Pentecost to indwell believers, and the disciples then understood the significance of Jesus' words regarding Himself and His death and resurrection. Though verse 13 was addressed specifically to the Twelve (v. 12), all believers may be similarly guided into the truth about Christ. Believers, however, are not automatically led by the Spirit to comprehend the truth of Scripture because, as already stated, obedience is necessary. Guidance implies obedience to the Guide and a willingness to be led. Only by the Holy Spirit can believers apply, that is, personally appropriate the Scriptures.

Fifth, the place of the Holy Spirit in interpreting the Bible means that He does not normally give sudden intuitive flashes of insight into the meaning of Scripture. Many passages are readily understood, but the meaning of others may come to light only gradually as the result of careful study. The Spirit's part in hermeneutics does not suggest some mysterious work that is unexplainable and unverifiable.

Sixth, the Spirit's role in interpretation means that the Bible was given to be understood by all believers. Its interpretation is not in the hands of an elite few scholars.[7]

However, these spiritual qualifications do not automatically mean that an individual's interpretations of the Bible are all correct. These are prerequisites, not guarantees.

Besides these spiritual qualifications, other qualifications are helpful in approaching the Bible. A willingness to study is essential. This may include a knowledge of Bible backgrounds, Bible history, and theology. As Ramm has explained, "Matters of fact cannot be settled solely by spiritual means. One cannot pray to God for information about the authorship of Hebrews and expect a distinct reply. Nor is it proper to pray for information with reference to other matters of biblical introduction expecting *a revelation* about *the revelation*."[8]

The Bible student must also approach the Scriptures with sound judgment and reason, seeking to be as objective in his approach to the Bible as possible, without coming to the Scriptures with prejudice or preconceived notions.

Does all this mean that the average layperson cannot comprehend the Bible? Must a person be educated in a Bible college or seminary to be able to interpret the Bible properly? No, the meaning of the pages of Scripture are not limited to a few. Made in the image of God, man is a rational (as well as an emotional and volitional) being. He has the intellectual capacity to understand the Bible. As a revelation of God, the Bible, written in human languages, is capable of being understood.

On the other hand, this does not mean that human teachers are not needed and that a person can be instructed by the Bible alone without any attention to what others believe about it.[9] Some have been given the gift of teaching (Rom. 12:7; 1 Cor. 12:28; Eph. 4:11). The 3,000 disciples saved on the Day of Pentecost "devoted themselves to the apostles' teaching" (Acts 2:42). Peter and John "entered the temple courts . . . and began to teach the people" (5:21). They continued "teaching the people" (v. 25) and "day after day . . . they never stopped teaching" (v. 42). "Barnabas and Saul . . . taught great numbers of people" in Antioch (11:26). In Corinth Paul was "teaching them the Word of God" for a year and a half (18:11). In Ephesus, Paul "taught . . . publicly and from house to house" (20:20). He was accused of teaching all men everywhere (21:28). Even when he was in Rome under house arrest he "boldly . . . taught about the Lord Jesus Christ" (28:31). If each individual believer could comprehend fully the Scriptures by himself apart from anyone else, then why were the apostles involved in teaching believers, and why is the gift of teaching given to some in the church today? Receiving the teaching of others can be in person or through written instruction in commentaries. Being open to the Spirit's leading of others can help Bible students avoid some of the dangers discussed earlier. This leads to the question of whether the Bible possesses clarity.

Can the Bible Be Understood?

Bible scholars sometimes refer to the perspicuity—or clarity—of the Scriptures. But if the Bible is clear, then why the need for rules or principles of interpretation? Why would any Christian coming to the Bible need the help of other teachers or written materials such as Bible commentaries, as just discussed?

Some people respond by saying it is impossible to understand the Bible. They read a Bible passage, determined that they will discover its meaning, but then find that the meaning eludes them. They conclude that if scholars who have studied the Bible for years cannot agree on how to interpret certain passages, how can they as laypersons do so? For them the Bible hardly seems to possess the quality of clarity.

If the Scriptures possess clarity, then why discuss interpretation at all?

Granted, some passages of the Bible, as already stated, are difficult to understand. And yet the basic message of the Bible is simple enough for any person to comprehend. The Scriptures are not obscure in themselves.[10] The teachings of the Bible are not inaccessible to the average person, as some have suggested. Nor is the Bible written as a puzzle, a book of secrets and riddles given in jumbled incommunicable form. The fact that the Bible is a book means that it is to be read and understood. As God's written revelation, the Bible *reveals* to us His character, plans, and standards. The human authors, whose writings were given by the inspiration of the Holy Spirit, wrote to be understood, not to confuse or bemuddle. As Martin Luther affirmed, the priesthood of all believers (1 Peter 2:5) means the Bible is accessible and understandable by all Christians. This opposed the alleged obscurity of the Bible, according to the Roman Catholic Church, which said that only the church could disclose its meaning.

Yet there are hindrances to communication. What was clear to the writer may not be immediately clear to the reader. This means that interpretation is necessary to help remove these obstacles to communication and to understanding. Exegesis and interpretation then are necessary to help expose the clarity that the Scriptures possess in themselves. As a divine Book in which God is communicating to man, the message is basically clear, and yet as God's Word it does include a profundity that can challenge the most diligent scholars.

CHAPTER TWO

Bible Interpretation —
Then and Now

When you drive an automobile, you need to keep your eyes open to various highway signs. Some signs give warnings: "Bump," or "Repair work ahead." Others give directions: "Detour," "Highway 31 — Exit right," or "One way only." Still other highway signs give information: "School zone," or "Speed limit — 30 m.p.h."

In a similar way understanding how individuals and groups have interpreted the Bible in the past can serve as signs to us, giving us warnings, direction, and information.

Like a warning signal, studying the history of Bible interpretation can help us see the errors of others in the past and the consequences of those errors, thus alerting us to guard against repeating them. As Mickelsen has written, "History shows that erroneous principles have often spoiled the exegetical work of fine men, some of whom are great saints. This should be a warning to us against careless interpretation. There is less excuse for us because we can profit by the lessons of the past."[1]

As a directional signal, knowing something of the development of Bible interpretation over the centuries can help us see the importance of correct Bible interpretations and what they involve. As an informational signal, the history of hermeneutics helps us see how certain interpretive issues have arisen, and how others in the past have dealt with them. It gives information on how we have arrived at where we are today in understanding the Bible.

As will be seen in this chapter, Bible students over the centuries have taken various approaches to the Scriptures: literal, allegorical, traditional, rationalistic, and subjective. (See the historical time line at the end of this chapter.)

Jewish Interpretation

Ezra and the Scribes

When the Jews returned from the Babylonian Exile, they were probably speaking Aramaic rather than Hebrew. This meant that when Ezra, the scribe (Neh. 8:1, 4, 13; 12:36) read the Law (8:3), it was necessary for the Levites (vv. 7-9) to translate from Hebrew to Aramaic. This may be the meaning of the phrase "making it clear" (v. 8). The Hebrew *pāras* means "to make distinct or interpret," possibly here meaning "to translate." In addition the Levites as they circulated among the people were "giving the meaning," that is, explaining or interpreting the Law "so that the people could understand what was being read" (v. 8).

Between the time of Ezra and the time of Christ, scribes not only taught the Scriptures but also copied them. They had great reverence for the text of the Old Testament, but this veneration for the text soon became excessive. For example Rabbi Akiba (A.D. 50?–132), who was the leader of a school for rabbis at Jaffa, Palestine, "maintained that every repetition, figure, parallelism, synonyme [*sic*], word, letter, particle, pleonasm, nay, the very shape of a letter, had a recondite meaning, just as every fiber of a fly's wing or an ant's foot has its peculiar significance."[2] Akiba taught that "as a hammer divides fire into many sparks, so every verse of Scripture has many explanations."[3] He said that meanings were to be found in every monosyllable of Scripture.

> If there is a superfluous "and" or "also," or sign of case, these are always to be specially interpreted. If in 2 Kings 2:14, it said of Elisha that "he also had smitten the waters" [KJV] it means that Elisha did more wonders at the Jordan than Elijah. If David says "Thy servant slew also the lion, also the bear," the meaning (by the rule of *inclusion after inclusion*), is that he slew three animals besides. If it is written that God visited Sarah, it means that . . . He [also] visited other barren women.[4]

Hillel and Shammai

Rabbi Hillel (70 B.C.?–A.D. 10?) was a prominent leader among the Jews of Palestine. He was born in Babylonia and established a school, which was named for him, in Jerusalem. He was known for his humility and love. He arranged under six topics the many rules that had developed among the Jews pertaining to the 613 commands in the Mosaic Law.

He also set forth seven rules for interpreting the Old Testament. Wood summarizes these seven as follows:

> The first has to do with inferences from the less to the more important and vice versa. The second is inference by analogy. The third is "constructing a family," that is, where a group of passages has a resemblance in contents, the group is regarded as having a common character derived from the meaning of the principal passage of the group. Thus, what is not explicit in any one of the passages may be interpreted in the light of the principal passage. The fourth is the same as the third but is limited to two passages. The fifth rule was based on a relation between the General and the Particular. The sixth was exposition by means of another similar passage. The seventh was a deduction from the context.[5]

Shammai, a contemporary of Hillel, differed from Hillel in both personality and hermeneutics. A man with a violent temper, he interpreted the Law rigidly. The teachings of these two rabbis often directly conflicted with each other. After the fall of Jerusalem in A.D. 70 the School of Hillel became prominent, and the School of Shammai receded in significance and influence.

Jewish Allegorization

Allegorizing is searching for a hidden or a secret meaning underlying but remote from and unrelated in reality to the more obvious meaning of a text. In other words the literal reading is a sort of code, which needs to be deciphered to determine the more significant and hidden meaning. In this approach the literal is superficial; the allegorical is the true meaning.

Jewish allegorization was influenced by the allegorizing of the Greeks. Greek philosophers, while appreciating the ancient Greek writings of Homer (ninth century B.C.) and Hesiod (eighth century B.C.), were embarrassed by the immoral conduct and by the anthropomorphisms of the fanciful gods of Greek mythology in those writings. For instance Phaedra fell in love with her stepson Hippolytus. Zeus had to defeat the three-headed Typhon. And Ares, the Greek god of war, delighted in slaughter. How could the Greek philoso-

phers revere these writings and at the same time accept the elements
in their writings "which were fanciful, grotesque, absurd, or immoral"?[6]

To get around this problem, the philosophers allegorized the
stories, looking for hidden meanings underneath the literal writings.
Theogenes of Rhegium, who lived around 520 B.C., may have been
the first Greek philosopher to have allegorized Homer. Another suggestion of the first philosopher to allegorize Homer is Pherecydes of
Syros, of the seventh century B.C.[7]

The allegorizing approach enabled Greek philosophers who
came along later, such as the Stoics, Chaeremon, and Cleanthes, to
promote their own ideas while claiming to be faithful to the writings
of the past. They could promote their own teachings under the guise
of allegorizing the mythology of Homer and Hesiod. The Greek
writers in this way were using allegorizing for apologetic purposes,
to keep the Greek poets from being ridiculed.

Jews in Alexandria, Egypt were influenced by Greek philosophy. But they too faced a problem: How could they accept the Old
Testament and also Greek philosophy, particularly that of Plato?
Their solution was to do the same as the Greek philosophers themselves, namely, to allegorize the Old Testament. The Alexandrian
Jews were concerned about anthropomorphisms and immoralities in
the Old Testament, just as the Greek philosophers were embarrassed
by those elements in Homer and Hesiod. Because of the many
Greeks living in Alexandria, the Jews were readily influenced by
them, and easily took up allegorizing the Old Testament as a way of
accepting it along with Greek philosophy. They too saw this as a
means of apologetics, a way to defend the Old Testament to the
Greeks.

The Septuagint, the Greek translation of the Old Testament
made in Alexandria about 200 years before Christ, makes deliberate
attempts to remove the anthropomorphisms of God. For example
the Hebrew of Exodus 15:3, "The Lord is a man of war" (KJV) is
rendered in the Septuagint by the words, "The Lord crushing wars."
"The form of the Lord" in the Hebrew of Numbers 12:8 is rendered
in the Septuagint "the glory of the Lord." In Exodus 32:14, "And
the Lord repented of the evil," the Septuagint reads, "And the Lord
was moved with compassion."[8]

Two names stand out in Alexandrian Jewish allegorization:
Aristobulus and Philo. Aristobulus, who lived around 160 B.C., believed that Greek philosophy borrowed from the Old Testament, and

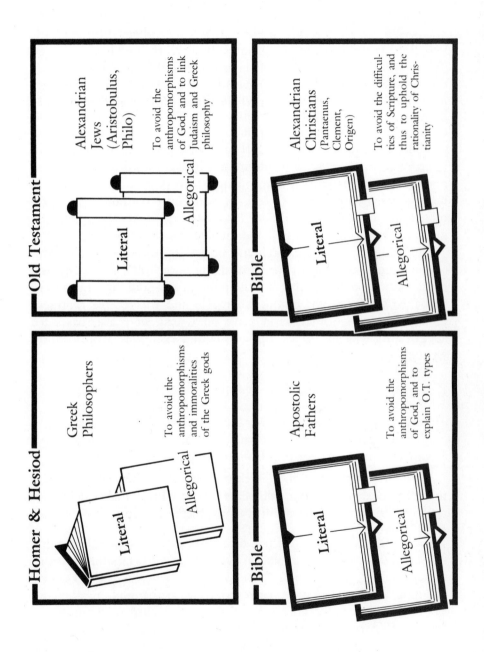

Old Testament

Alexandrian Jews (Aristobulus, Philo)

To avoid the anthropomorphisms of God, and to link Judaism and Greek philosophy

Literal

Allegorical

Bible

Alexandrian Christians (Pantaenus, Clement, Origen)

To avoid the difficulties of Scripture, and thus to uphold the rationality of Christianity

Literal

Allegorical

Homer & Hesiod

Greek Philosophers

To avoid the anthropomorphisms and immoralities of the Greek gods

Literal

Allegorical

Bible

Apostolic Fathers

To avoid the anthropomorphisms of God, and to explain O.T. types

Literal

Allegorical

that those teachings could be uncovered only by allegorizing.

The Letter of Aristeas, written by an Alexandrian Jew about 100 B.C., illustrates Jewish allegorizing. It said that the dietary laws really taught various kinds of discrimination necessary to obtain virtue, and that the chewing of the cud by some animals is referring to reminiscing on life and existence (Letter of Aristeas, 154).

Philo (ca. 20 B.C.–ca. A.D. 54) is the best known Alexandrian Jewish allegorizer. He too was influenced by Greek philosophy, yet because of his piety as a Jew he sought to defend the Old Testament to Greeks and, even more so, to fellow Jews. He was led to allegorize the Old Testament, rather than always following a literal method of interpretation, because of his desire to avoid contradictions and blasphemies. Philo stated that allegorizing is necessary to avoid seemingly unworthy statements of God, or seemingly contradictory statements in the Old Testament. He also said that allegorizing is necessary if the passage itself indicates that it is allegorical.

Philo taught that Sarah and Hagar represent virtue and education, Jacob and Esau represent prudence and folly, Jacob's resting on the stone speaks of the self-discipline of the soul, and the seven-branched candelabrum in the tabernacle and the temple represent seven planets. Synonyms and plays on words were also bases for allegorizing. Farrar gives the following examples from Philo's writings:

> If Scripture says that Adam "hid himself from God," the expression dishonors God who sees all things—and therefore it must be allegory. If we are told that Jacob sends Joseph to look after his brethren when he had so many servants, or that Cain had a wife or built a city, or that Potiphar had a wife, or that Israel is an "inheritance of God," or if Abraham be called "the father" instead of grandfather of Jacob—those are "contradictions," and therefore the passages in which they occur must be allegorized.[9]

Philo, however, did not totally set aside the literal meaning of Scripture. And yet he said it was the more immature level of understanding, corresponding to the body, whereas the allegorical meaning is for the mature, corresponding to the soul.

Some Jews became ascetics, forming exclusive communities, such as that of the Essenes at Qumran near the Dead Sea. They copied the Scriptures and wrote commentaries on some of the Old Testament books. They too were influenced by allegorizing. In the

Qumran commentary on Habakkuk 2:17 they wrote, "Lebanon stands here for the Communal Council, and 'wild beasts' for the simple-minded Jews who carry out the Law."

Early Church Fathers

Little is known about the hermeneutics of the earliest church fathers, those who lived in the first century A.D., but it is known that their writings were filled with Old Testament quotations, and that they saw the Old Testament as pointing toward Christ.

Clement of Rome lived around A.D. 30–95. He quoted at length from the Old Testament. He also cited the New Testament frequently as a means of fortifying his own exhortations.

Ignatius of Antioch in Pisidia (ca. 35–107) wrote seven letters to Rome, in which he alluded to the Old Testament frequently and emphasized Jesus Christ. Polycarp of Smyrna (70–155) also quoted the Old and New Testaments frequently in his letter to the Philippians.

The Epistle of Barnabas quotes the Old Testament 119 times. It also allegorizes frequently. A classic example is Barnabas' reference to the 318 servants with Abraham (Gen. 14:14). He said three Greek letters represent the number 318 and each has a meaning. The Greek letter t stands for 300 and represents the cross, and the letters i and $ē$ represent 10 and 8 respectively, and are the first two letters in *Iēsous,* the Greek word for Jesus. The 318 servants then become a type of Jesus on the cross. Barnabas wrote, God "knows that I never taught to anyone a more certain truth; but I trust that ye are worthy of it." This practice of seeing significance in numbers is known as *gematria.*

Barnabas' other interpretations are a bit farfetched. For example he said the sentence in Psalm 1:3, "He is like a tree planted by streams of water," speaks of both baptism and the cross. His leaf not withering means that the godly person will bring provision and hope to many people.

From these early church fathers it is obvious that while they may have started out well, they were soon influenced by allegorizing. And yet they viewed the Old Testament as having many types pointing ahead to Jesus Christ.

Justin Martyr of Samaria (ca. 100–164) quoted frequently from the Scriptures in his writings, usually for the purpose of showing that the Old Testament foretold Christ.

Justin was an enthusiastic lover and fearless defender of Christianity. He was a man of great learning, and delighted to use his knowledge of Greek philosophy to illustrate and enhance the teachings of Scripture. But his expositions are often fanciful, sometimes almost silly. He . . . carries the typical interpretation of the Old Testament to wild extravagance.[10]

Justin said Leah represents the Jews, Rachel is the church, and Jacob is Christ who serves both. When Aaron and Hur held up Moses' hands, that act represented the cross. Justin said the Old Testament is relevant to Christians, but its relevance, he argued, is seen by allegorizing.

In his *Dialogue with Trypho* he opposed Marcion, an early church writer who rejected the Old Testament and believed it has no relevance for Christians today. Marcion argued that even allegorizing could not give it Christian relevance.

Irenaeus lived in Symrna (now part of Turkey) and in Lyons (now in France). He lived around 130–202. In opposing Gnostics and their fanciful interpretations, Irenaeus stressed in his work *Against Heresies* that the Bible is to be understood in its obvious, natural sense. In opposition to other heretics, such as the Valentinians and the followers of Marcion, who rejected the Old Testament, Irenaeus stressed that the Old Testament is acceptable for Christians because it is full of types. In some cases, however, his typology became extreme to the point of allegory. For example he said that the three spies (not two!) hidden by Rahab were types of God the Father, God the Son, and God the Holy Spirit. In his five books "On the Detection and Overthrow of Knowledge Falsely So Called" he charged his opponents with two errors. First, they neglected the order and the context of Bible passages, taking isolated passages and words and interpreting them in the light of their own theories. Second, he charged the Valentinians with interpreting clear and obvious passages by the dark and obscure.[11] Irenaeus pointed out that one ambiguous statement in Scripture is not to be explained on the basis of another ambiguous statement.

The one standard of correct interpretation for Irenaeus is the rule of faith as preserved in churches in the apostolic succession.[12] He frequently appealed to tradition, saying that the true exposition of Scripture must be learned by elders who could claim apostolic succession.

Tertullian of Carthage (ca. 160–220) said that the Scriptures are the property of the church. The answer to heresy is "the rule of faith," that is, the teachings of orthodoxy held by the church. Tertullian believed that Bible passages must be taken in their original sense, interpreted according to the situation in which they were uttered or written.[13] And yet, like Irenaeus, his typology bordered on allegorizing. In Genesis 1:2 the Spirit's hovering over the waters refers to baptism, and Christ was teaching symbols when He told Peter to put away his sword.

Tertullian blamed the Gnostics for their allegorizing, and yet he allegorized whenever it suited his purposes. Symbols of the 12 Apostles are the 12 wells of Elim, the 12 gems on the high priest's breastplate, and the 12 stones taken from the Jordan River.[14]

Several observations may be made about these three apologists, Justin, Irenaeus, and Tertullian: (1) Allegorizing became apologetic, just as it had served that purpose for the Greek philosophers and the Alexandrian Jews. The problems of the Old Testament were readily solved, these men felt, by allegorization. (2) Typology easily slipped into allegorizing. (3) Church authority became a tool for opposing heresy. Unknowingly these apologists prepared the way for church tradition as a higher authority, a view that became dominant for centuries in the Middle Ages.

Alexandrian and Antiochene Fathers

Two schools of thought developed about 200 years or so after Christ, schools of hermeneutical views that had a strong impact on the church for centuries to come.

Alexandrian Fathers

Pantaenus, who died around 190, was the earliest known teacher of the Catechetical School in Alexandria, Egypt. He was the teacher of Clement (not to be confused with the Clement of Rome mentioned earlier).

It is not surprising that Clement (155–216), living in Alexandria, was influenced by the Jewish allegorist Philo. Clement taught that all Scripture speaks in a mysterious language of symbols. One reason is so that readers may become inquisitive and another is that it is not suitable for everyone to understand the Scriptures.

Clement said any passage from the Bible may have up to five meanings: (a) historical (the stories of the Bible), (b) doctrinal, with moral and theological teachings, (c) prophetic, which includes types and prophecies, (d) philosophical (allegories in historical persons such as Sarah representing true wisdom and Hagar representing pagan philosophy), and (e) mystical (moral and spiritual truths).

In his excessive allegorizing, Clement taught that the Mosaic prohibitions against eating swine, hawks, eagles, and ravens (Lev. 11:7, 13-19) represent respectively unclean lust for food, injustice, robbery, and greed. In the feeding of the 5,000 (Luke 9:10-17) the two fish represent Greek philosophy (*The Miscellanies* 6.11).

Origen (ca. 185–254) was a man of great learning and magnetic personality. In keeping with his veneration for the Scriptures, he developed the Hexapla, an arranging in six parallel columns of the Hebrew text and five Greek versions of the Old Testament. This immense work consumed about 28 years. He wrote a number of commentaries and homilies on most of the Bible, and also wrote several apologetic works including *Treatise against Celsus* and *De Principiis*. In this latter work he pointed out that since the Bible is full of enigmas, parables, dark sayings, and moral problems, the meaning must be found at a deeper level. These problems include the existence of days in Genesis 1 before the sun or moon were created, God's walking in the Garden of Eden, other anthropomorphisms such as the face of God, and moral problems such as Lot's incest, Noah's drunkenness, Jacob's polygamy, Tamar's seduction of Judah, and others. These and other problems used by enemies of the Gospel to oppose Christianity were readily answered by Origen through his allegorizing. In fact he said that Scripture itself demands that the interpreter employ the allegorical method (*De Principiis* 4.2.49; 4.3.1). He saw a threefold meaning in Scripture—literal, moral, and spiritual/allegorical. He based this on the Septuagint rendering of Proverbs 22:20-21, "Do thou thrice record them . . . that thou mayest answer with words of truth." This threefold sense is also suggested in 1 Thessalonians 5:23 by the body (literal), the soul (moral), and the spirit (allegorical). In reality he usually stressed only two meanings, the literal and the spiritual (the "letter" and the "spirit"). All Scripture has a spiritual meaning, he contended, but not all has a literal meaning.

In Origen's allegorizing he taught that Noah's ark pictured the church and that Noah represented Christ. Rebekah's drawing water at the well for Abraham's servant means we must daily come to the Scriptures to meet Christ. In Jesus' triumphal entry the donkey represented the Old Testament, its colt depicted the New Testament, and the two apostles pictured the moral and mystic senses of Scripture.

Origen so ignored the literal, normal meanings of Scripture that his allegorizing became unusually excessive. As one writer stated, it was "fantasy unlimited."[15]

Antiochene Fathers

Sensing the rampant disregard for the literal meaning of the Scriptures in the Alexandrian Fathers, several church leaders in Antioch of Syria emphasized historical, literal interpretation. They stressed the study of the Bible's original languages (Hebrew and Greek) and they wrote commentaries on the Scriptures. The basis for uniting the Old and New Testaments was typology and predictive prophecy rather than allegorizing. For them, literal interpretation included figurative language.

Dorotheus, by his teachings, helped prepare the way for the founding of the school at Antioch of Syria. Lucian (ca. 240–312) was the founder of the Antiochene school.

Diodorus, also of the Antiochene school (d. 393), wrote a work entitled *What Is the Difference between Theory and Allegory?* He used the word *theory* to mean the genuine meaning of the text, which he said includes metaphors as well as plain statements. He was the teacher of two other prominent Antiochene fathers, Theodore of Mopsuestia and John Chrysostom. Theodore of Mopsuestia is said to have been the greatest interpreter of the School of Antioch. In the last of his five books, *On Allegory and History against Origen*, he asked, "If Adam were not really Adam, how did death enter the human race?" Though Theodore denied the canonicity of several Bible books, he has been called the prince of ancient exegetes. Gilbert wrote, "The commentary of Theodore [of Mopsuestia] on the minor epistles of Paul is the first and almost the last exegetical work produced in the ancient church which will bear any comparison with modern commentaries."[16]

John Chrysostom (ca. 354–407) was archbishop of Constantinople. His more than 600 homilies, which are expository discourses with practical applications, led one writer to state that "Chrysostom is unquestionably the greatest commentator among the early fathers of the church."[17] His works contain about 7,000 quotations from the Old Testament and about 11,000 from the New.

Theodoret (386–458) wrote commentaries on most of the Old Testament books, and on the Epistles of Paul. His comments, according to Terry, are "among the best specimens of ancient exegesis."[18]

Late Church Fathers

Seven names are prominent among the late church fathers of the fifth and sixth centuries, though Jerome and Augustine are the best known of this group.

Jerome (ca. 347–419) originally followed Origen in his allegorizing. His first exegetical work, *A Commentary on Obadiah,* was allegorical. But later, after he was influenced by the Antiochene school and the Jewish teachers, he became more literal. His last commentary, on Jeremiah, was literal in its approach. He did believe, however, that a deeper meaning of Scripture was to be built on the literal sense. Or if the literal meaning were unedifying, he set it aside. For this reason he allegorized the story of Judah and Tamar (Gen. 38).

After traveling extensively, he settled in Bethlehem in A.D. 386, and in seclusion, he wrote commentaries on most of the Bible books and translated the Bible into Latin. This translation, the Vulgate, is clearly his greatest accomplishment.

As stated earlier, Tertullian helped prepare the way for church authority and tradition. Vincent, who died before 450, carried on this emphasis with greater clarity. In his *Commonitorium* (A.D. 434) he wrote that the Scriptures received their final exposition in the ancient church. "The line of the interpretation of the prophets and apostles must be directed according to the norm of the ecclesiastical and Catholic sense." This "norm" included the decisions of the church councils and the interpretations given by the Fathers. His hermeneutical authority was, "What has everywhere, always, by all been believed." Thus the three tests for determining the meaning of a passage were ecumenicity, antiquity, and common sense.

Augustine (354–430) was a leading theologian, with a great influence on the church for centuries. At first he was a Manichaean. The Manichaean movement, which began in the third century A.D., discredited Christianity by pointing up the absurd anthropomorphisms of the Old Testament. This approach posed problems for his understanding of the Old Testament. This tension was resolved, however, when at the cathedral in Milan, Italy he heard Ambrose, who often quoted 2 Corinthians 3:6, "The letter kills, but the Spirit gives life." This led Augustine to accept allegorizing as a solution to Old Testament problems.

In his work *De Doctrina Christiana* (*On Christian Doctrine*), written in 397, he pointed out that the way to determine if a passage is allegorical (and the way to solve exegetical problems) is to consult "the rule of faith," that is, the teaching of the church as well as Scripture itself. However, in the same work Augustine developed the principle of "the analogy of faith," by which he meant no interpretation is acceptable if it is contrary to the general tenor of the rest of Scripture. In book three of *On Christian Doctrine* he presented seven rules of interpretation by which he sought to give a rational basis for allegorization. They are as follows:

1. "The Lord and His body." What is said of Christ often applies also to His body, the church.

2. "The twofold division of the Lord, or the mixed church." The church may contain hypocrites as well as true believers, as seen in the good and bad fish in the net (Matt. 13:47-48).

3. "Promises and the Law." Some passages relate to grace and some to Law, some to the Spirit and some to the letter, some to works and some to faith.

4. "Species and genus." Some passages relate to the part (species) and some to the whole (genus). Believing Israelites, for example, are a species (a part) of the genus, the church, which is spiritual Israel.

5. "Times." Supposed discrepancies can be solved by including one statement within the other. For example the record of one Gospel which says the Transfiguration was six days after the scene at Caesarea Philippi, is included in the eight days recorded by another Gospel writer. And numbers often mean not the specific mathematical number but rather an extensive amount.

6. "Recapitulation." Some difficult passages may be explained by seeing them as referring back to a previous account. The second account of Creation in Genesis 2 is explained as a recapitulation of the first account in Genesis 1, not as a contradiction to it.

7. "The devil and his body." Some passages, such as Isaiah 14, which speak of the devil, relate more aptly to his body, that is, his followers.

In his approach to interpreting the Bible, Augustine said that the supreme test of determining whether a passage is allegorical is that of love. If a literal interpretation makes for dissension, then the passage is to be allegorized.[19] He emphasized that the task of the expositor is to determine the meaning of the Scriptures, not to bring a meaning to it. Yet he is guilty of this very thing he opposed, for he emphasized that "Scripture has more than one meaning and therefore the allegorical method is proper."[20] In his allegorizing Augustine taught that the four rivers in Genesis 2:10-14 are four cardinal virtues and that in the Fall the fig leaves represent hypocrisy and the skin covering is mortality (3:7, 21). Noah's drunkenness (Gen. 9:20-23) represents Christ in His suffering and death. The teeth of the Shulamite in Song of Songs 4:2 speak of the church "tearing men away from heresy."

John Cassian (ca. 360–435) was a monk from Scythia (modern Romania). He taught that the Bible has a fourfold meaning: historical, allegorical, tropological, anagogical. By tropological he meant a moral meaning. The Greek *tropē*, "a turn," suggests the turn of a word to a moral sense. By anagogical he meant a secret or heavenly meaning, from the Greek word *anagein*, "to lead up."

Cassian developed the four-line ditty that became famous throughout the Middle Ages:

Littera gesta docet,
Quid credas allegoria,
Moralis quid agas,
Quo tendas anagogia.

Translated this means the following:

The letter teaches events [i.e., what God and our ancestors did],
What you believe is [taught] by allegory,
The moral [teaching] is what you do,
Where you are heading is [taught] by analogy.

Mickelsen has suggested the following rough paraphrase to keep the metrical rhyme in English:

The *letter* shows us what God and our Fathers did;
The *allegory* shows us where our faith is hid;
The *moral* meaning gives us rules of daily life;
The *analogy* shows us where we end our strife.[21]

In this approach Jerusalem can have four meanings: historically, the city of the Jews; allegorically, the church of Christ; tropologically (or morally), the human soul; and anagogically, the heavenly city.

Eucherius of Lyons, who died around 450, sought to prove in his book *Rules for Allegorical Interpretation* the existence of symbolic language in Scripture. To justify this he argued that just as pearls are not thrown to swine so the truths of Scripture are kept from the unspiritual. Thus anthropomorphisms help the unlearned but others can see beyond them to the deeper meanings of Scripture. Yet Eucherius also saw a "historical discussion," that is, a literal sense, in Scripture.

Adrian of Antioch wrote a handbook on interpretation called *Introduction to Sacred Scriptures* around A.D. 425. In this work he stated that anthropomorphisms are not to be taken literally. He also discussed metaphorical expressions and rhetorical forms. He stressed that literalism is primary, but that Bible interpreters must go beyond the literal to deeper understandings.

Junilius wrote a manual of interpretation called *Rules for the Divine Law,* around 550. He said that faith and reason are not opposites. He, like Adrian, stated that interpretation of the Bible must begin with grammatical analysis, but must not be limited to it.

He saw four kinds of types in Scripture, illustrated by these examples: Christ's resurrection is a joyful type of our future joyful rising; Satan's sad fall was a type of our sad fall; Adam's sad fall was a type (by contrast) of our Saviour's joyful righteousness; and joyful baptism is a type of our Lord's sad death.[22]

It becomes clear from these late church fathers that Jerome, Vincent, and Augustine paved the way for two emphases that were to endure for more than a thousand years—allegorization and church authority. Cassian, Eucherius, Adrian, and Junilius built on Augustine's allegorical approach to Scripture, thus entrenching this approach to the Bible throughout the coming centuries of the Middle Ages.

Middle Ages

"The Middle Ages was a vast desert so far as biblical interpretation is concerned."[23] "There was no fresh, creative thinking about the Scriptures themselves."[24] Church tradition was prominent, along with the allegorizing of Scripture.

Common in the Middle Ages was the use of the catena, a chain of interpretations, pieced together from the commentaries of the church fathers. Most medieval catenas were taken from the Latin fathers, Ambrose, Hilary, Augustine, and Jerome.[25]

The beginning of the Middle Ages is usually identified with Gregory the Great (540–604), the first pope of the Roman Catholic

Church. He based his interpretations of the Bible on the church fathers. Not surprisingly, he justified allegorizing by saying, "What are the sayings of the truth if we do not take them as food for the nourishment of the soul? . . . Allegory makes a kind of machine for the soul far off from God by which it can be raised up to Him" (*Exposition of the Song of Songs*). Illustrations of his allegorizing include these: in the Book of Job the 3 friends are heretics, Job's 7 sons are the 12 Apostles, the 7,000 sheep are innocent thoughts, the 3,000 camels are vain notions, the 500 pair of oxen are virtues, and the 500 donkeys are lustful inclinations.

Venerable Bede (673–734), the Anglo-Saxon theologian, wrote commentaries that are largely compilations from the works of Ambrose, Basil, and Augustine. They too are largely allegorical. In the Parable of the Prodigal Son, the son, according to Bede, is worldly philosophy, the father is Christ, and the father's house is the church.

Alcuin (735–804), of York, England also followed the allegorizing method. In his commentary on John, he, like Bede, compiled the comments of others including Augustine and Ambrose.

Rabanus Maurus, a pupil of Alcuin, wrote commentaries on all the books of the Bible. In his allegorizing he wrote that the four wheels of Ezekiel's vision are the Law, the Prophets, the Gospels, and the Apostles. The historical meaning of the Bible is milk, the allegorical is bread, the analogical is savory nourishment, and the tropological is exhilarating wine.

Rashi (1040–1105) was a Jewish literalist of the Middle Ages, who had a great influence on Jewish and Christian interpretations by his emphasis on Hebrew grammar and syntax. He wrote commentaries on all the Old Testament except Job and Chronicles. He stated that "the literal must stand no matter what that might mean for the traditional."[26] The title Rashi is taken from the first letters of his name: *Ra*bbi *Sh*ilomo [Solomon] bar [son of] *I*saac.

Three writers at the Abbey of Saint Victor in Paris followed Rashi in his interest in the historical and literal sense of the Scriptures. These men — Hugo (1097–1141), Richard (d. 1173), and Andrew (d. 1175) — were known as the Victorines. Richard and Andrew were pupils of Hugo. The emphasis of the Victorines on the literal sense of Scripture was a bright light in the Dark Ages. Andrew disagreed with Jerome who had said that the first part of Jeremiah 1:5 refers to Jeremiah but that the last part of that verse refers to Paul. Andrew said, "What bearing does this have on Paul?" Richard, however, did give more attention than the other two to the mystical meaning of the Bible.

Bernard of Clairvaux (1090–1153), a leading monk, wrote extensively, including 86 sermons on only the first two chapters of the Song of Songs! His approach to the Scriptures was a typically excessive allegorizing and mysticism. As an example the virgins in Song of Songs 1:3 are angels, and the two swords in Luke 22:38 are the spiritual (the clergy) and the material (the emperor).

Joachim of Flora (1132–1202), a Benedictine monk, wrote that the time from Creation to Christ was the age of God the Father, the second age (from Christ to 1260) was the age of God the Son, represented by the New Testament, and the future age (to begin in 1260) was to be the age of the Holy Spirit. Joachim also wrote a harmony of the Gospels and commentaries on several of the prophets.

Stephen Langton (ca. 1155–1228), Archbishop of Canterbury, held that spiritual interpretation is superior to literal interpretation. Therefore in the Book of Ruth, the field is the Bible, Ruth represents students, and the reapers are the teachers. Langton is the one who made chapter divisions in the Vulgate Bible.

Thomas Aquinas (1225–1274) was the most famous theologian of the Roman Catholic Church of the Middle Ages. He held that the literal meaning of Scripture is basic, but that other senses are built on it. Since the Bible has a divine Author (as well as human authors), it has a spiritual sense. "The literal sense is that which the author intends, but God being the Author, we may expect to find in the Scripture a wealth of meaning. . . . The Author of Holy Scripture is God, in whose power it is to signify His meaning, not by words only (as man also can do) but also by things themselves. . . . That signification whereby things signified by words have themselves also a signification is called the spiritual sense, which is based on the literal and presupposes it" (*Summa Theologica*, I.1.10). Aquinas too held to the historical, allegorical, tropological, and anagogical meanings.[27]

Nicholas of Lyra (1279–1340) is a significant figure in the Middle Ages because he is a bridge between the darkness of that era and the light of the Reformation. In his commentaries on the Old Testament he rejected the Vulgate and went back to the Hebrew. But he did not know Greek. Luther was strongly influenced by Nicholas.

Though Nicholas accepted the fourfold sense of Scripture

common in the Middle Ages, he had little regard for it and stressed the literal. He was strongly influenced in that direction by Rashi.

John Wycliffe (ca. 1330–1384) was an outstanding Reformer and theologian, who strongly emphasized the authority of Scripture for doctrine and Christian living. Thus he opposed the traditional authority of the Catholic Church. He proposed several rules for Bible interpretation: (a) obtain a reliable text, (b) understand Scripture's logic, (c) compare parts of Scripture with each other, (d) maintain a humble, seeking attitude so that the Holy Spirit can instruct (*The Truth of Holy Scripture*, 1377, pp. 194–205). Stressing the grammatical, historical interpretation of Scripture, Wycliffe wrote that "all things necessary in Scripture are contained in its proper literal and historical senses." Wycliffe was the first English translator of the Bible. He has been called "the morning star of the Reformation."

The Reformation

In the Reformation the Bible became the sole authority for belief and practice. The Reformers built on the literal approach of the Antiochene school and the Victorines. The Reformation was a time of social and ecclesiastical upheaval but, as Ramm points out, it was basically a hermeneutical reformation, a reformation in reference to the approach to the Bible.[28]

The Renaissance, beginning in the 14th century in Italy and extending into the 17th century, was a revival of interest in classical writings, including an interest in Hebrew and Greek. John Reuchlin wrote several books on Hebrew grammar including *A Grammatical Interpretation of the Seven Penitential Psalms*. Desiderius Erasmus, the leading humanist of the Renaissance, edited and published in 1516 the first edition of the Greek New Testament. He also wrote and published *Annotations on the New Testament*, and paraphrases on the entire New Testament except Revelation. "These publications introduced a new era in biblical learning, and went far toward supplanting the scholasticism of the previous ages by better methods of theological study."[29]

Martin Luther (1483–1546) wrote, "When I was a monk, I was an expert in allegories. I allegorized everything. But after lecturing on the Epistles of the Romans I came to have knowledge of Christ. For therein I saw that Christ is no allegory and I learned to know what Christ is."

Luther denounced the allegorical approach to the Scriptures in strong words. "Allegories are empty speculations and as it were the scum of Holy Scripture." "Origen's allegories are not worth so much dirt." "To allegorize is to juggle the Scripture." "Allegorizing may degenerate into a mere monkeygame." "Allegories are awkward, absurd, inventive, obsolete, loose rags."[30]

Rejecting the fourfold sense of Scripture, which had been dominant throughout the Middle Ages, Luther stressed the literal sense (*sensus literalis*) of the Bible. He wrote that the Scriptures "are to be retained in their simplest meaning ever possible, and to be understood in their grammatical and literal sense unless the context plainly forbids" (*Luther's Works,* 6:509). His emphasis on the literal led to his stress on the original languages of the Scriptures. "We shall not long preserve the gospel without the languages. The languages are the sheath in which the sword of the Spirit is contained" (*Luther's Works,* 4:114-15). And yet the Bible student, Luther said, must be more than a philologist. He must be illumined by the Holy Spirit. Furthermore the grammatical, historical approach is not an end in itself; it is to lead us to Christ.

In his "analogia scripturae" ("analogy of faith") he, like Augustine, said that obscure passages are to be understood in light of clear passages. "Scripture is its own interpreter," he often stated. "This is the true method of interpretation which puts Scripture alongside of Scripture in a right and proper way" (*Luther's Works,* 3:334).

According to Luther, every devout Christian can understand the Bible. "There is not on earth a book more lucidly written than the Holy Scripture" (Exposition of the 37th Psalm). By this emphasis he was opposing the dependence of the common people on the Roman Catholic Church.

Though Luther vehemently opposed the allegorizing of Scripture, he too occasionally allegorized. For instance he stated that Noah's ark is an allegory of the church.

For Luther, Bible interpretation is to be centered in Christ. Rather than allegorizing the Old Testament, he saw Christ frequently in the Old Testament, often beyond what is legitimately provided for in proper interpretation.

Luther's rejection of the allegorizing approach to Scripture was revolutionary. Allegorizing had had a stronghold on the church for centuries. Though it developed in an effort to provide an answer to the Bible's anthropomorphisms and alleged immoralities, allegorizing was fraught with problems. Allegorizing becomes arbitrary. It has no objectivity or controls on one's imagination. It obscures the true meaning of Scripture. It has no authoritative message, for one person may say a passage teaches a certain truth allegorically, whereas another may see an entirely different teaching. It is a way of wresting the Scriptures from having any certain authority. "The Bible treated allegorically becomes putty in the hand of the exegete."[31] Allegorizing could also lead to pride, as some attempt to see in the Scriptures what they think is a meaning "deeper" in its spiritual, mystic sense from what others see.

However, did not the Apostle Paul use allegorizing? He wrote in Galatians 4:24-26, "This contains an allegory: for these women are two covenants, one proceeding from Mount Sinai bearing children who are to be slaves; she is Hagar. Now this Hagar is Mount Sinai in Arabia, and corresponds to the present Jerusalem, for she is in slavery with her children. But the Jerusalem above is free; she is our mother" (NASB). There is a difference, however, in interpreting allegories so designated in the Bible (see chapter 9 on "Probing the Parables and Analyzing the Allegories") and allegorizing much of Scripture. In Paul's allegory in Galatians 4, he, like other Bible writers who used allegories, clearly indicated what he was doing. Paul wrote, literally, "which things are allegorized." He used the word *allēgoreō*, which means "to speak so as to imply other than what is said." It is in addition to, not in place of the plain, grammatical meaning of the words. The following chart points up the difference between the allegorizing method of interpretation, common throughout centuries of the church, and Paul's use of an allegory.

Allegorizing	*Paul's Allegory*
1. The historical meaning is insignificant (if even true).	1. The historical meaning is significant and true.
2. The "deeper" meaning is the true meaning.	2. Parallels are drawn to make a point.
3. The "deeper" meaning is the "exposition" of the record.	3. Paul did not say the allegory was the "exposition" of Genesis 16.
4. Everything in the Old Testament may be allegorized.	4. When Paul allegorized, he said he was doing so.

Paul's allegory was an illustration or analogy in which he was pointing out that certain facts about Hagar correspond to non-Christians and that certain facts about Sarah correspond to facts about Christians.

Philip Melanchthon (1497–1560), Luther's companion, was thoroughly acquainted with Hebrew and Greek. That knowledge, along with "his calm judgment and cautious method of procedure, qualified him for preeminence in biblical exegesis."[32] Though at times he veered into allegory, in the main he too followed the grammatical, historical method.

John Calvin (1509–1564) has been called "one of the greatest interpreters of the Bible."[33] Like Luther, Calvin rejected allegorical interpretations. He said they are "frivolous games" and that Origen and many others were guilty of "torturing the Scripture, in every possible sense, from the true sense." Calvin stressed the Christological nature of Scripture, the grammatical, historical method, exegesis rather than eisegesis (letting the text speak for itself rather than reading into the text what isn't there), the illuminating ministry of the Holy Spirit, and a balanced approach to typology.

He, like Luther, emphasized that "Scripture interprets Scripture." Because of this he placed a strong emphasis on grammatical exegesis and the need for examining the context of each passage. Though well known for his theology (spelled out in his two-volume *Institutes of the Christian Religion*), he wrote commentaries on every book of the Bible except 14 Old Testament books and 3 New Testament books. Those books are Judges, Ruth, 1 and 2 Samuel, 1 and 2 Kings, 1 and 2 Chronicles, Ezra, Nehemiah, Esther, Proverbs, Ecclesiastes, Song of Songs, 2 and 3 John, and Revelation.

Calvin wrote in the preface to his commentary on Romans that "it is the first business of an interpreter to let his author say what he does say, instead of attributing to him what we think he ought to say." Calvin had an extensive knowledge of the Scriptures, evidenced by the fact that his *Institutes* include 1,755 quotations from the Old Testament and 3,098 from the New.

Ulrich Zwingli (1484–1531) was the Reformation leader in Zurich, whereas Calvin was the Reformation leader in Geneva. In Zwingli's break from Roman Catholicism he preached expository sermons, many of them on the Gospels. Rejecting the authority of the church, he wrote that "all who say that the gospel is nothing without the approval of the church err and cast reproach upon God" ("Sixty-seven Theses").

Zwingli emphasized the importance of interpreting Bible passages in light of their contexts. Pulling a passage from its context "is like breaking off a flower from its roots." In discussing the role of the Holy Spirit's illuminating ministry, he stated that "certainty comes from the power and clarity of the created activity of God and the Holy Spirit."

William Tyndale (ca. 1494–1536) is best known for his 1525 translation of the New Testament into English. He also translated the Pentateuch and the Book of Jonah. Tyndale too stressed the literal meaning of the Bible. "Scripture has but one sense, which is the literal sense."

The Anabaptist movement began in 1525 in Zurich, Switzerland by followers of Zwingli who felt he was not making a complete break with Catholicism on the issues of state control of the church and infant baptism. The three "founding fathers" of the Anabaptist movement were Conrad Grebel, Felix Manz, and Georg Blaurock. Other well-known leaders were Balthasar Hubmaier, Michael Sattler, Pilgram Marpeck, and Menno Simons. The Mennonites today are named after Menno Simons.

The Anabaptists believed that if a person had been baptized as a baby by the Reformed (Zwinglian) Church and then professed Christ as an adult, he should be rebaptized. For this reason their opponents dubbed them "Anabaptists," meaning "Rebaptizers." The early leaders in Switzerland called themselves "Swiss Brethren." They also stressed the ability of the individual to interpret Scripture aided by the Holy Spirit, the superiority of the New Testament to the Old, the separation of the church from the state, and faithful discipline and willingness to suffer for the name of Christ. They were vigorous in their concern for a purified New Testament church, loyalty to the Bible, and a life of humility, purity, discipline, and obedience to Christ.

In response to the Protestant Reformation the Roman Catholic Church convened the Council of Trent, which met at various times from 1545 through 1563. The reforms of the Catholic Church were known as the Counter Reformation. This Council affirmed that the Bible is not the supreme authority, but the truth is "in written books and in unwritten traditions." Those traditions include the church fathers of the past and the church leaders of the present.

The Council also affirmed that accurate interpretation is possible only by the Roman Catholic Church, the giver and protector of the Bible, not by individuals. The Council wrote, "No one—relying on his own skills shall 'in matters of faith and words pertaining to the edification of Christian doctrine—wresting the sacred Scriptures to his own sense, presume to interpret as according to that sense which the Holy Mother Church . . . hath held and doth hold; or even contrary to the unanimous consent of the Fathers.'"

The Post-Reformation

The 200 years of the 17th and 18th centuries were noted for several influential movements and activities. These include the confirming and spread of Calvinism, reactions to Calvinism, textual and linguistic studies, and rationalism.

Confirming and Spread of Calvinism

The Westminster Confession, approved by the English Parliament in 1647 and by the Scottish Parliament in 1649, spelled out the tenets of Calvinism for Britain. On the Scriptures, the Westminster Confession states, "The infallible rule of interpretation of Scripture is the Scripture itself; and therefore when there is a question about the true and full sense of any Scripture (which is not manifold but one), it must be searched and known by other places that speak more clearly."

Francis Turretin (1623–1687) taught theology at Geneva. Like Calvin, he taught that the Scriptures are inerrant and authoritative, and he stressed the importance of knowing the original text. These points are included in his work *Institutio Theologicae Elenctiacae*. In this work he discussed four major aspects of Scripture: its necessity, authority, perfection, and perspicuity.

Jean-Alphonse Turretin (1648–1737), the son of Francis Turretin, wrote *De Sacrae Scripturae Interpretandae Methodo Tractatus* (1728), in which he stressed these points pertaining to grammatical, historical exegesis:

1. Scripture is to be interpreted like any other book.

2. The interpreter must give attention to words and expressions in the Scriptures.

3. The objective of the exegete is to determine the purpose of the author in the context.

4. The interpreter should use the natural light of reason (in this he followed his father, who followed Aquinas on the place of reason) and should see nothing contradictory in the Scriptures.

5. The "opinions of the sacred writers" must be understood in terms of their own times (i.e., the cultural and historical background should be considered).

Johann Ernesti (1707–1781) has been called "probably the most distinguished name in the history of exegesis in the 18th century."[34] His work *Institutio Interpretis Nove Testamenti* (*Principles of New Testament Interpretation*) was a textbook on hermeneutics for more than 100 years. He stressed the importance of grammar in understanding the Scriptures, and he rejected allegorizing, emphasizing a literal approach to the Bible.

Reactions to Calvinism

Jacobus Arminius (1560–1609), a Dutch theologian, rejected a number of teachings by John Calvin, and taught that man has free will. In 1610 his followers set forth their views in a treatise called the "Remonstrance."

Mysticism, the view that man can have direct knowledge of and communion with God by his subjective experience apart from the Scriptures, grew in the post-Reformation under the influence of the writings of Jakob Boehme (1635–1705). Boehme prepared the way for Pietism with its emphasis on inner spirituality.

After the Council of Trent, Protestants began drawing up their own creeds in defense of their teachings. The post-Reformation period then became a time of theological dogmatism, "a period of heresy-hunting and rigid creedal Protestantism."[35]

Pietism developed as a reaction to the dogmatism of creedalism. Philipp Jakob Spener (1635–1705) is considered the founder of post-Reformation Pietism. A Lutheran, he reacted to dead formalism and a theology of mere words and creeds. In his works *Pious Longings* (1675) and *Spiritual Priesthood* (1677) he pointed out the need for holy living, the priesthood of every believer, and a life of Bible study and prayer.

August H. Francke (1663–1727) emphasized philology and the practical implications of Scripture for life. "Francke insisted that the entire Bible be read through frequently; that commentaries were to be used but with discretion so as not to take the place of the study of Scripture itself; and that only the regenerate could understand the Bible."[36]

Spener and Francke reacted against a textual approach to the Bible that dealt only with what they called the "outer shell."

Pietism influenced the Moravians, who in turn influenced John Wesley (1703–1791). Wesley stressed that the meaning of the Bible is plain, and that the Bible is to direct the reader to Christ. In reaction to rationalism, he distrusted human reasoning.

Textual and Linguistic Studies

In the 17th and 18th centuries "great strides were made in determining the original text of the Bible."[37] Louis Cappell has been called the first textual critic of the Old Testament, as seen in his work *Critica Sacra*, published in 1650. Johann A. Bengel (1687–1752) is known as "the father of modern textual criticism." He was the first scholar to recognize families or groupings of manuscripts based on common characteristics. In 1734 he published a critical edition of the Greek New Testament together with a critical commentary. In 1742 he wrote a verse-by-verse commentary on the New Testament called *Gnomen Novi Testamenti*, which emphasized the philological and also the spiritual and devotional.

Johnann J. Wettstein (1693–1754) corrected many New Testament manuscripts and published a two-volume Greek New Testament in 1751 with a commentary.

Rationalism

This movement stressed that the human intellect can decide what is true and false. The Bible, then, is true if it corresponds to man's reason, and what does not correspond can be ignored or rejected.

Thomas Hobbes (1588–1679) was an English philosopher who taught rationalism with a political bent. Hobbes was interested in the Bible as a book with regulations and principles for the English Commonwealth.

Baruch Spinoza (1632–1677), a Dutch Jewish philosopher, taught that human reason is free from theology. Theology (revelation) and philosophy (reason) have their separate spheres. Therefore he denied the miracles in the Bible. And yet he set forth several rules for interpreting the Bible, including the need for knowing Hebrew and Greek and the background of each Bible book. Reason is the all-embracing criterion for judging any interpretation of a Bible passage: "The norm of biblical exegesis can only be the light of reason, to all" (*Tractatus theologico-politicus*, 1670). The Bible is to be studied only for its historical interests.

The Modern Era

Nineteenth Century

Three elements may be considered in the 19th century: subjectivism, historical criticism, and exegetical works.

In the movement known as subjectivism, two names are

prominent: Friedrich D.E. Schleiermacher (1768–1834) and Søren Kierkegaard (1813–1855). Subjectivism is the view that knowledge comes by one's own experience, or that the supreme good is the realizing of a subjective experience or feeling.

Schleiermacher rejected the authority of the Bible and stressed the place of feeling and self-consciousness in religion. This was in reaction to rationalism and formalism. As stated in his *Monologues,* published in 1800, he stressed that Christianity should be viewed as a religion of emotions, not as a series of dogmas or a system of morals.

The Danish philosopher Kierkegaard, known as "the father of modern existentialism," relegated reason to the lowest level of human operation, rejected Christendom with its formal rationalism and cold creedalism, and taught that faith is a subjective experience in one's moments of despair.

In the 19th century, biblical criticism became prominent. It was rationalistic in its approach, with emphasis on the human authorship of the Bible and the historical circumstances surrounding the development of the biblical text. Being rationalistic, Bible students rejected the supernatural character of the Bible and its inspiration. With their philosophical bent toward naturalism, they explained away the miracles recorded in the Bible.

Benjamin Jowett (1817–1893) wrote in *Essays and Reviews* that "the Bible is to be interpreted like any other book," and this required knowing the original languages. However, to him this meant that the Bible is not supernatural for it has "a complicated array of sources, redactors, and interpolaters" which make it no different "from any other literary production."

According to Ferdinand C. Baur (1792–1860), the founder of the Tübingen School, Christianity developed gradually from Judaism into a world religion. Strongly influenced by Hegel's philosophy of thesis, antithesis, and synthesis, Baur taught that Peter and Paul directed two antagonistic groups but were finally synthesized in the ancient catholic (universal) church.

David F. Strauss (1808–1874) took a mythological approach to the Bible, which resulted in his denying grammatical, historical interpretation and miracles. Strauss was a pupil of Baur.

Julius Wellhausen (1844–1918) developed the view of Karl Graf and called it the Documentary Hypothesis. This views the Pentateuch as a work compiled by different authors—an author, designated as J, compiled the sections in the Pentateuch that use the name

"Jehovah" (hence J) for God, the E compiler put together the Elohim (hence E) sections, D was the Deuteronomist, and P, the latest, represents the Priestly code. Wellhausen believed that in Old Testament history the people developed from polytheism to animism to monotheism. Adolf von Harnack (1851–1930), another biblical critic, dissected the Bible much as a biologist examines a dead animal.

In contrast to the rationalistic, historical criticism of these and other leaders in the 19th century, a good many conservative scholars were writing exegetical commentaries on the Bible. Mickelsen says these include E.W. Hengstenberg, Carl F. Keil, Franz Delitzsch, H.A.W. Meyer, J.P. Lange, Frederic Godet, Henry Alford, Charles J. Ellicott, J.B. Lightfoot, B.F. Westcott, F.J.A. Hort, Charles Hodge, John Albert Broadus, and Theodor Zahn.[38] To these names could be added J.A. Alexander, Albert W. Barnes, John Eadie, Robert Jamieson, and Richard C. Trench.

Twentieth Century

Several strands of biblical interpretation have been present in the 20th century. Liberalism has continued much of the rationalistic and higher critical approach of the 19th century. Orthodoxy has taken a literal as well as a devotional approach to the Bible. Neoorthodoxy has said the Bible becomes the Word of God in man's existential encounters. Bultmannism has taken a mythological approach to the Bible.

Liberalism, strong in influence in the 19th century, has continued into the 20th century. It views the Bible as a human book not given by divine inspiration, and it teaches that supernatural elements in the Bible can be explained rationally. Liberal leaders include Nels Ferré, Harry Emerson Fosdick, W.H. Norton, L. Harold DeWolf, and others.

"The doctrines of sin, depravity, and hell offend the liberals' moral sensitivities so these doctrines are rejected."[39] Charles Darwin's theory of evolution is also applied to Israel's religion, in which Israel is seen as having evolved from polytheism to monotheism. Jesus is considered not as the Saviour from sin, but as a moral, ethical teacher.

Fundamentalism reacted strongly to liberalism, and promoted a literal approach to the Bible, a supernatural book. Today and in previous decades in this century many evangelical scholars hold to an orthodox view of the Bible, stressing grammatical, historical interpretation, thus following in the heritage of the Antiochene school, the Victorines, and the Reformers.

Karl Barth (1886–1968), in his *Commentary on Romans* in 1919, reacted strongly to dead liberalism. He did not agree with liberals that the Bible is merely a human document. Instead, in the Bible God speaks in divine-human encounters. In those encounters, revelation occurs and the Bible becomes the Word of God. The Bible is a record of and witness to revelation, not revelation itself. Other neoorthodox leaders include Emil Brunner (1889–1966) and Reinhold Neibuhr (1892–1971).

Neoorthodox theologians deny the inerrancy and infallibility of the Bible. The Creation of the universe, the creation of man, the Fall of man, the resurrection of Christ, and His second coming are interpreted mythologically. The Fall is a myth that teaches that man corrupts his moral nature. The Incarnation and the Cross teach us that the solution to the problem of human guilt must come from God. These events happened on a different level of history, a mythological level in contrast to actual history.

Rudolf Bultmann (1884–1976) taught that the New Testament should be understood existentially by "demythologization," that is, by eliminating mythological "foreign" elements, such as miracles, including the resurrection of Christ, which he said are unacceptable today. These "myths" expressed reality for people in Bible times, but for today these elements in the Bible are not literal. They are prescientific poetic devices for expressing transcendent "spiritual" truths. Jesus, for example, did not literally rise from the dead. His "resurrection" speaks instead of the new freedom His disciples experienced.

Influenced by the existentialism of Martin Heidegger (1889–1976), a German philosopher, Bultmannism takes an existential approach to the Bible, which means that the concern of leaders in this movement is to get to the religious-experience core of the Bible. This movement, called "the new hermeneutic," has been promoted by Ernest Fuchs, Gerhard Ebeling, and Hans-Georg Gadamer. In the new hermeneutic, the biblical text can mean whatever the reader wants it to mean. Like neoorthodoxy, the new hermeneutic denies propositional truth. Truth exists existentially, that is, as a person experiences it, not in written form. Therefore as Fuchs taught, we should not seek to determine the meaning of the biblical text. We should simply let it speak to us, letting it change our understanding of ourselves. Hermeneutics then is the process of self-understanding.

In this "word-event," as Ebeling called it, or flash of insight, the text speaks to our situation. The meaning of the Bible, Gadamer argues, can never be fully discovered. Because it was written so many centuries ago, people today cannot enter into that world. Therefore our world and the world of the Bible are held in tension.[40]

Demythologizing involves removing the myths, that is, the unscientific elements of the New Testament, and getting to the core of what the Bible is saying. The myths, while not acceptable scientifically to modern man, do say something. Therefore students of the New Testament need to determine what those myths are saying. They do this in existential encounters. Criticizing the approach of Bultmann and those in the new hermeneutic school, Pinnock notes that this movement imposes meanings on Scripture. "The *intent* of the text is secondary to the needs of the interpreter. The Bible no longer rules us; we rule it!"[41]

Conclusion

In addition to the literal approach to the Scriptures, four other approaches have been prevalent in various periods of church history: the allegorical, which largely neglects the literal; the traditional, which largely neglects the individual; the rationalistic, which neglects the supernatural; and the subjective, which neglects the objective. The chart on pages 56–57 gives a historical overview of these approaches and their major proponents throughout church history.

Many strands of thought regarding the Bible still exist today. Allegorizing is occasionally heard from pulpits. For example the Fish Gate in Nehemiah 3:3 is said to represent evangelism (since Jesus taught that His followers are to be fishers of men). The Old (or Jeshanah) Gate (v. 6) represents the old man (i.e., the sinful nature). And the Fountain Gate (v. 15) represents the Holy Spirit, who fills our lives with living water. However, no basis for this allegorizing is seen in Nehemiah 3.

The Roman Catholic Church still places the traditions of the church above the Bible, though occasionally one hears of Roman Catholics who are encouraged by their priests to read the Bible. In liberal pulpits, rationalism and human experience or subjectivism are still the norm. Man's reason is set above God's revelation, God is robbed of His supernatural character, and the Bible is robbed of its authority.

Neoorthodoxy is less prevalent today than a few decades ago,

HISTORICAL TIME LINE OF

	Early Church Fathers	*Apologists*	*Alexandrian and Antiochene Fathers*	*Late Church Fathers*
LITERAL	Clement of Rome Ignatius Polycarp	Justin Martyr Irenaeus Tertullian	Dorotheus Lucian Diodorus Theodore John Chrysostom Theodoret	
ALLEGORY	Barnabas		Pantaenus Clement Origen	Cassian Eucherius Adrian Junilius Jerome Augustine
TRADITION				Vincent
RATIONALISM				
SUBJECTIVISM				

MAJOR BIBLE INTERPRETERS

Middle Ages	Reformation	Post-Reformation	Modern Era
	Luther	Westminster	
Rashi	Melanchthon	Confession	
Hugo of Victor	Calvin	F. Turretin	Exegetical
Richard of Victor	Zwingli	John Wesley	commentators
Andrew of Victor	Tyndale	J.A. Turretin	Evangelical
	Anabaptists	Cappell	scholars
		Ernesti	
		Bengel	
		Wettstein	

Aquinas
Nicholas
Wycliffe

Bernard
Joachim
Langton

Gregory the
  Great
Venerable Bede
Rabanus Maurus
Alcuin

Council of Trent

		Post-Reformation	Modern Era
		Hobbes	Jowett
		Spinoza	Baur
			Strauss
			Wellhausen
			Harnack
			Peré
			Fosdick
			DeWolf
		Boehme	Schleiermacher
		Spener	Barth
		Francke	Kierkegaard
			Bultmann

having been replaced somewhat by the new hermeneutic of Bultmann.

Other systems of hermeneutics that have developed in recent years include, among others, structuralism, which ignores the historical background of biblical texts and views the Bible as having the same fundamental structural elements inherent in fictional narratives of all cultures and ages;[42] liberation theology, which interprets much of the bible from the vantage point of the economically and politically oppressed; feminist theology, which analyzes the Bible from the viewpoint of those oppressed by sexism; and ethnohermeneutics, which looks for supracultural meanings encoded in the Scriptures.[43]

This brief review of the history of hermeneutics shows that it is essential that evangelicals continue to stress the historical, grammatical, literary approach to the Bible. Only this approach, as developed in this book, enables believers to understand God's Word properly as the basis for godly living.

CHAPTER THREE

Whose View Is Valid?

In geometry an axiom is a self-evident truth, "a statement accepted as true for the sake of argument." In logic an axiom is a statement that does not need proof to substantiate its validity. An example of such an axiom is that things which are equal to the same thing are equal to each other. If A equals C and if B equals C, then it follows that A equals B. Another example of an axiom is that the whole is greater than any of its parts.

A corollary is a logical inference from an axiom. Given the truth of an axiom, certain logical statements may be inferred from them.

In approaching the Bible it is a self-evident truth that the Bible is a book. Like other books it is written in languages spoken by people for the purpose of communicating ideas from the writers to the readers.

Another obvious observation about the Bible is that it is a divine book. It is clear that the Bible, though like other books, is unique in that it has a divine origin.

From these two axioms — the Bible is a human book, and the Bible is a divine book — several corollaries can be drawn. I like to think of these corollaries as the basic principles of interpretation or hermeneutics. In other words the rules or principles for interpreting the Bible are not arbitrary. They are not imposed like laws over the Bible, for if that were so then some might conceive of the principles as having more authority than the Bible itself.

These hermeneutical principles, these corollaries drawn from axioms, are not the result of some unusual genius of a select few individuals. The principles of interpretation are not invented or learned but are part of the very nature of man. Man, as a communicator, has always sought to address other human beings in ways that would enable them to comprehend what the speaker was saying. When a person is addressed, he is automatically engaged in interpretation when he seeks to comprehend what is being communicated to him. This is a part of man's nature. Moses Stuart wrote along these lines in 1832.

> The principles of interpretation, as to their substantial and essential elements, are no invention of man, no product of his effort and learned skills; nay, they can scarcely be said with truth to have been discovered by him. They are coeval with our nature. Ever since man was created and endowed with the powers of speech and made a *communicative,* social being, he has occasion to practice upon the principles of interpretation, and has actually done so. From the first moment that one human being addressed another by the use of language down to the present hour, the essential laws of interpretation became and have continued to be, a practical matter. The person addressed has always been an *interpreter* in every instance where he has heard and understood what was addressed to him. All the human race, therefore, are, and ever have been interpreters. It is a law of their rational, intelligent communicative nature. Just as one human being was formed so as to address another in language, just so truly that other was formed to interpret and understand what is said. . . . Interpretation, then, in its basic or fundamental principles is a native art, if I may so speak. It is coeval with the power of uttering words. It is, of course, a universal art; it is common to all nations, barbarous as well as civilized. One cannot commit a more palpable error in relation to this subject than to suppose that the art of interpretation is . . . in itself wholly dependent on acquired skill for the discovery and development of its principles. Acquired skill has indeed helped to an ordinary exhibition and arrangement of its principles; but this is all. The materials were all in existence before skill attempted to develop them.[1]

In other words the principles for interpreting the Bible are simply descriptions of the way people think and read when they seek to understand the meaning of any writing. They are not inventions, they are discoveries. Rather than being created, they are observed. If

[handwritten margin note: coeval = of the same age]

they were arbitrarily devised by man, then each person could make up his own rules. But since these principles are part of the way man normally communicates, they are to be considered universal. They are not special rules applicable only to Bible study.

Knowing the rules is basic to playing a good game. For a player to ignore the rules or to devise his own would make for havoc. It would then be impossible for the game to be played in any meaningful fashion.

When we speak of Bible interpretation (hermeneutics) as a science and an art, we mean that as a science, there are rules to be employed, and as an art, those rules are to be observed properly.

Axiom One: The Bible Is a Human Book

Though the Bible is a supernatural work of God, as will be discussed in Axiom Two, the Bible is still a book. As with any other book, the Bible was written in languages that were intended to communicate concepts to its readers. The signs or symbols on the pages of the Bible were put there by writers for the purpose of communicating something to someone else. This is the purpose of a written communication: to help readers understand something, that is, to convey an idea, to communicate.

Communication, whether spoken or written, always involves three elements: (a) the speaker or writer, (b) the message, given in intelligible audible sounds or intelligible written symbols we call words, and (c) the hearers or readers. The purpose of the speaker or writer is to convey to the hearers or readers an idea he has in mind. He does this by means of linguistic symbols common to both the communicator and the ones receiving the communication. The desired result is that the hearers or readers will understand in their minds the ideas conveyed from the minds of the speaker or writer. A person can know the mind of a speaker or author only by what he says or writes. (As Paul wrote, believers can know God's plans only because He has revealed them to man by His Holy Spirit [1 Cor. 2:9-10].) Since the Bible is written in human languages, obviously its purpose is to convey truths from God, the ultimate Author, to human beings.

From this axiom—the Bible is a human book given as a written communication in human language to be understood by people—stem several corollaries.

1. *Each biblical writing—that is, each word, sentence, and*

book—was recorded in a written language and followed normal, grammatical meanings, including figurative language. This suggests that the Bible was not written in an unintelligible code to be deciphered by some magical formula. Since it was written in the languages of the people (Hebrew, Aramaic, Greek), it did not have to be decoded, deciphered, or translated. Those who read the Bible did not need to read into, beyond, or between words for some "deeper" or other-than-normal meaning. God communicated truths about Himself in the languages of the people who first read the Scriptures—languages they knew.

The words were immediately understandable. The readers knew immediately the concepts being conveyed by the sentences in the Bible. They understood them in the way they would normally understand other sentences written in their languages. They did not need to call on a wizard, a sorcerer, or a person with unusual spiritual insight or mystic intuition to convey its meaning.

Of course that language included idioms, unusual expressions unique to that language, and figures of speech.

> The basic presupposition of interpretation is that God is a *God of sense, not of nonsense.* By this, I mean that whatever God reveals through His ancient spokesmen must have made sense both to them and to their hearers. . . . The very fact that we have a Bible at all, from the human standpoint is an indication that it made real sense to the people. It spoke to them where they were.[2]

This corollary suggests that we should not go to the Bible with preconceived notions or ideas, but instead should let the Bible speak for itself. For example in the sentence, "The man rode the horse," the horse should be understood as referring to a four-legged domesticated animal, not "a spirit of vengeance." In Mark 5:1-20 the demons do not mean false doctrine nor do the swine represent the unconscious mind. Such an approach ignores this basic corollary since normal grammatical meanings are not considered.

Henrichsen notes,

> If you were to say to an audience, "I crossed the ocean from the United States to Europe," you wouldn't want them to interpret your statement to mean that you crossed life's difficult waters into the haven of a new experience. Likewise, no journalist

would like to write of the famine of a country such as India and have his words interpreted to mean that the people of India were experiencing a great intellectual hunger.[3]

Ramm points out that finding the literal sense of a writing is the normal approach to all literature.

Whenever we read a book, an essay, or a poem we presume the literal sense in the document until the nature of the literature may force us to another level. This is the only conceivable method of beginning or commencing to understand literature of all kinds.[4]

The Bible itself follows the normal or literal method of interpretation. For example the Old Testament prophesied that Christ would be born in Bethlehem (Micah 5:2), that He would ride on a donkey (Zech. 9:9), that He would be punished for our sins (Isa. 53:4-8). And He did all those things just as literally predicted. In quoting the Old Testament, the New Testament writers treated it as a normal, human instrument of communication. Of course the so-called literal or normal approach to Scripture includes figurative language, as discussed in chapter 7.

This corollary also suggests that the goal of Bible interpretation is to determine the original meaning of the text. This is called exegesis, reading the meaning out of the text, and is the opposite of eisegesis, reading a meaning into the text. If one person can make a Bible verse say what he wants it to say, and another person may say it means something else, something *he* wants it to mean, and if neither meaning is derived from the actual statement of Scripture, then we destroy the ability of the Bible to communicate as a normal piece of literature. Unless we accept the normal or natural sense of Scripture we have no controls in our approach to the Bible.

An issue sometimes discussed by biblical scholars is whether the goal of interpretation is to determine the intended meaning of the author or the intended meaning of the text. In one sense this is a fine distinction that some consider unnecessary. The "intended meaning of the author" or the "intended meaning of what the author wrote" would seem to be the same. However, can we really know what was in the mind of the biblical authors apart from what they have written? We cannot get *behind* a person's writings to know his intentions. All we can do is look at what he actually wrote; it is in this way that we know his intended meanings.

Speaking of "determining the intended meaning of the author" has become popular in some circles because of the influence of E.D. Hirsch, Jr. In his book, *Validity in Interpretation*,[5] he was responding to the view of Hans-Georg Gadamer and others who were teaching that a text can mean whatever the reader wants it to mean. The meaning, according to Gadamer, goes beyond what the author intended. Hirsch objects to this view by stating that meaning is to be seen in what the author intended. Hirsch certainly was correct in rejecting Gadamer's view, but he located the meaning in the author rather than in the text. In interpreting the Bible we seek to understand what the Bible says, not the human author's "intended meaning." We study the biblical text to understand its meaning.

2. *Each biblical writing was written by someone to specific hearers or readers in a specific historical, geographical situation for a specific purpose.* This corollary suggests that each portion of the Bible was originally written to address a certain reader or readers who were living in certain locations and times, and that that writing had a given purpose. This relates again to the point that exegesis is to discover the original meaning of the text. In other words what were the words conveying to their initial readers? Before we can determine their significance or relevance to us today, people who are not the original readers, we must first seek to determine what the words meant to those who originally read them. God told Noah to build an ark. But does that mean every Christian today should be engaged in ark-building? We must understand the command to Noah as being given in a specific historical, geographical situation. Jesus told His 12 disciples not to enter into any town of the Samaritans (Matt. 10:5). Obviously that does not mean that readers today are never to enter a town in Samaria.

Suppose you go to someone's house and you see a note on the door with the words, "Come in and wait." At first you may be tempted to go in, but then you ask yourself, Was this written to me? If not, who is the note for, and what problem or situation is being addressed by the note?

3. *The Bible is affected and influenced by the cultural environment from which each human writer wrote.* This means that the Bible interpreter needs to give attention to cultural matters. An ignorance of certain cultural customs may lead to faulty interpretations. These cultural areas include, among others, agricultural, architectural, geographical, military, and political aspects of life. These are discussed in chapter 4.

4. *Each biblical writing was accepted or understood in the light of its context*. Understanding a word or sentence in its context is another aspect of normal interpretation, of how we normally and usually approach any written material. A single word or even a sentence may have several meanings depending on the context in which it is used. The word *trunk* may mean a part of a tree, the proboscis of an elephant, a compartment at the rear of a car, a piece of luggage, the thorax of an insect, a part of the human body, or a circuit between telephone line exchanges. Obviously it cannot mean all these things or even several of them at once in a single usage. The reader can determine its meaning based on how it is used in the sentence.

The same is true of the sentence, "He is over the hill." The context may suggest that he is literally on the other side of a small mountain or that he figuratively is "over the hill" in the sense of having lived beyond middle age. Ignore the context and you lose a basic tool for interpretation.

As will be seen in chapter 5, even the words *saved* and *salvation* are used in the Bible to mean different things. The context in each case helps determine its meaning.

In Matthew 24:13, Jesus said, "He who stands firm to the end will be saved." At first glance such a statement may seem to contradict statements elsewhere in Scripture that man is saved by grace, not by works. A look at the context, however, shows that this is not the meaning of this verse. Jesus was speaking of the Tribulation period, as indicated by His reference to "the abomination that causes desolation" in verse 15, and He was speaking of Jews who in that time will be persecuted, for in verse 16 He refers to "those who are in Judea." Verse 13 then seems to be suggesting that those Jewish believers who live through the Tribulation and are not martyred will be delivered ("saved") at the end when Christ returns.

More than 400 years ago, Myles Coverdale wrote of the importance of noting the context, as well as other elements we have already discussed. "It shall greatly helpe ye to understande Scripture, if thou mark not only what is spoken or wrytten, but of whom, and to whom, with what words, at what time, where, to what extent, with what circumstances, considering what goeth before and what followeth."[6] More will be said on the subject of context in chapter 5.

5. *Each biblical writing took on the nature of a specific literary form*. Though our usual way of understanding a piece of literature is its ordinary, plain sense, we at the same time recognize differences in the kinds of literature. When we read a historical novel, we do not

expect all the details to be accurate historically. But when we read a physics textbook or a Latin grammar, we approach it differently from a novel. The way we read a board report differs from the way we read a cartoon. We do not read a recipe and a will the same way.

Since the Bible contains various kinds of literature, the unique characteristics of each form of literature need to be taken into consideration as we interpret the Bible. The Bible includes narratives, poetry, prophecy, letters, proverbs, drama, law, wisdom literature, apocalyptic visions, parables, and discourses. If we are not aware of these literary forms we may misinterpret statements in those sections.

6. *Each biblical writing was understood by its initial readers in accord with the basic principles of logic and communication.* When we approach a piece of literature, whether a drama, autobiography, or newspaper, we follow the normal principles of communication. We usually give a writer the benefit of the doubt and do not look for him to be contradicting himself. If it appears that one statement of his contradicts the other, then we look for some way of explaining the apparent contradiction. Some critics of the Bible give secular writers this benefit of the doubt, but do not do so with the Bible.

For example 1 John 1:8 reads, "If we claim to be without sin, we deceive ourselves and the truth is not in us." Then later in the same book the apostle wrote, "No one who is born of God will continue to sin, because God's seed remains in him; he cannot go on sinning, because he has been born of God" (3:9). The Bible interpreter looks for a way of putting those two verses together, assuming that the writer was following the principle of self-consistency (or noncontradiction). Many evangelicals explain these verses by saying that while no Christian is entirely free from sin (1:8), he does not *continually* sin (3:9) because he is a new creation, born of God. Other evangelicals say verse 9 is referring to the absence of sin in the believer's new nature.

These six corollaries suggest that in approaching the Bible we ask the following questions (which correspond to the six corollaries in order).

1. What did the words convey in the grammar of the original readers?

2. What was being conveyed by those words to the initial readers?

3. How did the cultural setting influence and affect what was written?

4. What is the meaning of the words in their context?

5. In what literary form is the material written and how does that affect what is said?

6. How do the principles of logic and normal communication affect the meaning?

Suppose we read the sentence, "That is some turkey!" How do we know what that sentence means? The word *turkey* can mean (a) a weird person, (b) a bird, (c) three strikes in a row in bowling, or (d) a failure in a theatrical production. To determine the meaning we can apply all six corollaries. First, we may ask, what is the normal, grammatical meaning? In this case the word *turkey* would normally refer to a bird. However, if the sentence is used in a figurative way, then any of the other definitions would apply. (In chapter 7 some suggestions will be made on how to determine if a word, phrase, or sentence is used in the Bible figuratively.)

Second, we may ask in what historical, geographical situation was the sentence about the turkey written? Who spoke the words and to whom? If this exclamation were spoken in a drama class, it is possible that the fourth meaning (a failure in a theatrical production) is intended. If it were mentioned in a sportscast, it might be the third definition or it could possibly be the first. If it were spoken by someone in a dining room, it might be number two or possibly one of the others. These various possibilities suggest that the other corollaries also need to be applied.

So the next question may then be asked: In what cultural setting were the words spoken? If the sentence were in a book written in 1920, then the first definition (a weird person) is probably not the meaning since *turkey* was not used in that way at that time.

Fourth, what is the context in which the sentence is used? This is probably the best clue to the meaning as the writer used the sentence about the turkey.

Fifth, what is the literary form in which it is used? If the sentence occurs in a book on how to produce drama, it may well refer to the fourth meaning. Or if it occurs in a rule book for bowling, it is most likely the third definition (three strikes in a row).

The sixth corollary on logic and communication does not help much in this case. Any four of the meanings might be intended.

Axiom Two: The Bible Is a Divine Book

As a means of communication, the Bible, as already seen, is a book like other books. Individuals were involved in recording the words.

Since these human instruments used human language in writing the books of the Bible, the first axiom suggests we pay attention to the common rules of grammar and syntax. (Grammar is the study of words and their functions in sentences, and syntax, as explained in chapter 5, refers to the way sentences are put together.)

Yet the Bible is like no other book. It is unique for it has come to us from God Himself. This is evident from its own claims to inspiration. Paul wrote, "All Scripture is God-breathed" (2 Tim. 3:16). Though human writers were used by God to record the Scriptures, using their own styles of diction and expressing their own personalities, their words were the "out-breathing" of God. Inspiration then is the supernatural work of the Holy Spirit whereby He guided and superintended the writers of Scripture so that what they wrote is the Word of God. This "breathing" into the writings, or superintending over the writings, was an act both verbal and plenary. It was verbal in that the Holy Spirit guided in the choice of the words, which cannot be separated from thoughts. The Bible's inspiration was also plenary in that it extended to every portion of the Bible. As a result it is infallible in truth and final in authority. The Greek word for "inspired" (2 Tim. 3:16, NASB) is *theopneustos,* literally "God-breathed" (as the NIV translates it). Because of its divine origin and nature, the Bible in its original writings was without error.

Second Peter 1:21 states the method the Holy Spirit used in the act of inspiration: "Men spoke from God as they were carried along by the Holy Spirit." The writers recorded their God-given words as they were carried along (*pheromenoi*) by the Holy Spirit. They were moved by the Holy Spirit in their writings, much as a sailboat is borne along by the wind. In inspiration, the Holy Spirit caused the writers to record God's revelation. They put in writing the truths God was unveiling about Himself and others. As I have written elsewhere:

> The Bible *is* revelation (not only a record of revelation), and inspiration is the act whereby God put the revealed truths into infallible written form. Revelation is the communication of truth which would not otherwise be known, whereas inspiration is the process whereby this information is presented accurately in written language. Revelation is the Spirit's disclosure of divine truth, whereas inspiration is the Spirit's superintending process of recording His revelation.[7]

Obviously then the word *inspiration* when used of the Bible refers to something other than the way the word is often used today. Music, art, and poetry are often referred to as being inspired. By this we simply mean they were composed as unique works that have an emotional effect on us.

When we speak of inspiration of the Bible, we do not mean that the *writers* were inspired but that the *words* themselves were inspired, that is, they were God-breathed. In some sense God infused His life into the words of the Bible so that they are actually His. This can be said of no other book in the world!

Many times we read in the Old Testament that the prophets introduced their messages with the words, "Hear the word of the Lord" or "Thus says the Lord." Scores of times their words are referred to as the Word of God. There can be no question that the Old Testament writers sensed they were speaking and recording the very words of God.

The New Testament frequently affirms the divine nature of the Old Testament. For instance Matthew wrote that the virgin birth of Jesus "took place to fulfill what the Lord had said through the prophet" (Matt. 1:22). Matthew affirmed that the words in Isaiah 7:14 were not merely Isaiah's words; they were what the Lord said, and Isaiah was the instrument through whom the Lord spoke. Matthew used similar terminology in Matthew 2:15: "And so was fulfilled what the Lord had said through the prophet," referring this time to the Lord speaking through Hosea. Matthew 15:4 reads, "For God said, 'Honor your father and mother' and 'Anyone who curses his father or mother must be put to death.'" In these two quotations from Exodus 20:12 and 21:17, it is noteworthy that Matthew did not say "Moses wrote," but rather "God said." Moses' words were God's words. In Matthew 4:14 the evangelist again referred to Isaiah as the instrument through whom God spoke: "to fulfill what was said through the Prophet Isaiah."

In responding to a question by the Pharisees, Jesus referred to David "speaking by the Spirit" (22:43). "Through the Prophet Daniel" are words by which Jesus referred to Daniel's mention of "the abomination that causes desolation" in Daniel 9:27; 11:31; 12:11 (Matt. 24:15). Jeremiah's prophecy about Jesus being betrayed by 30 silver coins is introduced in Matthew 27:9 by the words, "What was spoken by Jeremiah the prophet was fulfilled."

Jesus' recognition of the authority of the Old Testament is also indicated by His words, "It is written." He used these words five times in the Book of Matthew alone: 4:4, 7, 10; 21:13; 26:31. In these verses Jesus quoted from the Books of Deuteronomy, Isaiah, and Zechariah.

Our Lord recognized the divine nature of the Old Testament by quoting it with authority. For example in Matthew 22:37 He quoted Deuteronomy 6:5, and in Matthew 22:39 He quoted Leviticus 19:18. In Matthew 23:39 He quoted Psalm 118:26; in Matthew 11:10 He quoted Malachi 3:1; in Matthew 18:16 He quoted Deuteronomy 19:15. Several times in the Book of Matthew Jesus pointed to the divine authority of the Old Testament by introducing an Old Testament quotation by asking, "Haven't you read?" He did this as recorded in Matthew 19:4 (quoting Gen. 1:27), Matthew 21:16 (quoting Ps. 8:2), Matthew 21:42 (quoting Ps. 118:22-23), Matthew 22:31-32 (quoting Ex. 3:6 and Deut. 6:5).

From these observations in only the Book of Matthew, it is clear that Jesus recognized the divine nature of the Old Testament. The words He quoted were accepted by Him as words from God Himself. Other New Testament writers also acknowledged the divine origin of the Old Testament. In 1 Timothy 5:18 Paul quoted from Deuteronomy 25:4 and introduced the quotation with the words, "For the Scripture says." Interestingly in the same verse he also quoted from Luke 10:7, thus placing both quotations on the same level as Scripture, that is, as material written and accepted as from God.

Peter acknowledged the divine nature of Paul's writings by referring to his letters as Scripture (2 Peter 3:16). No wonder the Thessalonians acknowledged that what they heard from Paul was indeed not the word of men but the Word of God (1 Thes. 2:13). The apostles themselves recognized their own writings as being God's Word with His authority. For example Paul wrote, "What I am writing to you is the Lord's command" (1 Cor. 14:37). The scores of times the New Testament writers referred to the Old Testament point to their acceptance of it as Scripture, as the Word of God, given by the Holy Spirit.

It is thus clear that the Bible is from God. The affirmation, "The Bible is a divine book," is clearly an axiom, a self-evident truth. From this axiom stem four corollaries, which Bible interpreters should recognize as they approach the Scriptures.

1. *The Bible, being a divine book, is inerrant.* The logical inference from the Holy Spirit's inspiration of the Scriptures is that they are inerrant, that is, without error in their original writings.

(Inerrancy is not claimed for copies of the originals, for the copies include a few copyists' mistakes in the process of transmission.) There should be no problem in understanding that the manuscripts were inerrant, when inspiration is understood as the Holy Spirit's work of guarding and guiding the writers to write what He wanted recorded, word for word. The Holy Spirit's work of superintending guaranteed that what they wrote was protected from error. "If the Bible's original manuscripts contained even a few mistakes, how can we say that any of it is reliable? Since God is true (1 Thes. 1:9; 1 John 5:20) and cannot lie (Titus 1:2; Heb. 6:18), He can and did preserve His Word from error."[8] For more on the subject of inerrancy see Norman L. Geisler, ed., *Inerrancy* (Grand Rapids: Zondervan Publishing House, 1979), and Charles C. Ryrie, *What You Should Know about Inerrancy* (Chicago: Moody Press, 1981). As we come to the Bible to interpret it, we therefore accept it as a supernatural book that contained no errors in its original form.

2. *The Bible, being a divine book, is authoritative.* The authority of the Bible for what we believe and how we are to live stems from the fact that it is inerrant. Inerrancy in turn stems from the truth of the Holy Spirit's inspiration. Since the Bible comes from God, it has an intrinsic authority. Jesus' frequent quotations of the Old Testament, in which He recognized its supernatural origin, also indicate His acceptance of its authority. What He accepted as authoritative should certainly be authoritative for us. Because the Bible is our authority, and that authority is binding on us, we are challenged to be as accurate as possible in our interpretation of what the Bible says. As the Word of God, the Bible is trustworthy and authoritative. This behooves us to be reverent and diligent in our approach to understanding the Scriptures.

3. *The Bible, being a divine book, has unity.* Though recorded by approximately 40 human authors, the Bible, as discussed earlier, is the work of God Himself. Thus it can be expected to possess unity. This suggests several matters. First, the Bible will not contradict itself. Being from God, who is truth, the Scriptures are coherent and consistent. All the parts fit together. For example the prophetic portions of the Books of Daniel, Ezekiel, 2 Thessalonians, and Revelation, along with others, can all be correlated to give a comprehensive profile of God's plan for the future. The events prophesied in these passages are not contradictory; they correlate together. The four Gospels, though giving differing viewpoints on the life and ministry of Christ, are not contradictory.

Passages that seem to have discrepancies need to be interpreted in light of the harmony of the Scriptures. Peter's words, "Repent and be baptized, every one of you, in the name of Jesus Christ so that your sins may be forgiven" (Acts 2:38), should not be understood as teaching that salvation comes by water baptism. That view would contradict other Scriptures. However Acts 2:38 is interpreted, it must be understood in such a way that it does not contradict other verses which make it clear that water baptism is not the means of salvation. (See chapter 5 for a suggested interpretation of this verse.) Nor should Paul and James be pitted against each other as if they were contradicting each other. Both were writing under the inspiration of the Holy Spirit and therefore God was presenting noncontradictory truth through both men.

Second, because the Bible contains unity, its obscure and secondary passages are to be interpreted in light of clear and primary passages. When John Knox debated with Mary, Queen of Scots in Edinburgh in 1561, she said, "Ye interpret the Scriptures in one manner, and they [Roman Catholics] in another; whom shall I believe, and who shall judge?" John Knox replied, "The Word of God is plain in itself; And if there appear any obscurity in one place, the Holy Ghost, which is not contrarious to Himself, explains the same more clearly in other places."[9]

If there are two equally possible interpretations of a passage (and in a number of passages this is the case since we do not know with certainty how to interpret every verse), a general rule of thumb is, Accept the clear and sensible meaning. When Paul wrote in Colossians 1:6, "All over the world this Gospel is producing fruit and growing," he most likely meant the then-known world rather than people around the entire globe.

Third, another implication of the unity of the Scriptures is that the Bible often interprets itself. Martin Luther and John Calvin often said, "Scripture interprets Scripture." Some passages give light on other passages. And this is not surprising since the book possesses harmony and emanates from the mind of God Himself.

As we approach the Bible, we should interpret each part in light of the whole. Paul's word in 1 Corinthians 7:17, "Each one should retain the place in life that the Lord assigned to him," should not be construed to mean that if a man accepts Christ as his Saviour he can continue living with a woman in an adulterous relationship. This interpretation would contradict the whole of Scripture elsewhere and would ignore its unity and destroy its harmony. John

Stott quotes Sir Charles Ogers, who gives several rules for interpreting legal documents. His seventh rule is, "The deed is to be construed as a whole." He adds:

> Every part of the deed ought to be compared with the other and one entire sense ought to be made thereof. . . . The words of each clause should be so interpreted as to bring them into harmony with the other provisions of the deed if that interpretation does no violence to the meaning of which they are naturally susceptible.[10]

Fourth, accepting the unity of the Bible also means that we should acknowledge what is called the progress of revelation. This does not mean that biblical revelation progressed in an evolutionary sense. Instead it means that in later Scriptures God added to what He had given in earlier portions. This is not to suggest that what was recorded in earlier portions of the Bible was imperfect and that the later revelations were perfect. Nor does it suggest that earlier portions were in error and the later portions were truthful. Instead it means that what may have been given as partial information was then added to later so that the revelation is more complete. What Daniel, Ezekiel, Zechariah, and others prophesied about the end times is expanded in the Book of Revelation. What is said about death in the Old Testament is then elaborated in the New Testament. The Trinity in the Old Testament is presented in fuller statements in the New Testament. Recognizing this progress of revelation means that the interpreter will be careful not to read back into the Old Testament from the New. (The relationship of the Old Testament to the New is discussed in chapter 11.) Progressive revelation does not mean that the Old Testament is less inspired than the New nor that the Old Testament is less clear than the New.

Progressive revelation also means that some commands were changed later. Circumcision, enjoined on Abraham and his descendants in Genesis 17:10, was later rescinded (Gal. 5:2). The Law of Moses has been superseded, as indicated in 2 Corinthians 3:7-11 and Hebrews 7:11-19. In Matthew 10:5-7 Jesus gave the Twelve instructions that obviously differ from those He gave after His resurrection, as recorded in 28:18-20. Also Jesus told His disciples that the Holy Spirit, who was with them, would be in them (John 14:17). This is parallel to what John wrote in 7:39, "Up to that time the Spirit had not been given." This implies that the coming of the Holy Spirit was later, on the Day of Pentecost (Acts 2). Looking back on that event Peter said to those in the house of Cornelius, "the Holy Spirit came on them as He had come on us at the beginning" (11:15). These and other passages point to differences in God's revelation. As Ryrie has pointed out, "To fail to recognize this progressiveness in revelation would raise unresolvable contradictions between passages."[11]

4. *The Bible, being a divine book, has mystery.* It must be recognized that the Bible contains many things hard to understand. Bible students must acknowledge that they cannot always ascertain what a given passage means.

The Bible contains mystery in three areas. One is prophecy. The Bible includes predictions of future events, which no human could possibly predict by himself apart from divine revelation. This unique element needs to be taken into consideration as the Bible is interpreted. Liberal scholars tend to discount the predictive element in Scripture. They state, for example, that the Book of Daniel was written around 200 or 150 B.C. They assert this since they believe that Daniel could not have written prophecy. They say he wrote those events after they occurred and recorded them as if he had written them beforehand. Liberals do this because they start with the assumption that the Bible is not supernatural in origin.

Another aspect of the mystery of the Scriptures is its miracles. How can anyone explain how an axhead can float? How can anyone walk on water? How could a man rise from the dead? How could the earth be made out of nothing? No one of these is possible unless we allow for God's supernatural working. If we accept the divine nature of the Bible, we then can accept the record of these miracles as being true.

Another aspect of the mysterious nature of the Bible is its doctrine. A number of teachings in the Bible are difficult for the finite mind to comprehend. How can God exist as three Persons in one essence? How could Christ rise from the dead? How can He indwell each believer? How can God be omnipresent? How can God be sovereign and man still exercise his will?

In summary, accepting the divine nature of the Bible means we acknowledge its inerrancy, authority, unity, and mystery. If the Bible is looked on as merely a human book, then as we seek to interpret the Scriptures, we would not expect it to be inerrant, authoritative, harmonious, and to contain mystery.

The Bible then, according to these self-evident assertions, is a human book and is also a divine book. Neither can be denied. If we look on the book as only human, then we approach the Bible rationally. If we look on the book as only divine while ignoring its human elements, we approach the Bible as a mystical book. Seeing that the Bible is a book that is both human and divine, we seek to interpret it as we would any other book while at the same time affirming its uniqueness as a book of divine truth from the hand of God.

CHAPTER FOUR

Bridging the Cultural Gap

In the book *Through the Looking-Glass*, Humpty Dumpty said to Alice, "There are 364 days when you might get un-birthday presents." Alice agreed, and then Humpty Dumpty added, "And only *one* for birthday presents, you know. There's glory for you!"

Alice responded, "I don't know what you mean by 'glory.' "

Humpty Dumpty smiled. "Of course you don't—till I tell you. I meant 'there's a nice knock-down argument for you!'"

"But 'glory' doesn't mean 'a nice knock-down argument,'" Alice objected.

"When *I* use a word," Humpty Dumpty said scornfully, "it means just what I choose it to mean—neither more nor less."

"The question is," said Alice, "whether you *can* make words mean so many different things."[1]

Alice was concerned that Humpty Dumpty was taking the word *glory* and redefining it. Her concern stemmed from the fact that normally in communication a person does not redefine words to mean something vastly different from their commonly accepted meaning. And yet when a person explains what he means when he uses a word in a different way, the hearers can understand it.

If we take Humpty Dumpty's statement about a birthday being "glory for you" without his explanation, we are puzzled by what he means. And yet with the context, in which he explains the sentence, his meaning is clear.

People often do this with the Bible. They isolate a word or sentence or paragraph, and take it to mean what they think it means.

Disregarding the context is one of the greatest problems in Bible interpretation. By disregarding the "total surroundings" of a

Bible verse, we may completely misunderstand the verse. We need to take into consideration the sentences and paragraphs that precede and follow the verse and also to take into consideration the cultural setting in which the passage and even the entire book is written.

This is important because of the gap that exists between our culture in the West and those in Bible times. "Understanding the Bible properly requires that we clear our minds of all ideas, opinions, and systems of our own day and attempt to put ourselves into the times and surroundings of the Apostles and Prophets who wrote."[2] To the extent that we seek to transport ourselves into the historical situation of the Bible writers and disengage ourselves from our own cultures, to that extent the likelihood of our being more accurate in interpreting the Bible increases.

When the Reformers (Martin Luther, Philip Melanchthon, John Calvin, Ulrich Zwingli, and others) emphasized the need to get back to the Scriptures, they emphasized historical, grammatical interpretation. By "historical" they meant the setting in which the Bible books were written and the circumstances involved in the writing. By "grammatical" they meant determining the meaning of the Bible by studying the words and sentences of Scripture in their normal, plain sense. Another aspect of interpretation may be added to these two, namely, rhetorical. Rhetorical interpretation suggests studying how the literary quality of a portion of the Bible affects its interpretation. Putting these three together, we may speak of historical-grammatical-rhetorical interpretation. This chapter looks at historical interpretation, taking into consideration the circumstances of the writings and the cultural environment. Chapter 5 looks at the grammatical aspects of interpretation, and chapters 6 and 7 consider various aspects of rhetorical interpretation.

The context in which a given Scripture passage is written influences how that passage is to be understood. Context includes several things:
- the verse(s) immediately before and after a passage
- the paragraph and book in which the verses occur
- the dispensation in which it was written
- the message of the entire Bible
- the historical-cultural environment of that time when it was written.

Examples of the importance of knowing the immediate context of a verse and the context of the chapter or book in which the verse occurs will be discussed in the following chapter.

Most books on interpreting the Bible discuss the first several contexts first, followed by a discussion of the historical-cultural environment at the time the Bible authors wrote. I want to reverse this because the latter often has an influence on the other contexts.

It is important to know the circumstances of a given Bible book. This means looking for answers to these questions: Who wrote the book? At what time was it written? What prompted the author to write the book? That is, what problems, situations, or needs was he addressing? What is the book all about? That is, what is its main subject or subjects? To whom was the book written? That is, who were the first readers or hearers of the book? Answers to these questions can help us make more sense of what the Bible book says.

The major concern in this chapter is the cultural background from which the human authors of the Scriptures wrote. In any culture or age the writers of a document as well as the readers are influenced by their social setting. For example the Book of Nahum reflects the prophet's knowledge of the city of Nineveh, and the Book of Habakkuk reflects that prophet's knowledge of the Babylonians. A number of statements in the Book of Colossians seem to reflect the influence in Colosse of a philosophical-religious cult, possibly some beginning form of what later developed into Gnosticism. Much of the Book of Lamentations makes little sense unless the reader bears in mind that Jeremiah was writing a funeral dirge, bemoaning the destruction of the city of Jerusalem by the Babylonians. The treaties made by the Hittites with their vassals (conquered peoples) were written as covenants in a certain literary structure. This structure seems to be followed by Moses in his writing of the Book of Deuteronomy, and parts of Exodus.[3]

Noting the cultural background of a writing also helps us understand what that document meant to the people who first read it. Reading Great Britain's *Magna Charta* makes more sense when we understand the cultural environment of Britain in the 13th century.

Since a culture gap exists between our day and Bible times — and since our goal in Bible interpretation is to discover the original meaning of the Scriptures when they were first written — it is imperative that we become familiar with biblical culture and customs. As Sproul has written:

Unless we maintain that the Bible fell down from heaven on a parachute, inscribed by a celestial pen in a peculiar heavenly language uniquely suited as a vehicle for a divine revelation, or that the Bible was dictated directly and immediately by God without reference to any local custom, style or perspective, we are going to have to face the cultural gap. That is, the Bible reflects the culture of its day.[4]

What Do We Mean by Culture?

Webster defines "culture" as "the total pattern of human behavior [that includes] thought, speech, action, and artifacts," and as "the customary beliefs, social forms, and material traits . . . of a racial, religious, or social group." Thus culture includes what people *think* and believe, *say, do,* and *make.* This includes their beliefs, forms of communication, customs and practices, and material objects such as tools, dwellings, weapons, and so forth. An individual's culture includes several spheres of relationships and influences—his interpersonal relations with other individuals and groups, his role in his family, his social class, and the nation or government of which he is a part. Religion, politics, warfare, law, agriculture, architecture, business, economics, and the geography of where one lives and travels, what he and others have written and read, what he wears and the language(s) he speaks—all these leave their mark on how he lives, and if he is an author of a Bible book, on what he wrote.

When a missionary goes to a foreign land, he must know what the people in that culture think, believe, say, do, and make. He must understand their culture in order to comprehend them and thus communicate properly with them. If you have traveled to a foreign country, you have no doubt experienced some degree of "culture shock." This means you were jolted by the unfamiliar scenes and practices of the people in that nation. As you became more familiar with their unusual ways, the impact of the shock declined.

When we go to the Scriptures, it is as if we are entering a foreign land. Just as we may be puzzled by the way people do things in other countries, so we may be puzzled by what we read in the Bible. Therefore it is important to know what the people in the Bible thought, believed, said, did, and made. To the extent we do this we are then able to comprehend it better and communicate it more accurately. If we fail to give attention to these matters of culture, then we may be guilty of eisegesis, reading into the Bible our Western 20th-century ideas. "Context-concern forces us away from our private meanings back into the . . . framework of the author."[5]

In various countries today it is important to know local customs. In England automobiles are driven on the left side of the road.
If you forget that custom, you are definitely in trouble! As we read
much of the Bible, we "see" foreign customs. To interpret God's
Word properly, then, we must understand what those customs were
and what they meant. Attention to cultural studies in the Bible

> enables us to know the original, literal, socially designated
> meaning of the word, phrase, or a custom. . . . "literal interpre-
> tation" is crippled without the help of cultural studies. Again
> like biblical history, cultural matters are not niceties we may
> search out if we have the time but which we may ignore under
> the pressure of time and circumstances. They are indispensable
> for the accurate understanding of Holy Scripture.[6]

How Do Various Cultural Customs Affect the Interpretation of Certain Passages?

The four categories of culture—thoughts (and beliefs), speech, action, and artifacts—often overlap. What one thinks influences what
he does, and what he does or makes relates to what he believes, and
so forth. Another way to view various aspects of culture is to group
them in 11 categories: political, religious, economic, legal, agricultural, architectural, clothing, domestic, geographical, military, and
social.
     The following are examples of Bible passages whose interpre-
tations are affected by a knowledge of some aspects of the cultural
context.

Political (including national, international, and civil)
1. Why did King Belshazzar offer the third position in the Babylonian government to Daniel and not the second position? (Dan. 5:7,
16) This is because, as we know from secular history sources, Belshazzar was actually the second in command. His father Nabonidus
was out of the country for an extended period of time.
     2. Why did Paul refer in Philippians 3:20 to his readers'
citizenship in heaven? The city of Philippi was a colony of Rome.
The people living in Philippi were actually not citizens of Rome, but
the Roman Emperor Octavius Augustus granted the Philippians
"Italic rights," that is, he gave them the same privileges as if their
land was in fact in Italy. Knowing this fact, Paul wrote of an even

greater citizenship for the Christians in Philippi, namely, their citizenship in heaven. This would have had special meaning to the initial readers of this epistle.

3. Why did Jonah not want to go to the city of Nineveh? Secular sources inform us that the Ninevites were atrocious in the way they treated their enemies. They beheaded the leaders of peoples they conquered and piled up those heads. They sometimes placed a captive leader in a cage, treating him like an animal. Often they impaled their captives, thus giving them an agonizingly painful death. Other times they stretched out the legs and arms of a captive and skinned him alive. No wonder Jonah did not want to preach a message of repentance to the Ninevites! He felt they deserved judgment for their atrocities.

4. Why was Edom at such odds against Judah throughout its history? This may be puzzling to Bible readers, unless they remember the conflict between the twins Jacob and Esau. That conflict extended to their descendants. The nation Judah descended from Jacob, and the Edomites descended from Esau. This explains why Obadiah four times referred to the mountains of Edom as "the mountains of Esau" (Obad. 8-9, 19, 21).

5. Why did Boaz go to the city gate to talk with the town elders about Naomi's land? (Ruth 4:1) The city gate was the place where legal business was conducted and court cases were heard (Deut. 21:18-21; 22:13-15; Josh. 20:4; Job 29:7).

6. What did Jesus mean when He said, "If anyone would come after Me, he must deny himself and take up his cross daily and follow Me"? As we know from Jesus' own death, a person who carried his cross on the way to execution was considered a criminal. So to take up one's cross was to follow Jesus even to the point of death. Obviously then it did not mean putting up with hardships or unpleasant people or circumstances.

Religious

1. Why did Moses give the strange command, "Do not cook a young goat in its mother's milk"? (Ex. 23:19; 34:26; Deut. 14:21) This practice is referred to in writings discovered in the ancient city of Ugarit, near modern-day Ras Shamra in Lebanon. According to this archeological discovery, this practice was part of a Canaanite ritual. Apparently then God did not want the Israelites to participate in any religious practice of the Canaanites. An additional reason may be that God did not want the Israelites to confuse a substance that

sustains life (milk) with a process associated with its death (cooking). As Philo, a first-century Jewish philosopher, wrote, it is "grossly improper that the substance which fed the living animal should be used to season or flavor it after its death."[7]

2. Why did God bring on Egypt the 10 plagues? That is, why did He inflict those specific plagues on Egypt rather than other plagues? The answer seems to be that these were considered as polemics or acts that argued against the validity of the Egyptian gods and goddesses. In the plagues God was attacking and showing up the inadequacies and thus the falsehood of the Egyptian gods and goddesses. The following chart lists the gods being attacked by the plagues. These would have a great impact on the Egyptians. For instance the Egyptians believed that several gods and goddesses guarded the Nile River. But when God turned the Nile into blood, it showed their inability to fulfill the function assigned to them by the Egyptians. Why would livestock die (in the fifth plague) if the Egyptian god Hathor, with a cowhead, protected the cows, and why would livestock die in the presence of the Egyptian cow god Apis, a symbol of fertility? This plague was designed to show that Hathor and Apis were false gods. In the seventh plague, hail destroyed crops, showing that several goddesses and gods were unable to control the storms in the sky and prevent crop failure. These included the sky goddess Nut; Osiris, the god of crop fertility; and Set, the god of storms. In the tenth plague one of the leading goddesses, Isis, who supposedly protected children, was incapable of preventing the death of the firstborn child in each Egyptian home. Knowing these facts adds immensely to our understanding of the plagues.

3. Why did Elijah suggest Mount Carmel as the site of his contest with 450 Baal prophets? Followers of Baal believed Mount Carmel was a dwelling place of their god. So Elijah was letting them "play" on their "home field." If Baal could not bring lightning to a sacrifice in his home territory, his weakness would be evident. Also interestingly, the Canaanites viewed Baal as the god of rain, lightning, fire, and storms. Since a drought had existed for three and a half years before this dramatic event, obviously Baal was incapable of providing rain. His inadequacy was also demonstrated in that he could not cause the sacrifice to be consumed with fire.

4. Why did Paul write in Colossians 2:3 that Christ is the mystery of God "in whom are hidden all the treasures of wisdom and knowledge," and in verse 9 that "in Christ all the fullness of Deity lives in bodily form"? Paul stressed these facts about Christ because

The Plagues and the Gods and Goddesses of Egypt

Plagues	References	Possible Egyptian Gods and Goddesses of Egypt Attacked by the Plagues*
1. Nile turned to blood	Exodus 7:14-25	Hapi (also called Apis), the bull god, god of the Nile; Isis, goddess of the Nile; Khnum, ram god, guardian of the Nile; and others
2. Frogs	8:1-15	Heqet, goddess of birth, with a frog head
3. Gnats	8:16-19	Set, god of the desert
4. Flies	8:20-32	Re, a sun god; or the god Uatchit, possibly represented by the fly
5. Death of livestock	9:1-7	Hathor, goddess with a cow head; Apis, the bull god, symbol of fertility
6. Boils	9:8-12	Sekhmet, goddess with power over disease; Sunu, the pestilence god; Isis, goddess of healing
7. Hail	9:13-35	Nut, the sky goddess; Osiris, god of crops and fertility; Set, god of storms
8. Locusts	10:1-20	Nut, the sky goddess; Osiris, god of crops and fertility
9. Darkness	10:21-29	Re, the sun god; Horus, a sun god; Nut, a sky goddess; Hathor, a sky goddess
10. Death of the firstborn	11:1–12:30	Min, god of reproduction; Heqet, goddess who attended women at childbirth; Isis, goddess who protected children; Pharaoh's firstborn son, a god

*Some gods and goddesses had more than one function or area of responsibility. Also in ancient Egyptian religion many of the gods and goddesses who were worshiped in one city or location and/or at one period of time were believed to have assimilated the gods and goddesses of other areas and time periods. Their religion was thus often complex and at times even contradictory.

Sources: *Encyclopaedia Brittanica,* under the word "Egypt"; Lionel Casson, *Ancient Egypt* (New York: Time-Life Books, 1965); Pierre Montet, *Egypt and the Bible* (Philadelphia: Fortress Press, 1968).

From *The Bible Knowledge Commentary,* Old Testament (Victor Books, 1985), p. 120.

the false teachers in Colosse were teaching that Christ is only partly God. Paul's statements then are a direct refutation of that false view.

5. What was the point of meat being sacrificed to idols, which Paul discussed in 1 Corinthians 8? No one today sits down to a meal in the home of a guest and asks if the meat had been sacrificed to idols. Obviously this custom pertained to a cultural setting different from today. The point is that people in Corinth would buy meat in the marketplace, offer some of it to pagan idols in one of several temples, and then take the rest of it home for dinner. Therefore some Christians felt that eating such meat involved them in idol worship.

6. Why did the Herodians, Sadducees, and a scribe ask the questions they asked of Jesus in Mark 12:13-28? The questions related to their separate occupations and beliefs. The Herodians were supported by Herod and the Romans, and so they debated with Jesus about paying taxes to a foreign power (v. 14). The Sadducees did not believe in resurrection, and so they sought to silence their opponent by a hypothetical question about a woman who had seven husbands (v. 23). The Jewish scribes were concerned about Old Testament commandments and so one of them asked Him which commandment was the most important (v. 28).

Economic

1. In Job 22:6 why did Eliphaz accuse Job of demanding "security from your brothers for no reason"? In Old Testament times this practice was considered a despicable crime. If an individual owed someone some money but was unable to pay, the debtor would give his coat to the creditor as a pledge or guarantee of forthcoming payment. However, the creditor was to return the coat at night so that the person, presumably caring for sheep out in the cold at night, would have his coat for a blanket. To take a pledge from someone for no reason was sinful. Job was not guilty of this action, as he explained later (31:19-22).

2. Why did Elimelech's closest relative give his sandal to Boaz? (Ruth 4:8, 17) According to the Nuzi tablets, discovered in present-day Iraq, in excavations from 1925 to 1931, such an action symbolized releasing one's right to land he walked on. This was done when a sale of land was completed.

Legal

1. In 2 Kings 2:9 when Elisha said to Elijah, "Let me inherit a double portion of your spirit," was he asking for twice as much

spiritual power as Elijah had? No, he was stating that he wanted to be his heir in the sense of being his successor. According to Deuteronomy 21:17 the firstborn in a family was to receive a double share of his father's estate.

2. Does "Firstborn over all creation" in Colossians 1:15 mean that Christ was created? No, this means that He is the Heir of all creation (Heb. 1:2), much as a firstborn son had a special place of honor and privilege in a family. The Greek word for firstborn is *prōtotokos*. Had Paul intended to convey the idea that Jesus was the first created being, he would have used a different Greek word, *prōtoktisis*. But that Greek word is never used of Jesus.

Agricultural

1. What is so unusual about Samuel calling on the Lord for rain at the time of the wheat harvest in 1 Samuel 12:17? The wheat harvest took place in May or June. This was soon after the six-month dry season started, extending from April through October. If rain were to come in the dry season, this would obviously show the Lord's unusual working.

2. Why does Psalm 1:4 compare the wicked to chaff? This was to depict that the wicked have no security. When farmers winnow wheat, the chaff, light in weight, blows away. No farmer tries to retain and use the chaff because it is useless. The wicked, like the chaff, have no security and are worthless.

3. Why did Amos call the women of Bethel "cows of Bashan" in Amos 4:1? The cows in Bashan, a fertile area northeast of the Sea of Galilee, were known for being fat. Like these cows, the women of Bethel were wealthy and lazy, doing little besides sitting around eating and drinking.

4. Why did the Lord say to Job in Job 39:1, "Do you know when the mountain goats give birth?" The goat referred to is probably the Ibex, which hides in the mountains when it gives birth to its young. Naturalists have sought to observe the birthing of this animal but have been largely unsuccessful. They have seen the Ibexes copulating or giving birth to their young in the mountains of Judea only 4 times in 30 years.[8] God, of course, was pointing up Job's ignorance of much of what goes on in the world of nature.

5. In Matthew 13:31-32 did Jesus make an error when He said the mustard seed is the smallest? Some people answer yes to this question because as they point out, the orchid seed, not the mustard seed, is the smallest of all seeds. Jesus, however, referred to the

mustard tree as a *garden plant* and in His day the mustard seed was in fact the smallest garden-variety seed in Palestine. Obviously no orchid seeds were in Palestine at that time. Mustard seed is so small that approximately 750 seeds are needed to weigh a mere gram (1/28 of an ounce). This means that approximately 21,000 seeds would be needed to weigh 1 ounce. And yet, given this unusual small size, the mustard plant can grow to a height of 12 to 15 feet in one year!

6. In Luke 13:32 did Jesus call Herod a fox because He meant Herod was sly and cunning? No, a fox in those days was considered a treacherous animal, and so Jesus was suggesting that Herod was known for his treachery.

7. Why did Jesus denounce a fig tree for having no fruit when it was not even the season for figs? (Mark 11:12-14) In March fig trees in Israel normally produce small buds followed by large green leaves in April. The small buds were edible "fruit." The time when Jesus "cursed" the fig tree was the Passover, that is, April. Since the tree had no buds it would bear no fruit that year. But "the season for figs" was late May and June, when the normal crops of figs ripened. Jesus' denouncing of the tree symbolized Israel's absence of spiritual vitality (like the absence of the buds) in spite of her outward religiosity (like the green leaves).

Architectural

1. How could Rahab have her house on a wall? (Josh. 2:15) The walls in Jericho were double walls with space between where dirt was built up so that houses could be built between them and yet be near the top of the walls.[9]

2. How could four men let a paralytic man down through a roof? (Mark 2:1-12) Most houses in the Western world are built with slanted roofs, but in Bible times roofs were flat and often were made of tiles. Therefore it would be no problem for these men to stand on the roof, remove some of the tiles, and let the man down.

3. Why did the disciples meet in an upper room? (Acts 1:13) This is because rooms on an upper level were often larger than the rooms below. The upper room would therefore more comfortably accommodate the 11 disciples.

Clothing

1. What is meant by the clause, "scoop fire into his lap"? (Prov. 6:27) The word for lap may refer to a fold in a person's garment

used much like a pocket for carrying things.

2. What is meant by the command, "Gird up your loins" in Job 38:3; 40:7; and 1 Peter 1:13? (NASB) When a man ran, worked, or was in battle, he would tuck his robe under a wide sash at his waist so that he could move about more easily. The command thus means to be alert and capable of responding quickly.

Domestic

1. What is meant in Hosea 7:8, "Ephraim is a flat cake not turned over"? Sometimes a flat cake would get overcooked on one side if it were not turned over. This seems to be Hosea's way of saying that Ephraim was imbalanced, giving too much attention to some things and inadequate attention to others.

2. Was it not rude for John at the Last Supper to be leaning on Jesus? (John 13:23) No, they were seated on couches rather than in chairs when they ate, and therefore in that culture for someone to lean back against another was not considered rude.

3. Why did James say to anoint a sick person with oil? (James 5:14) In Greek two words are used for rubbing or anointing. The first is *chriō*, which means to anoint in a ritual. This is not the word James used. The word in James 5:14 is *aleiphō*, which means to rub with oil. What James was referring to, then, was not a ritual. Instead it was a refreshing and encouraging act for an ill or discouraged person. (*Aleiphō* is also used in Matt. 6:17 with reference to rubbing oil on one's own head [to refresh himself] and in Luke 7:46, with reference to the sinful woman rubbing perfume on Jesus' feet.)

4. Why did the man in Luke 9:59 say he wanted to go bury his father before he could follow Jesus? He did not mean that his father had just died. Instead he meant he felt obligated to wait until his father died even if it meant several years, probably so that he would then receive his father's inheritance. This explains the man's reluctance to follow Jesus.

5. Why did Job say, "Why were there knees to receive me"? (Job 3:12) A newborn child was placed on its grandfather's knees as a symbol that the child was in his line (Gen. 48:12; 50:23). In grief, Job was questioning why he was even born.

6. Why were the five virgins foolish for having taken lamps but no extra oil? (Matt. 25:1-13) The reason is that a marriage ritual could last as long as three hours and so the oil could have been used up from their lamps. The five wise virgins, however, "took oil in jars . . . with their lamps" (v. 4), thus showing their preparedness.

7. Why did the Lord refer to grass being thrown into the fire? (Matt. 6:30) Earthen ovens, on which thin pancake-like bread was baked, were heated by burning dry grass.

Geographical

1. Why did Jesus have to "go through Samaria"? (John 4:4) Since the Jews did not associate with Samaritans (v. 9), the Jews normally went around Samaria when going from Judea in the south to the area north of Samaria. They would take a highway near the Jordan River or the Mediterranean Sea. Jesus, however, went directly through the province of Samaria to the town of Sychar in order to meet the woman whom He in His omniscience knew would be there.

2. Why did David escape to En Gedi? (1 Sam. 23:29) He knew that because of the difficult terrain on the way to En Gedi, south of Jericho and west of the Dead Sea, it would be hard for Saul to follow him there. Also caves were there and this too would make it difficult for Saul to find him. Furthermore a cool, refreshing waterfall is there. These factors made it a logical place for David's escape.

3. Why did the message to the Laodicean church in Revelation 3:16 say that the people in the church "were lukewarm — neither hot nor cold"? This statement reflected the fact that the people in that local assembly were spiritually like the water in their city. Water was channeled to Laodicea in pipes, six miles from Heirapolis. When the water left the hot springs in Heirapolis it obviously was hot, but by the time it reached Laodicea it was lukewarm.

4. Why did Jesus speak of a man going "down" from Jerusalem to Jericho when Jericho is located northeast of Jerusalem? (Luke 10:30) The elevation drop in the 14 miles from Jerusalem to Jericho is more than 2,000 feet. Obviously going from Jerusalem to Jericho then was to go down in elevation.

Military

1. Why did Habakkuk say that the Babylonians "heap up rubble to capture [cities]"? (Hab. 1:10, NASB) This does not suggest that they were collecting trash. Instead this points to the building of earthen ramps against a city wall. Since many cities were built high on hills, the only way an enemy could get to the city was to pile up dirt and debris against the hill to lower the elevation grade.

2. Why did Paul say in 2 Corinthians 2:14 that God "always

leads us in triumphal procession in Christ"? In the Roman Empire, a general, returning home from a victorious battle, would march through the streets of his hometown with his own soldiers behind him, followed by his captives. Similarly God is leading us in a triumphal procession spiritually by our being "in Christ."

Social

1. Why did people in Bible times sometimes throw dust on their heads? (Job 2:12; Lam. 2:10; Ezek. 27:30; Rev. 18:19) They were demonstrating that they felt so deeply grieved that it was as if they were in the grave, under the dirt.

2. Why did God say in Malachi 1:2-3, "I have loved Jacob, but Esau I have hated"? Two explanations are possible. One is that in the ancient Near East a person would use the word *love* in his will to designate the person chosen to inherit his estate, and he would use the word *hate* to mean a legal rejection of any rival claim. (In a similar fashion to despise or hate wisdom, as in Prov. 1:7, is to reject it.) Another explanation is that this is a form of comparison, in which the Lord was saying He loved Jacob more than He loved Esau. A parallel to this is seen in Genesis 29:30-31 in which Jacob is said to have loved Rachel and not to have loved (i.e., to have hated) Leah.

3. Why did Joseph shave before he went to see Pharaoh? (Gen. 41:14) Did not the Hebrews normally wear beards? The Egyptian custom was not to wear beards, so Joseph was simply following the custom of that country.

4. What is the significance of a "covenant of salt"? (Num. 18:19; 2 Chron. 13:5) How the salt was used in making such a covenant is not known, but the fact that it was a preservative seems to suggest that the parties desired that their friendship continue.

5. Why did Jesus tell the disciples not to greet anyone on the road? (Luke 10:4) Rather than suggesting an antisocial attitude, Jesus was suggesting that they not be delayed in their mission. Greetings would often take a long period of time in which the people would bow several times, repeat their greetings, and then discuss the affairs of the day.

In summary it is apparent that ignorance of these customs could result in misunderstanding the meaning of the passages. The Bible student confronts many other customs as he reads the Bible. It is wise, therefore, to be alert to unusual customs referred to and to determine what the passages meant to the people in those original settings.

Commentaries often help explain these customs. Helpful books on Bible customs are William L. Coleman, *Today's Handbook of Bible Times & Customs* (Minneapolis: Bethany House Publishers, 1984); Madeline S. and J. Lane Miller, *Harper's Encyclopedia of Bible Life,* rev. ed. (San Francisco: Harper and Row, Publishers, 1978); James I. Packer, Merrill C. Tenney, and William White, Jr., eds., *The Bible Almanac* (Nashville: Thomas Nelson Publishers, 1980); J.A. Thompson, *Handbook of Life in Bible Times* (Downers Grove, Ill.: InterVarsity Press, 1986); and Fred H. Wight, *The New Manners and Customs of Bible Times,* rev. Ralph Gower (Chicago: Moody Press, 1986).

To What Extent Are Passages of the Bible Limited by the Culture?

One of the most important issues Bible interpreters face is the question of culturally conditioned Bible passages. That is, are some passages of the Bible limited to that day by the cultural setting and therefore not transferable to our culture, or is everything we read in the Scriptures normative for today? To what extent is the relevance of the Bible limited by the cultural setting? If some passages are limited in this way, then how do we determine which ones are transferable to our culture and which ones are not?

Some argue, for example, that since we no longer have slaves and masters and the command to slaves in Ephesians 6:5 is irrelevant for today, then in the same context the command for wives to submit to their husbands is also equally irrelevant and nonbinding for today. This view, however, overlooks the fact that while slavery may not exist today as it did in Bible times, there may be some way in which the principle behind that command can be applied to employer-employee relations. Furthermore nowhere in the Bible are the commands for wives to submit to their husbands rescinded. Two other questions this issue raises are whether the command in 1 Timothy 2:12 for women not to teach men is culturally limited, and whether the words in the Bible about homosexual conduct were limited to Bible times.

The issue of cultural relevance is an important one because of the two tasks of the interpreter: to determine what the text meant to its immediate readers in that cultural setting, and to determine what the text means to us now in our context.

It should be immediately evident that all practices in the

Bible are not transferable to the present day. If that were true, then when you buy a house, the former owner should take off one of his sandals and give it to you, the buyer, following the practice in Ruth 4:8.

To illustrate the problem, read each of the following items and circle the "P" (for permanent) or the "T" (for temporary) after each sentence.[10]

1.   Greet one another with a holy kiss (Rom. 16:16).   P   T
2.   Abstain from meat that has been sacrificed to idols
     (Acts 15:29).   P   T
3.   Be baptized (Acts 2:38).   P   T
4.   Wash one another's feet (John 13:14).   P   T
5.   Extend the right hand of fellowship (Gal. 2:9).   P   T
6.   Ordain by the "laying on of hands" (Acts 13:3).   P   T
7.   Prohibit women from speaking in a church assembly
     (1 Cor. 14:34).   P   T
8.   Have fixed hours of prayer (Acts 3:1).   P   T
9.   Sing songs, hymns, and spiritual songs (Col. 3:16).   P   T
10. Abstain from eating blood (Acts 15:29).   P   T
11. Slaves should obey their earthly masters (Eph. 6:5). P   T
12. Observe the Lord's Supper (1 Cor. 11:24).   P   T
13. Do not make any oaths (James 5:12).   P   T
14. Anoint the sick with oil (James 5:14).   P   T
15. Permit no woman to teach men (1 Tim. 2:12).   P   T
16. Preach two by two (Mark 6:7).   P   T
17. Go into Jewish synagogues to preach (Acts 14:1).   P   T
18. Eat what is set before you asking no questions of con-
     science (1 Cor. 10:27).   P   T
19. Prohibit women from wearing braided hair, gold, or
     pearls (1 Tim. 2:9).   P   T
20. Abstain from fornication (Acts 15:29).   P   T
21. Do not seek marriage (1 Cor. 7:26).   P   T
22. Be circumcised (Acts 15:5).   P   T
23. Women should pray with their heads covered (1 Cor.
     11:5).   P   T
24. Drink Communion from a single cup (Mark 14:23).   P   T
25. Take formal religious vows (Acts 18:18).   P   T
26. Avoid praying in public (Matt. 6:5-6).   P   T
27. Speak in tongues and prophesy (1 Cor. 14:5).   P   T
28. Meet in homes for church (Col. 4:15).   P   T

29.	Work with your hands (1 Thes. 4:11).	P T
30.	Lift your hands when praying (1 Tim. 2:8).	P T
31.	Give to those who beg from you (Matt. 5:42).	P T
32.	Pray before meals (Luke 24:30).	P̸ T
33.	Support no widow under 60 years old (1 Tim. 5:9).	P T
34.	Say "Amen" at the end of prayers (1 Cor. 14:16).	P T
35.	Fast in connection with ordination (Acts 13:3).	P T
36.	Wear sandals but not an extra tunic (Mark 6:9).	P T .
37.	Wives should submit to their husbands (Col. 3:18).	P T
38.	Show no favoritism to the rich (James 2:1-7).	P T
39.	Use unleavened bread for Communion (Luke 22:13, 19).	P T
40.	Cast lots for church officers (Acts 1:26).	P T
41.	Owe no man anything (Rom. 13:8).	P T
42.	Have seven deacons in the church (Acts 6:3).	P T
43.	Do not eat meat from animals killed by strangulation (Acts 15:29).	P T
44.	Allow no one to eat if he will not work (2 Thes. 3:10).	P T
45.	Give up personal property (Acts 2:44-45).	P T
46.	Have self-employed clergy (2 Thes. 3:7-8).	P T
47.	Take collections in church for the poor (1 Cor. 16:1).	P T
48.	Men should not have long hair (1 Cor. 11:14).	P T

These illustrate the frequency with which Bible students confront the problem of cultural relevance. Readers will differ in the way they answer these questions. How can we determine which ones should be considered permanent and thus relevant for us today and which ones should be considered temporary and cultural? That is, what guidelines can be used to decide one's answers?

The following principles may be useful in determining which cultural practices and situations, commands, and precepts in the Bible are transferable to our culture and which ones are nontransferable.

1. *Some situations, commands, or principles are repeatable, continuous, or not revoked, and/or pertain to moral and theological subjects, and/or are repeated elsewhere in Scripture, and therefore are permanent and transferable to us.* We need to ask if the Scriptures treat the situation, command, or principle as normative. Sometimes a reason is given for a command. Capital punishment is considered a permanent command because, after being given in Genesis 9:6, it is nowhere revoked, and the reason given in that verse is that man is

made in God's image. The command in Proverbs 3:5-6 to trust the Lord is certainly repeated, though stated in various ways throughout Scripture. The command to believers to put on the armor of God (Eph. 6:10-19) is in no way revoked. Nor has God withdrawn the command for humility, as stated in 1 Peter 5:6. The command for men to pray with hearts of purity is universal as suggested by the words "men everywhere" (1 Tim. 2:8).

A Nazarite was to let his hair grow as a sign of his dedication to the Lord (Jud. 13:5; 1 Sam. 1:11). But in the New Testament long hair for any man is considered dishonorable (1 Cor. 11:14). The New Testament has thus revoked the Nazarite practice, which was part of the Old Testament Mosaic Law. As McQuilkin has stated, "All Scripture should be received as normative for every person in all societies of all time unless the Bible itself limits the audience."[11] "When the Bible clearly gives a command and nowhere else nullifies that command, it must be accepted as the revealed will of God and a mandate to mold our personal and group behavior (our 'culture') in the form of this instruction."[12] This means that the Bible is its own authority, including the authority to set limits on which practices are culture-bound and which ones are not. One way we can determine which commands are to be repeated is by examining whether the command or situation is paralleled in Scripture elsewhere.

2. *Some situations, commands, or principles pertain to an individual's specific nonrepeatable circumstances, and/or nonmoral or nontheological subjects, and/or have been revoked, and are therefore not transferable to today.* Paul's instructions to Timothy in 2 Timothy 4:11-13 to bring his cloak and scrolls is obviously limited to Paul's situation. Nowhere are Christian fathers commanded to sacrifice their sons as Abraham was told to do (Gen. 22:1-19); that command was only for that occasion in the patriarch's life.

Hebrews 7:12 and 10:1 indicate that the Aaronic priesthood and in fact the entire Mosaic Law have been done away.

In the Old Testament, incest was punished by stoning (Lev. 20:11), but in the New Testament incest is treated by excommunication (1 Cor. 5:1-5).

3. *Some situations or commands pertain to cultural settings that are only partially similar to ours and in which only the principles are transferable.* Five times the New Testament refers to greeting others with a holy kiss (Rom. 16:16; 1 Cor. 16:20; 2 Cor. 13:12; 1 Thes. 5:26; 1 Peter 5:14). Since that was the normal form of greeting in that day, and since that is not the normal form of greeting in our

Western culture, it follows that this practice need not be carried over to today. Instead the principle behind it should be followed, namely, to express friendliness and love to others. In Latin America the same principle is expressed by a hug rather than a kiss, and in America a handshake is sometimes accompanied by a hug or a pat on the back.

Another example is Deuteronomy 6:4-9. Certainly parents are to love the Lord and to teach His commandments to their children at various times. However, the command in verse 9 to "write them on the doorframes of your houses and on your gates" seems to have a cultural setting similar but not identical to today. Perhaps the modern-day counterpart is having Bible verses on plaques hung on the wall. Obviously the principle still holds true that parents should keep the Scriptures before their children.

Though meat we purchase has not been sacrificed to idols, the principle of 1 Corinthians 8 holds true, namely, that we ought not be involved in any practice that would be a stumbling block to weak believers.

4. *Some situations or commands pertain to cultural settings with no similarities but in which the principles are transferable.* A sinful woman expressed her love to Jesus by pouring perfume from an alabaster jar on Jesus' head (Matt. 26:7-8). There is obviously no way in which we can do this to Jesus now, but the principle holds that we can express our love to Him sacrificially. When Moses stood in God's presence on holy ground, he removed the sandals from his feet (Ex. 3:5). Does this mean that a person today must remove his shoes when he is in God's presence?

Regarding the third and fourth principles above, Virkler remarks that, "Behavior that has a certain meaning in one culture may have a totally different significance in another culture."[13]

A frequently discussed passage pertaining to the question of "culturally conditioned" biblical material is 1 Corinthians 11:2-16. Does this passage refer to a woman's hair as a covering or to a separate head covering over the hair? It seems to mean the latter, based on the statements in verses 4-7. The head covering is more likely a shawl, which extended from the back over the head something like a parka, rather than a veil over the face. Archeologists have uncovered sketches and sculptures of this kind of head covering in the Greco-Roman world. In first-century Judaism and in the Greco-Roman world, wearing a head covering in public was in fact a sign of a woman's submission to her husband. Not to wear it was an indication of insubordination or rebellion. This is mentioned in

3 Maccabees 36 and in the writings of Plutarch, a Roman statesman. Assuming that the head covering is a shawl, there are four options in interpreting how the passage relates, if at all, to today.

One view is that women today should wear shawls in church as a sign of their submissiveness to their husbands. If this view is held, then principle 1 above is being followed—the view that the cultural situation and the principle behind it are both repeatable and relevant for today.

A second view is that the passage has no relevance at all for women today. This view illustrates the second principle above, namely, that neither the cultural situation nor the principle behind it are repeatable. According to this view, women may disregard these verses altogether as having application to them today because the cultural situation has no correspondence to our culture today.

Other Bible interpreters hold a third view—that women today should wear hats in church as a sign of their submission to their husbands. Approaching the passage in this way, they are following the third principle, which sees the situation in Corinth as being partially similar to our culture today, and that the principle is transferable and permanent. The thought is that since women today normally do not wear shawls in praying, they should wear something comparable such as hats.

A fourth view is that women today need not wear hats in church, but that they are to be submissive to their husbands. This corresponds with the fourth principle above. The cultural setting is seen as being entirely different, but the principle is transferable. In the Corinthian culture, a woman's shawl was a symbol of her husband's authority and she was thereby showing that she was placing herself under that authority. In Corinth, sacred prostitutes, that is, those associated with pagan temples, did not wear shawls. It is also noteworthy that Jewish women did not wear a head covering until they were married. There was no need to do so since they were not under the authority of a husband. Yet the principle of submission seems to be permanent and transferable to all present-day cultures since Paul referred to Creation (1 Cor. 11:9) and the presence of the angels (v. 10). I favor the fourth view in light of the significance of the shawl in the New Testament Age. Also when women today wear hats to church, are they consciously depicting their being under their husband's authority or are they simply being fashionable? (On the meaning of the presence of the angels, see *The Bible Knowledge Commentary*, New Testament, p. 529.)

Want an interesting exercise? Consider the subject of foot-washing. This is mentioned 19 times in the Bible — Genesis 18:4; 19:2; 24:32; 43:24; Exodus 30:19; 40:31; Judges 19:21; 1 Samuel 25:41; 2 Samuel 11:8; Song of Songs 5:3; Luke 7:44; John 13:5-6, 8-10, 12, 14; and 1 Timothy 5:10. Look up these verses and see if you can determine the way in which this cultural practice was carried out and what it meant in Old and New Testament times. Then look at the four principles discussed earlier and determine which one applies to foot-washing. Think of these questions as you study this issue: Is foot-washing needed today as it was in biblical times? Why or why not? Do the Scriptures command us to practice foot-washing as an ordinance in the church? Why or why not? To whom are Jesus' words in John 13:15 being addressed? Are those words to be followed by believers today? Why or why not? What reasons for the practice with the disciples did Jesus give in John 13? See particularly verses 1, 7, 12, and 16.

Guidelines for Determining Whether Bible Practices Are Culture-bound or Transcultural

Sometimes it is difficult to determine whether principle 3 or 4 discussed earlier should be followed in determining the question of cultural versus transcultural practices. Perhaps the following steps may be helpful.

First, see if the behavior in the biblical culture means something different in our culture. This would seem to be the case with shawls and the holy kiss. Wearing a shawl in church today and greeting others with kisses have meanings today that differ from their initial significance in Bible times. Related to this step is determining if the practice is missing entirely from our culture. Foot-washing is considered by many to be an example of this.

Second, if the behavior does mean something different in our culture, then determine the timeless principle expressed in that practice.

Third, determine how the principle can be expressed in a cultural equivalent. Paul wrote in 1 Timothy 2:1-2 that we are to pray for kings. But what about believers who live in countries, such as in the United States, that have no kings? Is this passage irrelevant to them? It would seem that the cultural setting is at least partially similar in that believers could follow the principle by praying for governmental leaders, whether they are presidents or premiers. James wrote that a Christian was discriminating and sinning if he gave his seat in a church gathering to a wealthy Christian and told a poor believer to stand or sit on the floor (James 2:1-4). Does that mean today that rich parishioners should be seated on the floors of churches so that the poor may be seated on pews? No, this is not a requirement for today because the cultural situation is different. However, the principle of humility remains and Christians ought not discriminate against each other in any way based on their economic status.

Should women today wear shawls on their heads in church? No, because the significance of women wearing shawls in the Greco-Roman world no longer holds true in our culture. The act does not carry the symbolism it once had. But is there a principle here to be followed, and to be expressed in a modern-day cultural equivalent? The principle of subordination (not inferiority!) of the wife to her husband still holds because that truth is stated elsewhere in Scripture (e.g., Eph. 5:22-23; Col. 3:18; 1 Peter 3:1-2). A possible modern cultural parallel, some have suggested, is the wife's wedding ring (and changing her last name to that of her husband) which shows that she is married and thus is under her husband's authority.

Also believers today need not remove their shoes when they come in God's presence in church or in private prayer, but they should express their reverence before the Lord.

Spiritual discernment and careful study of the Scriptures are important in considering the impact of cultural matters on Bible interpretation.

CHAPTER FIVE

Bridging the Grammatical Gap

A hallmark of the Reformation was a return to the historical, grammatical interpretation of Scripture. This was in direct opposition to the approach to the Bible that had been in vogue for hundreds of years—the view that ignored the normal meaning of words in their grammatical sense and let words and sentences mean whatever the readers wanted them to mean.

In the Middle Ages words, phrases, and sentences in the Bible had taken on multiple meanings, losing all sense of objectivity. How, then, the Reformers asked, could the Bible be a clear revelation from God?

They responded that God has conveyed His truth in written form, using words and sentences that are to be understood by man in their normal, plain sense. Therefore the better we understand the grammar of Scripture and the historical setting in which those sentences were first communicated, the better we can understand the truths God intended to convey to us.

The Reformers were seeking to return people to the way the Bible had been treated by the early church fathers, including Clement of Rome, Ignatius, Polycarp, and Irenaeus, and the leaders in the Antiochene School, including Lucian, Diodorus, Theodore of Mopsuestia, John Chrysostom, and Theodoret.

Why Is Grammatical Interpretation Important?

Several factors point to the importance of giving attention to the grammar of Scripture (the meanings of words and sentences and the way they are put together).

The Nature of Inspiration

If we believe the Bible is *verbally* inspired, as discussed in chapter 1, we believe every word of Scripture is important. Some words and sentences may not hold the same degree of importance other words or sentences have in the Bible, but all words and sentences in the Bible serve a purpose. Otherwise why would God have included them?

Only grammatical interpretation fully honors the verbal inspiration of Scripture. If a person does not believe the Bible is verbally inspired, then it is inconsistent or at least strange for him to give much attention to the words of Scripture.

The Goal of Exegesis

The aim of biblical exegesis is to determine what the text of Scripture itself says and means, and not to read something into it. As John Calvin stated, "It is the first business of an interpreter to let his author say what he does, instead of attributing to him what we think he ought to say."

Thoughts are expressed through words, and words are the building blocks of sentences. Therefore to determine God's thoughts we need to study His words and how they are associated in sentences. If we neglect the meanings of words and how they are used, we have no way of knowing whose interpretations are correct. The assertion, "You can make the Bible mean anything you want it to mean," is true only if grammatical interpretation is ignored.

The Problem of Communication

Someone has noted that the average person in America speaks 30,000 words a day in ordinary conversation. That is a lot of talk! The more a person speaks the greater the possibility of his being misunderstood. A speaker or writer can be misunderstood if his hearers or readers do not know exactly what he meant by some word or words. Sometimes in conversation, a person will say to another, "Oh, I thought you meant such and such." Further words given by the speaker help communicate his meaning.

Our task in Bible study is to discover as precisely as possible what God meant by each of the words and sentences He included in the Scriptures. This problem is compounded for many readers because the Bible is written in other languages. How then can we know exactly what the Scriptures mean unless we know Hebrew, Aramaic, and Greek?

Suppose you picked up a German Bible and noticed these words: "Denn also hat Gott die Welt geliebt, dass er seinen eingebornen Sohn gab, auf dass alle, die an ihn glauben, nicht verloren werden, sondern das ewige Leben haben." If you do not know German and you want to know what these words say, you have two choices. One choice is to learn German. The other is to ask someone who knows German to translate these words for you. Either choice will lead you to know that they are John 3:16.

The same holds true for the study of the Bible. We want to get as close to the original as possible in our understanding of the Scriptures. This means, therefore, that we should learn the original languages, or if that is not possible, then we need to rely on others who do know the languages. Bible students, commentators, teachers, and preachers who know Hebrew, Aramaic, and Greek can be useful sources of information in helping us know the meaning of the Scriptures in their original languages.

This is not to suggest that a person cannot know, appreciate, and teach the Bible without knowing those languages. Many capable Bible expositors who have not known Hebrew, Aramaic, or Greek have been greatly used of God in preaching and teaching the Bible. And many people have been greatly blessed in their spiritual lives by studying a translation of the Bible in their own native language without knowing the Bible's original languages. The point, however, is that greater precision is available as one learns the biblical languages. This was the burden of the Reformers: to seek to understand as precisely and accurately as possible what God is communicating to man in His written revelation. For that reason, attention to the principles of grammatical interpretation is extremely important.

What Is Grammatical Interpretation?

When we speak of interpreting the Bible grammatically, we are referring to the process of seeking to determine its meaning by ascertaining four things: (a) the meaning of words (lexicology), (b) the form of words (morphology), (c) the function of words (parts of speech), and (d) the relationships of words (syntax).

In the meaning of words (lexicology), we are concerned with (a) etymology—how words are derived and developed, (b) usage—how words are used by the same and other authors, (c) synonyms and antonyms—how similar and opposite words are used, and (d) context—how words are used in various contexts.

In discussing the form of words (morphology) we are looking at how words are structured and how that affects their meaning. For example the word *eat* means something different from *ate,* though the same letters are used. The word *part* changes meaning when the letter *s* is added to it to make the word *parts.* The function of words (parts of speech) considers what the various forms do. These include attention to subjects, verbs, objects, nouns, and others, as will be discussed later. The relationships of words (syntax) are the way words are related or put together to form phrases, clauses, and sentences.

How Do We Determine the Meaning of Words?

Four factors influence the meaning of a given word: etymology, usage, synonyms and antonyms, and context.

Examine the Etymology of the Words

Etymology refers to the root derivation and development of words. In etymology the aims are (a) to get back to the root meaning of the word and (b) to see how the word developed.

Sometimes the component parts of a compound word help reveal its meaning. This can be seen in the English word "hippopotamus," which is derived from two Greek words—*hippos* for horse and *potamos* for river—and thus this animal is a kind of river horse. The Greek word *ekklēsia,* usually translated "church," comes from *ek* ("out of") and *kalein* ("to call or summon"). Thus it came to refer in the New Testament to those who are called out from the unsaved to form a group of believers. Originally *ekklēsia* referred to an assembly of citizens in a Greek community who were summoned by a town crier for transacting public business.

The Greek word *makrothymia,* translated "patience" or "long-suffering," consists of two Greek words *makros,* which means "long," and *thymia,* which means "feeling." In putting the two words together the letter *s* was dropped and the word means long-feeling, that is, having control of one's feelings for a long period of time. "Patience" is a suitable translation.

In the 18th century Johann Ernesti (1707–1781) warned against following etymology as a reliable guide. He wrote:

> The fluctuating use of words, which prevails in every language, gives rise to frequent changes in their meaning. There are but

few words in any language which always retained [their] primary meaning. Great care therefore is necessary in the interpreter, to guard against rash etymological exegesis; which is often very fallacious.[1]

Sometimes a word in its development takes on an entirely different meaning from what it originally meant. The root derivation of a word is often an unreliable guide for the meaning of a word, because meanings change. For example the word *enthusiasm* in its etymology means "to be possessed by a god." Obviously the derived meaning today differs significantly from its root meaning, in which the two words *in* and *god* were put together. Also the English *good-bye* is a derivation of "God be with you," and yet few people think of its original meaning when they tell someone "good-bye."

The English word *regard* was derived from "guard," but obviously *regard* and *guard* differ substantially in their meaning.[2] The English word *nice* from the Latin *nescius* originally meant "simple" or "ignorant," hardly related to its present-day meaning! As Cotterell and Turner have written, in the 13th century the word *nice* added the meaning of "foolish" or "stupid," in the 14th century, "wanton," and in the 15th, "coy" or "shy." But each of these is now obsolete. Even the 16th-century idea of *nice* as "subtle, precise, minutely accurate" is only occasionally seen today, as in the phrase "a nice distinction."[3] After Christopher Wren completed St. Paul's Cathedral in London, Queen Anne saw it and said, "It is awful, amusing, and artificial." Those words today hardly sound complimentary. But in 17th-century England, her words meant the cathedral was full of awe ("awful"), delightful ("amusing"), and artistic ("artificial"). Over time the meanings of those words have changed extensively.

The Greek word *eirēnē* originally meant peace from war, then it came to mean peace of mind or tranquility, then well-being, and in the New Testament it is often used to refer to a right relationship with God. Obviously then, "the etymology of the word is not a statement about its meaning but about its history."[4]

Sometimes a word means something entirely different from its component parts. The word *broadcast* means something different from its original meaning, which was to sow seed by "casting it abroad." When a person pulls dandelions from his yard, he most likely does not have in mind lion's teeth. And yet that is the original meaning of the French words *dent de lion,* from which we have "dandelion" in English. A butterfly has little relevance to the words *butter* and *fly*, and a pineapple only vaguely resembles a pine and an apple.

A biblical word should not be explained on the basis of its *English* etymology. This is to read back into Scripture what is not there. For example the biblical word *holy* is not derived from the English word *healthy*. Etymologically the Hebrew and Greek words for holy do not mean being spiritually healthy. Nor does the Greek word *dynamis* ("power") mean dynamite. To say that Paul had in mind dynamite when he wrote Romans 1:16, "I am not ashamed of the Gospel, because it is the dynamite of God for the salvation for everyone who believes," is to be guilty of "reverse etymology."[5] Dynamite seems inappropriate for what Paul had in mind because "dynamite blows things up, tears things down, rips out rock, gouges holes, destroys things."[6] Instead *dynamis* means a dynamic, active, living, spiritual force.

Sometimes Bible interpreters note the meaning of a Greek word in classical Greek and then suggest that the same meaning carries over into the New Testament. That procedure, however, can sometimes lead to inaccurate meanings. For example *euangelion* was used in classical Greek in the sense of "reward for good news" given to a messenger. Also the classical writers Socrates and Xenophon used the word to refer to a "sacrifice for a good message," and still later the word came to suggest "the good message." Then in the New Testament it took on the special sense of "the good news of salvation" in Jesus Christ.[7]

Discover the Usage of the Words

As already stated, often the etymology of a word does not help determine its meaning. Therefore we need to determine its current established usage by the writer. This practice is called *usus loquendi* (literally, the use by the one speaking). In other words what was the customary meaning of the word when the writer used it? How he used the word in its context often helps determine its meaning.

This is especially important because a word carries different meanings depending on how it is used. For example the word *left* takes on different meanings in these four sentences: "He left," "He left these," "He went left," "He is left." The verb *run* can refer to many things that move or operate. We say our feet run, noses run, rivers run, machines run, a sore runs, time runs (or runs out or down), a watch runs, a manager runs a business, a woman's hosiery may run, colors run, and papers run stories. A person may run a fever, run into trouble, run up bills, run out of money or patience, run for office, or run over a stick. Each usage connotes a slightly different idea. The word *board* is also used in a variety of ways. As Terry wrote, *board* can refer to a piece of timber, a table on which food is served, food itself (as in paying for room and board), a board of directors (men who gather around a table to transact business), and the deck of a boat (hence the words "on board" or "overboard").[8] Think of the numerous ways the word *break* can be used.

In the New Testament the word *called* is used at least two ways. In the Synoptic Gospels, God's "call" means His invitation, whereas when Paul used the word to refer to God's call, he meant God's act of giving him a title and a commission ("called to be an apostle," Rom. 1:1), or God's work in giving believers salvation (8:28, 30), or God's inviting believers with a strong urging ("called as to a holy life," 2 Tim. 1:9).

The Greek word *pneuma* ("spirit") is derived from *pneō* ("to breathe"), but in the Bible the word *pneuma* only occasionally means breath. It also means wind, attitude, emotions, spiritual nature, inner being (in contrast to the physical body), immaterial beings such as angels or demons, and the Holy Spirit. A study of the word *sarx* ("flesh") reveals that it too has a variety of meanings including humanity (Rom. 3:20, NASB), the human body (2 Cor. 12:7), muscles of the human body (Luke 24:39), or man's sinful nature or disposition (Rom. 8:6-7, 13; Eph. 2:3).

As will be discussed later, the immediate context often, though not always, helps determine the meaning of a word. It is important to note several kinds of usage.

First, note the usage of a word by the same writer in the same book. If the immediate context does not make clear the meaning of a word, it is sometimes helpful to ask, how did the writer use this elsewhere in this same book? In Ephesians 2:20 does the word *prophets* refer to Old Testament prophets or New Testament prophets? As one examines the other ways Paul used *prophets* in Ephesians — in 3:5 and 4:11 — it becomes clear that in those verses he was referring to New Testament prophets. Therefore it is likely that he meant the same thing in 2:20.

Second, note the usage by the same writer in his other books. In studying John's use of *light* and *darkness* in 1 John, it is helpful to note how he uses those words in his Gospel and in the Book of Revelation.

Third, note the usage by other writers in the Bible. Sometimes a writer's use of the word in the immediate context may not reveal its precise meaning, and he may not even use the word elsewhere in the same book or other writings. Therefore it is helpful to examine how the word is used in other Bible books. In seeking to determine the meaning of the Hebrew word 'almâh (whether it means "young woman" or "virgin") in Isaiah 7:14, it is helpful to study the eight other occurrences of that word in the Old Testament (Gen. 24:43; Ex. 2:8; 1 Chron. 15:20; Ps. 68:25; Prov. 30:19; Song 1:3; 6:8; and in the title to Ps. 46).

This is not to suggest, however, that the meaning of a word is the same in all its occurrences. In 2 Peter 3:10 stoicheia means elements, that is, basic components of the universe. In Hebrews 5:12, however, stoicheia means elementary or basic truths, hardly basic components of the physical universe. The same word may take on again a slightly different meaning in Galatians 4:3, 9 and Colossians 2:8, 20.

Fourth, note how the word is used by writers outside the Bible. In the Hebrew Old Testament approximately 1,300 words occur only one time.[9] They are called hapax legomena, meaning, literally, "once spoken." And about 500 words in the Old Testament occur only twice. Therefore the meaning of these words cannot be determined by comparing them with usage elsewhere in the Bible. The way these words are used in other writings outside the Bible can sometimes help us ascertain their meaning. In Proverbs 26:23 the Hebrew word sprg, a hapax legomenon, is rendered "silver dross" in the NASB. Based on the use of the same word in Ugaritic, a language closely related to Hebrew, the NIV translated the word "glaze," which seems to make more sense in the verse. Bible scholars have also found that Arabic and Aramaic usages of words corresponding to Hebrew Old Testament words have sometimes helped us understand their meaning.

The use of words in koinē (common) Greek outside the New Testament sometimes is helpful in ascertaining a New Testament word meaning. For example the word ataktos is translated "disorderly" in 2 Thessalonians 3:6, 11 in the KJV. This is probably because of the influence of this word in classical Greek, where it is used of soldiers who broke rank, and who were thus considered disorderly. However, in the papyri, which are more current with the writing of the New Testament, the word ataktos is used of a boy playing hooky from school. Therefore in the verses cited above the word more likely means "idle," not "disorderly."

Discover the Meanings of Similar Words (Synonyms) and Opposite Words (Antonyms)

Seeing how a word differs from its synonyms can help narrow down the meaning of that word. It is important not to read back into a given word the meaning of its synonyms, but rather to seek to find how the words carry varying shades of meaning. Sometimes these will not always be clear, for synonyms sometimes become almost identical in meaning. However, in Romans 14:13 Paul referred to both a "stumbling block" and an "obstacle." The stumbling block (*skandalon* in Greek) means a serious kind of offense, something causing another person to fall. An "obstacle" (*proskomma*), on the other hand, means a slight offense, something that disturbs another. Paul obviously was stating that he did not want to disturb another believer in either a serious or a minor way.

In Colossians 2:22 *commands* suggests laws to be obeyed and *teachings* (i.e., doctrines) imply truths to be believed.

Seeing how a word differs from its exact or near opposite can assist in determining its meaning. In Romans 8:4-9 does "flesh" (KJV) mean the physical body (in contrast to the human spirit) or does it mean the sinful nature (in contrast to the Holy Spirit)? The answer is found by noting how "flesh" contrasts with the word "spirit." Verses 6, 9, and 11 suggest that "spirit" means the Holy Spirit rather than the human spirit. Therefore "flesh" in verses 4-9 probably means the sinful nature.

In 6:23 "death" means spiritual death, not physical death because it is contrasted to eternal life.

Consider the Context

Considering the context is extremely important for three reasons. First, words, phrases, and clauses may have multiple meanings, as already discussed, and examining how they are used in a given context can help determine which of several meanings is more likely. Second, thoughts are usually expressed by a series of words or sentences, that is, in association, not isolation. "The meaning of any particular element is nearly always controlled by what precedes and what follows."[10] Third, false interpretations often arise from ignoring the context. Psalm 2:8, "Ask of Me, and I will make the nations Your inheritance, the ends of the earth Your possession," is sometimes used by missionaries to speak of anticipated conversions on their mission fields. The preceding verse, however, makes it clear that these words are spoken by God the Father to God the Son.

Several kinds of contexts should be considered in Bible interpretation. First is the *immediate context.* Often the sentence in which a word is used clarifies the meaning. The use of the word *pen* by itself might mean fountain pen or pig pen, but most likely the sentence in which is it used would clarify which is meant.

Cotterell and Turner list seven senses for the Greek word *kosmos,* usually translated "world."

a. The whole created universe, including the earth, the heavens, heavenly bodies, etc.

b. "Earth" as opposed to heaven or the heavens

c. "Mankind," that is, the "world" of people

d. The condition of mortal life; "life in the world"

e. The beings (human and supernatural) in rebellion against God, together with the systems under their control, viewed as opposed to God

f. The system of earthly and social structures (including its joys, possessions, and cares)

g. "Adornment" or "adorning."

Cotterell and Turner then cite the following six verses, pointing out that only one of these senses is viable in each verse and that the immediate context of the sentence itself normally clarifies the meaning.[11]

a. "For God so loved the *kosmos* that He gave His one and only Son, that whoever believes in Him shall not perish but have eternal life" (John 3:16).

b. "Do not love the *kosmos* or anything in the *kosmos.* If anyone loves the *kosmos,* the love of the Father is not in him. For everything in the *kosmos*—the cravings of sinful man, the lust of his eyes, and the boasting of what he has and does—comes not from the Father but from the *kosmos*" (1 John 2:15-16).

c. "Your beauty should not come from outward *kosmos,* such as braided hair and the wearing of gold jewelry and fine clothes" (1 Peter 3:3).

d. "And now, Father, glorify Me in Your presence with the glory I had with You before the *kosmos* began" (John 17:5).

e. "Those who use the things of the *kosmos,* as if not engrossed in them. For this *kosmos* in its present form is passing away" (1 Cor. 7:31).

f. "For we brought nothing into the *kosmos,* and we can take nothing out of it" (1 Tim. 6:7).

For an interesting exercise match one of the seven meanings

of *kosmos* with the usage of that word in each of the six verses. (For Cotterell and Turner's answers see the section "Answers to Exercises" near the end of the book.)

The point here is that as a general rule each occurrence of a word will normally have only one of its possible senses, and that meaning is usually determined by the context, and in these verses by the immediate context.

For another example the word *faith* can mean trust or confidence in God, faithfulness, a body of truth, or intellectual assent. Jude 3 and Galatians 1:23 use *faith* in one of these four meanings, Romans 3:3 in another one of the senses, Romans 1:17 and Ephesians 2:8 in another of the four meanings, and James 2:19 in another sense. Look up these verses and seek to determine the meaning for each of these occurrences of *faith*.

As mentioned earlier the word *salvation* or *saved* does not always mean deliverance from sin. The following are five ways these words are used:

    a. Safety or deliverance from difficult circumstances

    b. Physical and/or emotional health

    c. Israel's national release from oppression by her enemies

    d. Deliverance from the penalty of sin by the substitutionary death of Christ

    e. Final deliverance from the presence of sin.

Look up each of the following verses and write on the line before each verse the letter corresponding to the definition above.

    _____ Exodus 14:13

    _____ Luke 1:71

    _____ Luke 18:42 (The words "has healed you" in the NIV are literally "has saved you.")

    _____ John 3:17

    _____ Acts 15:11

    _____ Acts 16:30

    _____ Acts 27:20

    _____ Romans 5:9

    _____ Romans 13:11

    _____ Philippians 1:19 ("Deliverance" is literally "salvation.")

    _____ James 5:15 (The words "will make the sick person well" in the NIV are literally "will save the sick person.")

Bible students will also want to keep in mind that the word *law* has several meanings, which can usually be ascertained from the way the word is used in the sentence. In Romans 2:14 and 8:2 *law* means a principle. In John 1:17, 45 the word means the Pentateuch, the first five books of the Bible. *Law* in Matthew 22:40 probably means all the Old Testament except the Prophets. The same word in Romans 2:12 and 8:3 means the Mosaic system.

As another example, the phrase "in the last days" (and "the last hour") is often assumed to refer to the same era each time it is used. And yet in Hebrews 1:2; 1 Peter 1:20; and 1 John 2:18 the phrase seems to suggest the *entire* present Church Age, whereas the phrase in 1 Timothy 4:1; 2 Timothy 3:1; 2 Peter 3:3; and Jude 18 seems to suggest the *final* days of the Church Age.

The Greek word *parousia* is often assumed to refer always to the Rapture. The contexts show how its etymological meaning of "presence" is related to three things: (a) the personal presence of individuals (1 Cor. 16:17; 2 Cor. 7:6-7; 10:10; Phil. 1:26; 2:12), (b) Christ's presence in the air at the Rapture (1 Cor. 15:23; 1 Thes. 2:19; 4:15; 5:23; 2 Thes. 2:1; James 5:7-8; 2 Peter 3:4; 1 John 2:28), or (c) Christ's presence on the earth with His saints immediately after the Tribulation (Matt. 24:3, 27, 37, 39; 1 Thes. 3:13; 2 Thes. 2:8-9; 2 Peter 1:16; 3:12).

The context of the *paragraph or chapter* is sometimes helpful in clarifying a word, phrase, or sentence that is not made clear in the sentence in which it is used. For example in John 2:19 Jesus spoke of destroying "this temple," and in verse 21 John explained that the temple of which Jesus was speaking was His body. In 7:37-38 Jesus said that "streams of living water will flow from within" a believer. In the following verse John explained that Jesus meant the Holy Spirit.

Does *fire* in Matthew 3:11 ("He will baptize you with the Holy Spirit and with fire") mean spiritual dynamics? That is, was John the Baptist saying that Jesus would give people spiritual fervor? The fact that fire is used in both the verse before and the verse after (vv. 10, 12) suggests that literal fire is referred to also in verse 11. This would then suggest that Jesus would baptize some with the Holy Spirit, at the moment of conversion (1 Cor. 12:13), and that others would suffer eternal judgment in hell.

Another context to consider in interpretation is the context of the Bible *book* in which the word, phrase, or sentence occurs. For example 1 John 3:6-10 cannot mean that a Christian never sins, in view of what John wrote in that same epistle in 1:8, 10 and 2:1. Understanding that throughout the Book of James the apostle is emphasizing evidences of true faith helps us understand his discussion of faith and works in 2:12-25. James' point was that true faith is evidenced by works, at least at some point in a believer's life. If his so-called "faith" has resulted in no works whatsoever in his entire life, then obviously that "faith" was not genuine and cannot save him. Faith "without deeds" (v. 20), that is, head belief that is not followed by life change, is a so-called faith and is useless or dead (vv. 20-26).

Parallel passages also serve as helpful contexts for ascertaining the meaning of certain words or sentences. Parallel passages may be verbal parallels, in which the same or similar words, phrases, or sentences occur, or idea parallels, in which the same or similar ideas are expressed but in different words. Close parallels exist between parts of 1 and 2 Kings and 1 and 2 Chronicles, between a number of the accounts in the Gospels, between parts of Romans and Galatians, between portions of Ephesians and Colossians, between verses in 2 Peter and Jude, between some parts of Daniel and Revelation, and between single passages (e.g., cf. Isa. 2:2-4 with Micah 4:1-3; Rom. 4:3 with Heb. 11:8-19; and Matt. 11:12 with Luke 16:16).

Another context to be considered is *the entire Bible.* For example Galatians 5:4, "You have fallen away from grace," may at first glance seem to teach that a Christian can lose his salvation. But this contradicts the entire tenor of Scripture, which is inspired by God "who does not lie" (Titus 1:2). The same is true of Philippians 2:12 ("work out your salvation") which may at first seem to suggest that a person can attain salvation by works. The KJV translates the Hebrew word *'anûš* in Jeremiah 17:9 as "desperately wicked." The use of this word elsewhere in the Old Testament, however, suggests that the word means incurably sick or diseased. (See 2 Sam. 12:15; Job 34:6; Isa. 17:11; Jer. 15:18; 30:12, 15; Micah 1:9.) Therefore, based on this evidence in the context of the entire Old Testament, the NIV is correct in translating the verse as follows: "The heart is deceitful above all things and *beyond cure.* Who can understand it?" (italics added)

Does Ecclesiastes 9:5, "The dead know nothing," teach soul sleep, the view that the dead have no consciousness till they are resurrected? No, because that view would contradict other verses in the Bible that teach that the dead are conscious (Luke 16:23-24; 2 Cor. 5:8; Phil. 1:23). Interpreted in the light of all Scripture, the verse in Ecclesiastes does not mean unconscious existence. How then is it to be understood? The context of the paragraph suggests that the dead will no longer have personal knowledge or firsthand experience of the things they experienced in this life, including the emotions of love, hatred, and jealousy and the happenings of daily life (Ecc. 9:6), and rewards for accomplishments (v. 5).

Two corollaries of this principle of noting the context of the entire Bible are these:

1. An obscure or ambiguous text should never be interpreted in such a way as to make it contradict a plain one. The words "baptized for the dead" in 1 Corinthians 15:29 should not be interpreted to mean that a person can be saved after he has died. This would contradict the plain teaching of Hebrews 9:27 and other verses.

2. A complex, ingenious, or devious interpretation should not be given preference over a simple and more natural explanation. When Jesus said in Matthew 16:28, "I tell you the truth, some who are standing here will not taste death before they see the Son of man coming in His kingdom," He was obviously not referring to the coming millennial kingdom, because all those to whom He addressed those words experienced death. Instead the more natural and simple explanation is that He was referring to a foretaste of His kingdom evidenced in His appearance on the Mount of Transfiguration, which occurred only six days later (17:1-13). The normal understanding of the statement "God sent forth His Son" (Gal. 4:4) is that Jesus was the Son of God from all eternity, not that He *became* the Son at His birth or His baptism.

In view of this section on the meaning of words (lexicology) the following principles should be kept in mind.

1. A word does not usually mean what it originally meant, nor is its meaning often determined by its component parts.

2. The meanings of words in English should not be read back into the biblical meanings.

3. The same word may have different meanings in its various occurrences in the Bible.

4. Each word or phrase normally has only one meaning, which is indicated by its usage in the sentence and/or one of several contexts.

5. The same word in the Bible does not always mean the same thing.

6. A word should not be given all its shades of meaning in any one occurrence. The context of an utterance usually designates the one sense which is intended from among the various possible

meanings of a word. On the other hand it must be recognized that occasionally ambiguity is present.

John wrote in John 1:5 that "the darkness has not understood" the light. The NIV suggests in a footnote that "understood" may also be rendered "overcome." The Greek word *katalambanō* can mean either "to comprehend" or "to overcome." This may be a case of deliberate ambiguity on John's part, suggesting that both meanings may be present. A similar example is the word *anōthen* (3:3), which can mean "from above" or "again." It is conceivable that a *double entendre* is intended here,[12] that the new birth is both from above (i.e., from God) and is "again" (i.e., a second spiritual birth in contrast to one's first physical birth). When Paul wrote that a "woman who prays or prophesies with her head uncovered dishonors her head" (1 Cor. 11:5), what did he mean was being dishonored—her husband (who is her head, v. 3) or her physical head? Could he have used a *double entendre* here, meaning that both her husband (vv. 7-12) and her own literal head (vv. 13-15) were dishonored? These observations about ambiguity do not overturn the principle of a single meaning, as already discussed. We should assume one meaning unless there is strong reason in the context to suggest otherwise.

How Do the Forms of Words (Morphology) and the Functions of Words (Parts of Speech) Relate to Bible Interpretation?

Morphology refers to the way words are inflected, that is, formed or put together. For instance adding an "s" at the end of the noun "fuse" makes it plural, but adding "re" at the beginning of "fuse" makes it the verb "refuse," or changing the "e" at the end to "al" makes it a noun "refusal." The pronoun "he" is in the nominative case, but "him" is in the accusative case. The verb "run" is in the present tense, but changing the "u" to "a" makes the verb "ran," the past tense. The way words are put together obviously reflects their meaning. The word "overhang" differs greatly in meaning from "hangover." A single letter can alter the meaning of the word significantly as in "hate," "heat," and "heart."

In Greek and Hebrew the meanings of words are changed similarly by inflections at the beginning, middle, or end of the words.

Morphology is an important part of the grammatical approach to interpretation, which seeks to give attention to every detail of the Scriptures because of their verbal inspiration.

Since grammatical interpretation is concerned with the grammar of the Scriptures, it is helpful to know the *parts of speech*. They are eight, grouped in two families. The "noun" family includes nouns, pronouns, adjectives, and prepositions. The "verb" family includes verbs, adverbs, conjunctions, and interjections.

The "Noun" Family

A *noun* is a word that names something, such as a person (Jesus), a place (Ephesus), a thing (blood), a concept or idea (redemption, grace, blessing, peace), or an action (ascension). In number, nouns may be singular (heart) or plural (eyes). In gender, nouns may be masculine (Jesus), feminine (woman), or neuter (ointment).

A *pronoun* is a word that substitutes for a noun, referring to items named or understood. Pronouns may be personal (I, you, he, she, it, we, they), relative (who, which, that, what), intensive (himself), or reciprocal (one another).

An *adjective* is a word that modifies (qualifies in some way) a noun or pronoun. It may refer to extent (a *large* city; *five* loaves) or a quality or characteristic (a *wonderful* Saviour; a *rich* salvation; a *fervent* prayer).

A *preposition* is a word that goes with a noun to form a "prepositional phrase." Prepositions may point to any number of relationships as seen in the following, all taken from Ephesians:

Means: *by* His blood
Accompaniment: *with* Jesus
Location: *in* Him; *on* the earth; *at* Ephesus
Benefit: *for* His glory
Motion: *to* heaven; *from* the dead
Direction: *toward* us
Origin: the Word *of*[3] God
Characteristic: the Father *of* glory; the Holy Spirit *of* promise; the day *of* redemption
Identity: pledge *of* our inheritance
Position: *over* all; *at* His right hand
Permeation: *through* all
Entrance: *into* the lower parts
Opposition: *against* the devil's schemes
Conformity: *according* to the flesh
Time: *before* the foundation of the world.

The "Verb" Family

A *verb* asserts something about what a noun or pronoun is or does. Verbs have tense (past, present, or future), voice (active or passive), and mood (indicative, interrogative, imperative, or optative).

An example of the past tense is "ran." Examples of the present tense are "run," "runs," and "is running." An example of the future tense is "will run." A number of examples of the past tense can be seen in Ephesians 1:3-9: "has blessed us," "chose us," "predestined us," "has freely given us," "lavished on us," "made known," "purposed." (The word "us" in many of these examples is not part of the verb but is a pronoun which is the object of the verb.)

Paul used the present tense when he wrote in 3:14, 17, "I kneel," "I pray." "Will be able to understand" in verse 4 is an example of the future tense.

The "voice" of a verb indicates whether the action is active or passive. In the sentence, "God sent His Son," the verb "sent" is in the active voice. In the sentence, "The Son was sent by God" the verb "was sent" is in the passive voice. In "He chose us" (Eph. 1:4) the verb is in the active voice, and in "We were also chosen" (v. 11) the verb is in the passive voice.

Mood suggests the kind of action, whereas tense suggests the time of action. For instance "ran" is a statement (indicative mood). "Is running?" is a question (interrogative mood). "Run!" is a command (imperative mood). "Please run" is a wish or request (optative mood). In Ephesians 4:1 Paul made a statement, "I urge you," and in the next verse he gave several commands, the first of which is, "Be completely humble and gentle."

Adverbs are another part of speech in the verb family. An adverb is a word that modifies or qualifies in some way a verb, adjective, or a phrase. An adverb may suggest manner or quality, telling how: he spoke *softly;* he prayed *earnestly;* he ran *fast.* Adverbs may also suggest place, indicating where, as in the sentences "he went *away,*" "he ran *ahead,*" "he ran *around* the block." An adverb may suggest degree, indicating how much, as in "he ran *enough.*" Adverbs may also indicate time, telling when: "he came *early,*" "you were *formerly* darkness," "he ran *yesterday.*" Adverbs may suggest purpose or result, indicating why, as in the example "he ran *to lose weight.*" (In this case "to lose weight" is a phrase called an infinitive and it is used adverbially to describe the verb "ran.") An example of an adverb in Ephesians 1 is "freely" (v. 6). In 4:2 "completely" is an adverb modifying "humble." In verse 25 "truthfully" modifies the imperative verb "speak," telling how one should speak. Adverbs may also give a negative: "Do *not* give the devil a foothold" (v. 26), "*Never* will I leave you" (Heb. 13:5), "I will *not* be afraid" (v. 6).

Conjunctions are connectives that join words, phrases, or clauses. The following are examples of the many kinds of conjunctions, all taken from Ephesians.

Contrast: *but* (2:4, 13)

Comparison: *just as* (4:32; 5:25)

Correlation: *as . . . so* (5:24)

Reason: *because* (2:4; 6:8); *for* (2:8); *for this reason* (1:15; 3:1, 14)

Result: *therefore* (2:11); *consequently* (v. 19); *then* (4:14)

Purpose: *that* (4:28); *in order that* (1:12, 18); *so that* (v. 17)

Conclusion: *then* (4:1); *so* (v. 17)

Time: *when* (1:13); *until* (4:13); *finally* (6:10)

Addition: *also* (1:18); *in addition* (6:16)

Concession: *although* (3:8)

Interjections are single words that express a negative (not, nor), interrogation (why), affirmation (certainly, indeed), or exclamation (surely, oh, ouch, phooey).

Why Know the Parts of Speech?

The grammatical function of a word in a phrase or sentence influences its meaning. By itself the word "cutting" could be a noun, verb, or adjective. In the sentence, "The *cutting* of the grass took time," the word is a noun. In the sentence, "He was *cutting* the grass," the word is part of the verb "was cutting." In the sentence, "He made a *cutting* remark," the word is an adjective. The ability of a word like "cutting" to convey different meanings is called polysemy. Another example of polysemy is the word "with" which has three distinct meanings in these sentences: "he ate his food *with* his wife," "he ate his food *with* a fork," and "he ate his food *with* delight." In the first sentence "with" suggests accompaniment; in the second, means; and in the third, emotion.

The following examples may demonstrate how knowing certain facts about the parts of speech in phrases and sentences in the Bible can be helpful in interpretation.

1. In Job 21:2-3a the verbs *listen* and *bear* (with me) are in the plural and the pronoun *you* is in the plural and so Job was addressing the three friends. But in verse 3b the Hebrew verbal form

translated *mock* is singular (i.e., "You [sing.] mock") and so he was speaking to Zophar.

2. The singular *seed* in contrast to the plural *seeds* is important in Paul's argument in Galatians 3:16.

3. In the phrase "the apostles and prophets" in Ephesians 2:20 only one article *the* occurs. It is not repeated before the word "prophets." Therefore there is one foundation consisting of both apostles and prophets, not two foundations.

4. Does 1 Corinthians 3:9 mean that "we are God's fellow workers" or that as workers together with each other we belong to God? The answer is the latter because the phrase *of God* in Greek is in the genitive (possessive) case. It reads literally, "Of God we are fellow workers."

5. In Revelation 3:10 the Greek preposition *ek* means "out from," not "out through," as some suggest it should be rendered, and thus is a strong argument for the pretribulation Rapture.

6. The antecedent of the pronoun *he* in Daniel 9:27 is "the ruler who will come" (v. 26), not the Messiah. Thus the one who will make a covenant with many is the Antichrist (the view of premillennialism), not Christ (the view of amillennialism).

7. In Ephesians 2:13-22 the aorist (past) tense is used for what has been accomplished by the death of Christ ("have been brought near," v. 13; "made the two one," v. 14; "destroyed the barrier," v. 14; "preached peace," v. 17). But the present tense is used for the effect of that death for believers ("making peace," v. 15; "we both have," v. 18; "is joined together," v. 21; "are being built together," v. 22).

8. The present tense may refer to something that is permanently true ("In Christ all the fullness of the Deity lives in bodily form," Col. 2:9), continuous ("We eagerly await a Saviour . . . the Lord Jesus Christ," Phil. 3:20), repeated ("When you see a cloud . . . you say," Luke 12:54), habitual ("No one who is born of God will continue to sin," 1 John 3:9), or future ("They divide My garments," Ps. 22:18).

9. In Romans 3:23 the first verb "have sinned" is in the aorist tense (undefined past action) and could therefore be rendered "all sin" to express action which is true at any time. The second verb "fall short" is in the present tense and should be rendered "are continually coming short" or "come short."

10. The perfect tense in Hebrew expresses completed action, whether past, present, or future (but usually past). (The imperfect

expresses incomplete action.) Why then is the perfect often used when speaking of prophetic events? Because those events are so certain of fulfillment (of being completed) that the perfect tense is appropriate. This is called the "prophetic perfect." These verbs are often translated in the past tense, as in, for example, Isaiah 53:2-9.

11. The importance of conjunctions is seen in Ephesians 4:11. The first four occurrences of the word "and" (NASB) is the same Greek word (*de*), but the fifth occurrence of "and" (between "pastors" and "teachers") is a different word (*kai*), and can best be rendered by a hyphen ("pastor-teachers").

12. The conjunction "for" introduces a reason for the preceding statement(s). In Romans 8, "for" (Greek, *gar*) occurs 15 times. In 1:15-18 (NASB) one reason builds on another: Paul was "eager to preach the Gospel" (v. 15), "for" he was "not ashamed" (v. 16), "for it is the power of God for salvation" (v. 16) "for in it the righteousness of God is revealed" (v. 17).

How Do the Relationships of Words (Syntax) Help in Interpreting the Bible?

The word "syntax" comes from the Greek *syntassein,* which means "to place in order together." According to Webster's Dictionary "syntax" is "the way in which words are put together to form phrases, clauses, or sentences." It is a branch of grammar.

Single words by themselves seldom convey a complete thought. Like bricks in a building, words are single elements that together make sentences, the basic units of thought. The single words "man," "hard," "ball," and "hit" do not convey a meaningful thought. Therefore they need to be put together. However, the way they are arranged can change the meaning, as seen in these sentences.

"The man hit the ball hard."
"The ball hit the man hard."
"The man hit the hard ball."
"The hard man hit the ball."
"The hard ball hit the man."

Phrases

A *phrase* consists of a short grammatical group of words without a verb. In our study of prepositions we saw a good number of examples of prepositional phrases. Examples of prepositional phrases in Colossians 1:2 are: "*to* the holy and faithful brothers," "*in* Christ," "*at* Colosse," "*to* you," "*from* God our Father."

Another kind of phrase is the participial phrase. A participle is a word usually ending in "ing." It is verbal in nature and is dependent on a main clause. Examples in Ephesians are "*speaking* the truth in love" (4:15), "*making* the most of every opportunity" (5:16), and "*giving* thanks to God" (v. 20). Examples in Colossians are "*admonishing* and *teaching* everyone" (1:28), "*overflowing* with thankfulness" (2:7), and "*nailing* it to the cross" (v. 14).

A question of interpretation pertaining to a prepositional phrase is in Ephesians 1:4-5. The question is, Does the prepositional phrase "in love" go with the thought of verse 4, describing the fact that God chose us in Him in love, or does the phrase "in love" go with the thought in verse 5, modifying the words "He predestined us"? Some Bible versions place the phrase with the thought in verse 4 and others place it with the thought in verse 5. The NIV is probably correct in linking the words with God's work of predestination (v. 5) so that the sentence begins, "In love He predestined us."

Clauses

A *clause* is a grammatical unit of words comprised of a subject (the person, place, thing, concept or idea, or action) being discussed and a predicate (the verb indicating action, state, or condition). The two words "Christ died" are a clause because they are a single grammatical unit with a subject (Christ) and a predicate (died). Many clauses also have an object, as in the words "He chose us" (Eph. 1:4).

These two examples — "Christ died" and "He chose us" — are called independent clauses. This means that each thought stands alone and is complete in itself. Also there are dependent clauses, which "depend" on independent clauses for their full meaning. In Colossians 1:3 Paul has both kinds of clauses. "We always thank God" is an independent clause. The subject is "We," the predicate or verb is "thank," "always" is an adverb, and "God" is a noun, the object of the verb "thank." The words "when we pray for you" are a dependent clause because by themselves they do not make a complete thought. They depend on the independent clause for their meaning. You can always tell a dependent clause by the fact that you cannot say it by itself and make a complete sentence. Dependent clauses are of various kinds.

Causal: "We always thank God . . . *because* we have heard" (vv. 3-4).

Concessive (in which a thought is conceded): "*Though* I am

absent from you in body, I am present with you in spirit" (2:5).

Comparative: "*Just as* you have received . . . continue to live in Him" (v. 6).

Conditional: "*Since* you died with Christ . . . why . . . do you submit to its rules?" (v. 20)

Purpose: "We pray this *in order that* you may live a life worthy" (1:10).

Result: "Pray . . . *so that* we may proclaim" (4:3).

Temporal: "*When* you were dead in your sins . . . God made you alive with Christ" (2:13).

Sentences

Sentences, as to their structure, may be simple, compound, or complex. A *simple sentence* has only one independent clause (at least a subject and a predicate). An example is in Colossians 3:2, "[You] set your mind on things above." A *compound sentence* has at least two independent (and coordinate) clauses. An example is seen in verse 19: "Husbands, love your wives and do not be harsh with them." A *complex sentence* has at least one independent clause and one dependent clause. "We always thank God" (1:3) is an independent clause, and "because we have heard" (v. 4) is a dependent clause.

For a helpful exercise indicate whether the following sentences from Colossians are simple, compound, or complex.

1. "Let the peace of Christ rule. . . . And be thankful" (3:15). _____

2. "When Christ . . . appears, then you also will appear with Him in glory" (v. 4). _____

3. "Clothe yourselves with compassion" (v. 12). _____

4. "For in Christ all the fullness of the Deity lives . . . and you have been given fullness in Christ" (2:9-10). _____

5. "Be wise in the way you act toward outsiders" (4:5).
_____

6. "Here there is no Greek or Jew . . . but Christ is all" (3:11). _____

7. "Since, then, you have been raised with Christ, set your hearts on things above" (v. 1). _____

Indicate which kind of dependent clause is in each of the following complex sentences from Colossians. Indicate whether they are causal, concessive, conditional, purpose, result, or temporal.

1. "Children, obey your parents . . . *for* this pleases the Lord" (3:20). _____

2. "*Since,* then, you have been raised with Christ, set your hearts on things above" (v. 1). _____

3. "Do not lie to each other, *since* you have taken off your old self" (v. 9) _____

4. "I tell you this *so that* no one may deceive you" (2:4).
_____

5. "*When* you were dead in your sins . . . God made you alive with Christ" (v. 13). _____

6. "Let your conversation be always full of grace . . . *so that* you may know how to answer everyone" (4:6). _____

7. "Epaphras . . . is always wrestling in prayer for you, *that* you may stand firm in all the will of God" (v. 12). _____

Sentences, as to their purposes, may be as follows:

A statement—to assert a fact, opinion, complaint, emotion, observation, and so forth. Statements may be affirmations (mentioning a positive side) or negations (giving a negative side).

A question—to raise an inquiry.

A command—to give an order or charge. (A command in the negative is a prohibition.)

A request—to ask for something.

A wish—to express a desire.

In the interpretation of certain verses it is important to note whether they are statements, questions, or commands, or serving some other purpose. (You will recall that this has been referred to as the mood of a verb.)

In John 5:39 Jesus said, "Search the Scriptures" (NASB). Is this a statement or a command? In 12:27 Jesus said, "Father, save Me from this hour" (NASB). Is this a statement or a question?

An example of the importance of various aspects of syntax is seen in Acts 2:38, a verse that is interpreted in various ways, and which may seem to suggest that water baptism is required for salvation. An important observation, which can be seen only in Greek, is that the verb *repent* is in the plural, as is the word *your* which precedes the word *sins.* Interestingly, however, the words *baptized* and the first occurrence of *you* in the verse are in the singular. This seems to suggest that the words "and be baptized, every one of you [sing.], in the name of Jesus Christ," should be set apart as a parenthetical statement. The main thought then is, "Repent [pl.] so that your [pl.] sins may be forgiven." This is a command that corresponds with many similar commands in the New Testament. Then the instruction to be baptized is directed to individuals, suggesting that any individual who does repent should then submit to water baptism. Seen in this way, the verse then does not conflict with other passages of Scripture.[14]

Word Order and Repetition

The order of words is also a significant part of syntax, which should not be overlooked in Bible interpretation. In English the order of words takes on significance. "God is love" and "Love is God" are sentences with the same words, but the order changes the meaning.

In Greek, emphasis can be given to words, phrases, or clauses by placing them at the beginning of a sentence (and sometimes at the end) in contrast to the normal word order of subject, verb, and object. For example "In Him" is at the beginning of Ephesians 2:21 and thus is emphasized, whereas normally the prepositional phrase would follow the verb "is joined together."

In 1 Corinthians 1:17 the word "not" is placed at the beginning of the sentence in Greek, in order to emphasize the negative idea.

In Hebrew the normal word order is verb, subject, object. Thus if the subject or the object comes first, that is emphasized. In Isaiah 1:14 the order is object, verb, subject, thus stressing the object: "Your New Moon festivals and your appointed feasts My soul hates." Emphasis in Hebrew is also given by repetition. An example is "Holy, holy, holy is the Lord Almighty" (6:3).

Summary

Grammatical interpretation means giving attention to the words of Scripture and how they are used. While this may sometimes seem a bit involved or technical, it is essential if we are to understand the Bible properly.

The following is a summary outline of the procedures suggested for proper grammatical interpretation.

A. Procedure in discovering the meaning of a word

1. Examine the etymology of the word, including its original meaning and any different meanings that develop from it.

2. Discover the usage of the word.

a. By the same writer in the same book

b. By the same writer in other Bible books

c. By other writers in the Bible

d. By other writers outside the Bible

3. Discover how synonyms and antonyms are used
4. Consider the contexts
   a. The immediate context
   b. The context of the paragraph or chapter
   c. The context of the book
   d. The context of parallel passages
   e. The context of the entire Bible
5. Decide which one of several possible meanings best fits the thought of the passage.

B. Procedures for discovering the meaning of a sentence

1. Analyze the sentence and its elements, noting its parts of speech, the kind of sentence it is, the kind of clauses it has, and the word order.

2. Discover the meaning of each key word (see the five points above under "Procedure in Discovering the Meaning of a Word") and how they contribute to the meaning of a sentence.

3. Consider the influence of each part of the sentence on the thought of the whole.

CHAPTER SIX

Bridging the Literary Gap

In 1973 our family moved to Dallas. Three months before our move, my wife and I flew to Dallas to look for a house. As we looked, we faced the problem many prospective home buyers face: either we liked the house but could not afford it or if we could afford it we did not like it. However, on the fourth day of looking we saw a house we liked, and one we felt we could afford. It was under construction at the time. The outside walls were up, the inner frames were in, and the roof was on. But it was difficult to sense exactly what it would be like when finished, so the builder showed us one similar to it down the street, a house that was already finished and sold but not yet occupied.

In the next 24 hours, we signed a contract, and chose paint colors, light fixtures, wallpaper, and carpeting.

As we looked for a house and as we chose those colors, fixtures, and fabrics, we had to keep in mind the furniture we already owned. We wanted those features to match the furniture. That, of course, is a basic principle in interior design—having things correlated (with the same elements) or having different things coordinated. Interior designing is concerned with the details of structure so that the overall effect is both pleasing and functional.

Unity (coordination), variety, and utility (function) are important. In choosing and positioning furniture, homeowners and interior designers consider color, position, pattern, fabric, and shape. Interior designers and wise homemakers consider the same elements when selecting window coverings, wall coverings, floor coverings, and accessories such as pictures, lamps, and knickknacks. When you step into a well-designed room, these elements tell you something about the purpose and the character of the room.

So it is with the Bible. Its "interior designing" is fabulous. The more you know of the patterns, styles, and forms of the various units in a book of the Bible the more you will know of that book's purpose and unique character, and the better you will understand it. This aspect is often neglected in Bible study and interpretation. In a sense this is understandable because a good design does not call attention to itself. But when examined closely you see the wisdom behind the designing. This chapter, along with the following one, discusses rhetorical interpretation, the style and form of the Scriptures.

What Is Rhetorical Interpretation?

Some of the definitions Webster's Dictionary gives of the word "rhetoric" are these: "style of language" and "the art of writing or speaking as a means of communication with concern for literary effect."

"Rhetorical interpretation" refers then to the process of determining how the *style* (particular verbal elements or ways of expression) and *form* (organizational structure) influence how it is to be understood. Rhetorical interpretation is the process of determining the literary quality of a writing by analyzing its genre (kind of composition), structure (how the material is organized), and figures of speech (colorful expressions for literary effect) and how those factors influence the meaning of the text.

Consideration of these elements ought to be included in Bible study and interpretation because, as suggested in chapter 3, the Bible is a book and therefore is a literary product. "Literature is an interpretive presentation of experience *in artistic form.*"[1]

Asking about the literary genre or kind of composition of a given portion of the Bible is like an interior designer asking, What kind of room is it? Is it a living room, dining room, den, bedroom, kitchen, breakfast nook, or playroom? You will normally know the kind of room by what you see in it. Similarly, observing the contents of a Bible book can help you determine its genre or kind of composition.

Discussing structure is like asking, How is the dining room put together? What are its component parts? How does it differ from other dining rooms? Two dining rooms may differ in color, size, style of furniture, floor covering, arrangement, and yet they are both dining rooms. The literary genre of the first four books of the New

Testament is Gospels, but obviously not all the Gospels are alike. They are structured differently.

So in rhetorical interpretation we are looking at various kinds of literary rooms (genre) and then seeing how they are put together (structure and style).

Pictures on walls, accessories on shelves, flower arrangements on tables — these and other niceties add color, interest, and sparkle to a room. Likewise, figures of speech, which are colorful ways of expressing ideas, add to the interest of the Scriptures. Unless figures of speech are recognized, some passages may be misinterpreted.

Does the Bible Have Literary Luster?

This question can be answered in the affirmative for two reasons.
First, the Bible presents people as real, live people.

> Biblical literature is replete with adventure, marvelous events, battles, supernatural characters, villains . . . brave heroes, beautiful and courageous heroines . . . dungeons, quests, rescue stories, romantic love, boy heroes. . . . Biblical literature is alive. Biblical scholars have too often given the impression that biblical literature is a dry-as-dust document to be cut up and put on display as a relic of ancient cultures.[2]

As literature, the Bible records human experiences. It speaks of people's emotions and conflicts, victories and defeats, joys and heartaches, imperfections and sins, spiritual losses and gains. Intrigue, suspense, excitement, foibles, disappointment, reversals — these and many other experiences of mankind are seen in the Bible.

Second, the Bible presents authors as capable literary writers. Hardly any Bible scholars today agree with the comment of Dibelius that "what they [the Gospel writers] wrote down was either completely unliterary . . . or else half-literary."[3] Many have thought that Amos was a rustic, uneducated person who knew little of how to write. But the more you study the Book of Amos, the more you see its high literary quality. Ryken correctly asserts that the Bible contains a "literary artistry of the highest order." He adds,

> Biblical authors wrote in well-understood literary conventions and with a grasp of literary principles. They knew how to tell stories with well-made plots. They knew how to tell stories that

are unified by the principle of tragedy or satire. . . . Biblical poets knew how to invent apt metaphors and how to put statements into parallel form. . . . Most of them were masters of style.[4]

Plays, poems, newspapers, novels, short stories, autobiographies, science fiction, documentaries—these kinds of literary products have various features that influence how we understand their content. Likewise we must recognize different types of composition in the Bible (both on the scale of entire books and the smaller units within them) such as history, law, narrative, poetry, prophecy, Gospels, Epistles, Wisdom literature, etc. Whether the material is an epistle or a narrative, or whether it is poetic or prophetic makes a difference. "Since parts of the Bible are literary in form, a literary approach is necessary to understand what is being said."[5] The Bible's artistry in form and style makes it a literary masterpiece. Its stories and poems are "products of verbal and imaginative skill,"[6] making it a book of outstanding literary excellence.

Literary Genre in the Bible

What Is Literary Genre?

Genre, a French word from the Latin genus, means a literary type. "Literary genre" refers to the category or the kind of writing characterized by a particular form(s) and/or content. Distinguishing the various genres (kinds of literature) in Scripture helps us interpret the Bible more accurately. "We do this with all kinds of literature. We distinguish between lyric poetry and legal briefs, between newspaper accounts of current events and epic poems. We distinguish between the style of historical narratives and sermons."[7] Marshall makes some interesting observations along this line:

> If I were to write an account of what I did on Christmas day, the style in which I would do so would vary depending on whether I was writing a letter to my aunt, or producing a report for a newspaper, or writing a Christmas story for children based on my experiences, or composing a poem about it, or even writing a song about it. These are different styles for these different occasions.[8]

In this connection it is of interest to note that 4 of the 25 affirmations included in the Chicago Statement on Biblical

Hermeneutics refer to literary form.

"We affirm that Scripture communicates God's truth to us verbally through a wide variety of literary forms" (Article X). "We affirm that awareness of the literary categories, formal and stylistic, of the various parts of Scripture is essential for proper exegesis, and hence we value genre criticism as one of the many disciplines of Biblical study" (Article XIII). "We affirm that the Biblical record of events, discourses, and sayings though presented in a variety of appropriate literary forms, corresponds to historical fact" (Article XIV). "We affirm the necessity of interpreting the Bible according to its literal or normal sense. The literal sense is the grammatical-historical sense — that is, the meaning which the writer expressed. Interpretation according to the literal sense will take account of all figures of speech and literary forms found in the text" (Article XV).[9]

What Are Some Literary Genres in the Bible?

1. *Legal.* Whereas the term *law* often refers to the first five books of the Bible, legal material, that is, the body of material that includes commandments for the Israelites, is included in Exodus 20–40, the Book of Leviticus, portions of the Book of Numbers (chaps. 5–6, 15, 18–19, 28–30, 34–35), and almost all the Book of Deuteronomy. Two kinds of legal material are included. One is apodictic law. These are direct commands that usually begin with the words "you shall not," as in the Ten Commandments (Ex. 20:3-17) or "do not" (as in Lev. 18:7-24; 19:9-19, 26-29, 31, 35). These laws are not necessarily exhaustive. In 19:14 the Lord told Moses to tell the people not to curse a deaf person or put a stumbling block in front of the blind. Suppose an Israelite harmed a dumb, crippled, or retarded person. It would seem obvious that this verse was suggesting that the principle of concern for deaf or blind people should also be applied to other kinds of handicapped individuals.

A second kind of legal material in these Old Testament books is casuistic law. This means case-by-case law. In these commands a condition setting forth a specific situation introduces the laws. Examples are seen in Leviticus 20:9-18, 20-21 and Deuteronomy 15:7-17. Exodus 23:4-5 presents a single casuistic law, set in the midst of several apodictic laws in verses 1-2, 6-9. Again these are not exhaustive. The instruction in those verses refers to an enemy's ox or donkey. But what if an enemy owns a camel or sheep that wanders off? Obviously the example of the ox or donkey is not intended to exclude reference to other animals.

2. _Narrative._ A narrative is of course a story, but a biblical narrative is a story told for the purpose of conveying a message through people and their problems and situations. Biblical narratives are selective and illustrative. The biblical narratives are not intended to be full biographies giving every detail of individuals' lives; the writers carefully selected the material they included (obviously doing so under the inspiration of the Holy Spirit) to accomplish certain purposes. Second Samuel, for example, includes selected material from David's life to show in the first 10 chapters how he established and extended his kingdom. Then chapters 11 and 12 record his sin with Bathsheba and Uriah. Chapters 13–21 point up David's many personal and national sins. The final three chapters (22–24) record his song of praise, his last words, a listing of his mighty men, his numbering of his soldiers, and the building of an altar. The events recorded in chapters 13–21 are selected to illustrate—without the writer stating it explicitly in so many words—that sin results in devastating consequences.

On the other hand 1 and 2 Chronicles do not include some of that material. Those books omit any reference to the sins of David, and instead they include extensive material on David as king, and on the priests and the temple. Why is this? When the Jews returned from the Babylonian Captivity under Zerubbabel (538 B.C.) and Ezra (458 B.C.), the people were saying, in essence, "Our temple is puny (cf. Hag. 2:3) and we have no king." First and 2 Chronicles were written therefore to encourage the people to recognize that the line of David would continue and that the temple would continue. The first of these speaks of hope for the future and the second points to their heritage from the past. In view of these two facts the people reading 1 and 2 Chronicles would have been encouraged to be faithful and to trust the Lord.

In the Book of Ruth why did the writer include a genealogy in 4:17-21, when this could have just as easily been left out of the book? It seems that the entire book is pointing implicitly to the fact that Ruth and Boaz, being faithful to the Lord, are an important link in the ancestry of King David. The genealogy in Ruth 4 refers to David twice (vv. 17, 21).

Narratives usually follow a pattern in which a problem occurs near the beginning of the narrative, with increasing complications that reach a climax. And then the narrative moves toward a solution to the problem and concludes with the problem solved.

As the problem develops, suspense usually intensifies and

issues and relationships become more complicated until they reach a dramatic climax. The following chart illustrates this narrative pattern.[10]

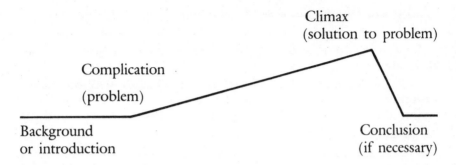

Climax
(solution to problem)

Complication

(problem)

Background
or introduction

Conclusion
(if necessary)

Suspense

Cotterell and Turner call the climax "peaking." "In narrative stories it is common to find a peak toward which the narrative advances, and from which there is a rather rapid descent."[11] As you read narratives in the Bible, look for this pattern.

Narratives may be of six kinds.

a. *Tragedy*. A tragedy is a story of the decline of a person from verity to catastrophe. Samson, Saul, and Solomon are examples of tragedy narrative.

b. *Epic*. An epic is a long narrative with a series of episodes unified around an individual or a group of people. An example of this is Israel's wilderness wanderings.

c. *Romance*. A romance is a narrative in which the romantic relationship between a man and a woman is narrated. The Books of Ruth and the Song of Songs are illustrations of this kind of narrative.

d. *Heroic*. A heroic narrative is a story built around the life and exploits of a hero or a protagonist, an individual who sometimes is a representative of others or an example for others. Examples are Abraham, Gideon, David, Daniel, and Paul.

e. *Satire*. A satirical narrative is an exposure of human vice or folly through ridicule or rebuke. The Book of Jonah is a satire because Jonah, as a representative of Israel, is ridiculed for his refusal to accept God's universal love. Ironically he was more concerned about a plant than he was about the pagans in Nineveh. Also it is ironic that God had compassion on Jonah, though the prophet did not have compassion on the Ninevites. Many readers of the Book of

Jonah have noted that it ends in an abrupt way with the problem of the prophet's anger seemingly unresolved. The reason for this is that this is often the way a satire concludes. Jonah's humiliation is an appropriate ending for a satire, and the Israelites would be challenged to see themselves and their own attitude toward pagan nations in Jonah's attitude. (The fact that the Book of Jonah is written as a satire in no way nullifies the book's historicity.)

f. *Polemic.* A polemic narrative is an aggressive attack against or refuting of the views of others. Examples of this are Elijah's "contest" with the 450 Baal prophets (1 Kings 18:16-46), and the 10 plagues against the gods and goddesses of Egypt.

3. *Poetry.* The Books of Job, Psalms, Proverbs, Ecclesiastes, and Song of Songs are the five major poetical books of the Old Testament. However, poetry is included in many of the prophetic books. The NIV presents the material in poetic style so that the distinction between poetry and prose is more readily noticeable. Poetry is also included in earlier portions of the Old Testament, including Exodus 15; Judges 5; and 1 Samuel 2. In the New Testament, Mary's song is in poetic form (Luke 1:46-55) as are the words of Zechariah (vv. 67-79). A distinct feature of the poetry of the Bible is that two (and sometimes three or four) lines are stated in parallel form. This contrasts with English poetry which is usually characterized by meter and rhyme, neither of which occurs as a regular feature of Hebrew poetry. Scholars have debated extensively over the question of meter in Hebrew poetry. Their inability to come to a consensus on the issue points to the absence of a recognized meter in the Bible's poetry. Occasionally rhyme occurs in some poetic verses, but this is rare. The kinds of poetic parallelism are discussed later in this chapter.

Of course the Psalms are written in poetry. Several kinds of psalms are generally recognized: lament of the people, lament of the individual, declarative praise of the people, declarative praise of the individual, and descriptive praise. A *lament of the people* usually has an introductory petition, the lament itself, a confession of trust, and a petition for the psalmist to be heard and delivered, and a vow of praise. Examples are Psalms 12, 44, 80, 94, 137. A *lament of the individual* usually includes an introduction (with an address to and/or a turning to God, and a cry for help), the lament itself (which refers to the psalmist's enemies, the psalmist himself, and God), a confession of trust, a petition to be heard and delivered, an expression of confidence that the psalmist has been heard, and a vow of praise. Sometimes a report of deliverance is also included. Examples are Psalms 3, 22, 31, 39, 42, 57, 71, 120, 139, 142. A *declarative praise of the people* includes an exhortation, words of praise, reflection on past need, and the report of deliverance. Examples are Psalms 65, 67, 75, 107, 124, 136.

In *a declarative praise of the individual,* proclamation is given, an introductory summary is included, reflection on past need is cited, and the report of deliverance follows, with a renewed vow of descriptive praise and/or instruction. Examples include Psalms 18, 30, 32, 34, 40, 66, 92, 116, 118, 138. The *descriptive praise* psalm includes a call to praise (including a hallelujah prologue and an invitation for the readers to praise the Lord), a statement of the cause for praise (citing God's greatness in creation and His grace in history and specific illustrations), and a conclusion which gives either a renewed call to praise, a restatement of cause for praise, or a statement of blessing. Some descriptive praise psalms are 8, 19, 104, 148 (exalting Him as Creator), 66, 100, 111, 114, 149 (praising Him as the Protector of Israel), and 33, 103, 113, 117, 145–147 (praising God as the Lord of history). In addition some psalms are called *songs of Zion* (46, 48, 76, 84, 87, 122), several others are *wisdom psalms* (36–37, 49, 73, 112, 127–128, 133), and 10 are *songs of trust* (11, 16, 23, 27, 62–63, 91, 121, 125, 131).[12]

In studying and interpreting the psalms it is important to (a) look for these categories of psalms and the elements within each category, (b) recognize that many figures of speech are included (see chapter 7 on figures of speech), (c) note the kinds of parallelisms in the verses (see p. 138 on poetic parallelism), (d) study the historical background of the psalms, and (e) find the central idea or unifying message or thought in the psalm.

The Psalms should be seen as a *guide to worship*. Like the psalmist, we can use the Psalms to enable us to praise God, to make appeals to Him, and to remember His benefits. Also we can learn from the Psalms to *relate honestly* to God in expressing joy, disappointment, anger, or other emotions. The Psalms can also be used to encourage us to reflect and meditate on what God has done for us.[13]

4. *Wisdom literature*. The Wisdom books are Job, Proverbs, and Ecclesiastes. (Some also include the Song of Songs in this group.) All Wisdom literature is poetry, but not all poetic material is Wisdom literature. Two kinds of Wisdom literature are seen in these books. One is proverbial literature, seen in the Book of Proverbs. The proverbs or maxims are general truths based on broad experi-

ence and observation. These are guidelines which are normally true in general. They are guidelines, not guarantees; precepts, not promises. For example, while it is generally true that a person who is lazy will experience poverty, a few exceptions to that general maxim may be observed in life. Also godliness generally results in a person leading a long life, as a number of proverbs state, but some exceptions to this have been observed.

A second kind of Wisdom literature is reflective. This involves a discussion of mysteries in life, as in Job and Ecclesiastes.

5. *Gospels.* Some people approach the four Gospels as historical narratives, as if the books were written simply to record biographical information on the life of Christ. Obviously they are not biographies in the normal sense in that they exclude much material from the life of Christ which one would normally expect to find in a historical biography. The Gospels include a good bit of biographical material on Christ, but they are more than biographies. They are both doctrine and narrative, presented to set forth information on the person of Jesus Christ. Jesus' teachings in parables and in direct discourse are interspersed with the records of His miracles and encounters with individuals.

"The Gospels are collections of stories, far more packed with action than is customary in narrative. The overriding purpose of the Gospel stories is to explain and praise the Person and work of Jesus . . . . through His actions, through His words, and through the responses of other people to Him."[14]

In studying the Gospel of John it is striking to note the many responses of belief and unbelief, of acceptance and rejection of Christ, recorded in that book.

Acceptance and Rejection of Jesus
in the Gospel of John

Acceptance	People Divided	Rejection
2:11		
		2:18 Questioned His authority
2:23		
4:41		
		5:16, 18 Tried to kill Him
		5:18 Accused Him of blasphemy
6:14		
	6:52	

Acceptance	People Divided	Rejection
		6:66 Withdrew from Him
		7:1 Tried to kill Him
		7:20 Accused Him of having a demon
		7:30 Tried to seize Him
7:31		
		7:32, 44 Tried to seize Him
	7:40-43	
		8:13 Accused Him of lying
		8:19, 22, 25 Questioned Him
8:30		
		8:37, 40 Tried to kill Him
		8:48, 52 Accused Him of having a demon
		8:53, 57 Questioned Him
		8:59 Tried to stone Him
	9:16	
9:38		
		9:40 Questioned Him
	10:19	
		10:20 Accused Him of having a demon
	10:21	
		10:31 Tried to stone Him
		10:33 Accused Him of blasphemy
		10:39 Tried to seize Him
10:42		
		11:8 Tried to stone Him
11:27		
11:45		
		11:53 Tried to kill Him
		11:57 Tried to seize Him
12:9, 11, 13		
		12:34 Questioned Him
		12:37 Did not believe in Him
12:42		
16:30		
		19:7 Accused Him of blasphemy
		19:16-18 Crucified Him

6. *Logical discourse.* This genre of biblical literature is also called epistolary literature and refers to the epistles of the New Testament, Romans through Jude. The Epistles generally include two kinds of material: (a) expository discourse, which expounds certain truths or doctrines, often with logical support for those truths, and (b) hortatory discourse, which includes exhortations to follow certain courses of action or to develop certain characteristics in light of the truths presented in the expository discourse material.

In form, the Epistles usually begin by naming the author, the recipients (the person or persons being addressed), words of greetings, and often, though not always, expressions of thanks for some aspect of the readers' conduct or character. The Epistles obviously differ from private letters, in that they are presented as messages from God with some of the writers directly affirming that they were writing under the inspiration of God the Holy Spirit; the material is given with apostolic authority; and the material is intended to be read in the churches. This latter point is even true of a supposedly private letter like 2 Timothy, because in 2 Timothy 4:22 the word *you,* with which the epistle concludes, is in the plural. This may have been a subtle suggestion on Paul's part that Timothy share the letter with others. (Again, this illustrates the importance of noting fine points of grammar, as discussed in chapter 5.)

Many of the Epistles were addressed to specific local groups of believers, or individuals (such as Timothy, Titus, and Philemon). This fact raises the question as to how we should relate the Epistles and the specific situations addressed in them to us today. This matter is discussed in more detail in chapter 12, but it may be helpful to mention at this point that the Bible interpreter should note instructions given in the Epistles that are obviously universal and therefore applicable for all ages and cultures. In addition it is important to distinguish between principles and specific applications. This point also relates to the matter of culturally conditioned versus transferable commands, discussed in chapter 4.

7. *Prophetic literature.* Prophetic literature is material that includes predictions of the future at the time of the writing of the material with injunctions often included that those who hear the prophecy adjust their lives in light of the predictions. In the Old Testament, for example, the people of Israel were told to prepare their hearts for the coming of the Messiah, Jesus Christ. Repentance from sin often accompanied predictions about the Lord's return and accompanying events.

A special form of prophetic literature is apocalyptic material, which focuses specifically on the end times, while presenting the material in symbolic form. Prophetic literature is discussed in chapter 10.

How Does an Awareness of Literary Genre Help in Understanding the Bible?

An awareness of the literary genre or kind of literature of a given Bible book helps more in synthesis than detailed analysis. It helps give a sense of the overall thrust of the Bible book, so that verses and paragraphs can be seen in light of the whole. This helps prevent the problem of taking verses out of context. It also gives insight into the nature and purpose of an entire book, as seen, for example, in the Book of Jonah.

Structural patterns help us see why certain passages are included where they are. Also attention to literary genre keeps us from making more of the passage than we should or from making less of the passage than we should.

Structural Analysis

Different structures or patterns give different effects. We see this in interior design as well as in the Bible. Suppose you have a lamp, a chest of drawers, and a mirror. You could position the mirror horizontally over one side of the chest of drawers with the lamp on another side. Or to give a different effect you could hang the mirror vertically. Or you may not wish to include a mirror at all. How you arrange these three items depends on your purpose and the desired effect.

This is "structure," or the relationships of parts. "Structural analysis" of the Bible is the effort to analyze the relationships that exist in the network of structural elements in self-contained portions (both large and small) of Scripture.

Larger Structural Patterns

The following are given as examples of structural arrangements of Bible books. These examples show the variety of structural arrangements in the Bible.

The Book of Acts may be divided into three parts, based on the three geographical areas Jesus mentioned in Acts 1:8, "You will be My witnesses in Jerusalem, and in all Judea and Samaria, and to the ends of the earth."

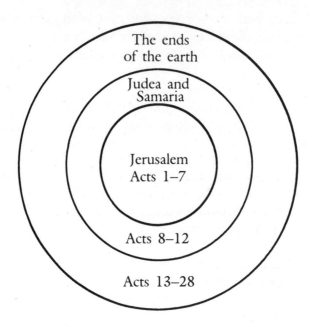

The Book of Revelation may be divided into three parts based on Jesus' words in Revelation 1:19 to record "what you have seen, what is now and what will take place later."

Revelation 1 – What You Have Seen (Past)
Revelation 2–3 – What Is Now (Present)
Revelation 4–22 – What Will Take Place Later (Future)

The structure of the Book of Ruth shows some interesting parallels in a pattern called inversion, illustrated as follows:

A. Family history and ties of kinship, and the women of Bethlehem (chap. 1)

B. Boaz and Ruth (chaps. 2–3)

A.́ Family history and ties of kinship, and the women of Bethlehem (chap. 4)

Chapters 2 and 3 are parallel in the following ways:

Chapter 2	Chapter 3
1. Ruth receives permission from Naomi to go to the fields.	1. Ruth receives instruction from Naomi to go to the threshing floor.
2. Ruth goes to the fields.	2. Ruth goes to the threshing floor.

Chapter 2	Chapter 3
3. Boaz asks Ruth's identity.	3. Boaz asks Ruth's identity.
4. Boaz accepts, praises, and feeds Ruth.	4. Boaz accepts, praises, and feeds Ruth.
5. Ruth reports to Naomi and receives counsel.	5. Ruth reports to Naomi and receives counsel.

The structure of the Book of Job is unique. It may be outlined as follows:

I. Prologue (Job 1–2)
II. Dialogue (Job 3–41)
    A. Job's opening lamentation (Job 3)
    B. First cycle of speeches (Job 4–14)
        1. Eliphaz and Job (Job 4–7)
        2. Bildad and Job (Job 8–10)
        3. Zophar and Job (Job 11–14)
    C. Second cycle of speeches (Job 15–21)
        1. Eliphaz and Job (Job 15–17)
        2. Bildad and Job (Job 18–19)
        3. Zophar and Job (Job 20–21)
    D. Third cycle of speeches (Job 22–37)
        1. Eliphaz and Job (Job 22–24)
        2. Bildad and Job (Job 25–31)
        3. Elihu (Job 32–37)
    E. Jehovah's closing intervention (Job 38–41)
III. Epilogue (Job 42)

In his Gospel, Matthew repeated a certain sentence five times. This gives a clue to the way the book may be structured. The sentence is, "When Jesus had finished saying these things" (7:28) or a slight variation of that wording. Matthew 11:1 reads, "After Jesus had finished instructing His twelve disciples"; 13:53 has, "When Jesus had finished these parables"; 19:1 says, "When Jesus had finished saying these things"; and 26:1 reads, "When Jesus had finished saying all these things."

Based on these sentences the book may be outlined as follows:

I. Preparation of the Messiah (Matt. 1:1–4:11)
II. Proclamation of the Messiah (4:12–7:29)
III. Manifestation of the Messiah (8:1–11:1)
IV. Opposition of the Messiah (11:2–13:53)
V. Withdrawal of the Messiah (13:54–19:2)
VI. Presentation and Rejection of the Messiah (19:3–26:2)
VII. Crucifixion and Resurrection of the Messiah (26:3–28:20).

Smaller Structural Patterns

A great variety of structural patterns of verses and passages within Bible books adds to the luster and colorful effect of the Bible's literary quality.

1. *Parallel patterns.* As stated earlier, Bible poetry is expressed in thought patterns. Several kinds of patterns are used. One is *comparison.* In this form of parallelism, the second line repeats the thoughts of the first line using synonyms. An example is Psalm 1:5, "Therefore the wicked will not stand in the judgment, nor sinners in the assembly of the righteous." The first line includes the word "wicked" whereas the second line has "sinners." The words "the judgment" in the first line are paralleled by the words "the assembly of the righteous" in the second line.

In *contrast* parallelism, the second line contrasts with the first. The second line is usually introduced by the word "but." Verse 6 is an example: "For the Lord watches over the way of the righteous, but the way of the wicked will perish."

A third kind of poetic parallelism may be called *completion.* In this pattern the second line completes the idea of the first line or vice versa. In verse 3 the phrase "which yields its fruit in season" is not a complete thought in itself but it does complete the thought begun in the first line of that verse, "He is like a tree planted by streams of water."

In verse 4 a fourth kind of parallel pattern is used. This may be called *figurative* parallelism, in which the second line illumines the first by a figure of speech or vice versa. Saying that the wicked are "like chaff" indicates that they are without security and worth.

Another less frequent parallel pattern is the *stairstep* parallelism. In this form the second line repeats a part of the first line and then adds something to make the sentence complete. Psalm 29:1 is an example: "Ascribe to the Lord, O mighty ones, ascribe to the Lord glory and strength."

2. *Ring pattern.* In a ring pattern a central portion is preceded and followed by parallel material. Genesis 37 records the story of Joseph being sold into Egypt. Chapter 38 speaks of Judah and Tamar, and chapter 39 resumes the story of Joseph. In a sense, then, chapters 37 and 39 form a ring around chapter 38, the purpose of which is to set off by contrast the awfulness of Judah's sin over against Joseph's purity.

3. *Chiasm pattern.* A chiasm pattern is a form frequently seen in the Scriptures. In a chiasm, elements one and four in one or more verses are parallel in thought, and points two and three are parallel in

thought. Psalm 137:5-6 reads, "If I forget you, O Jerusalem, may my right hand forget its skill. May my tongue cling to the roof of my mouth if I do not remember you." Note that lines one and four each begin with "if," and lines two and three begin with the words "may my right hand" and "may my tongue."

Another example of chiastic structure is Matthew 7:6. "Do not give dogs what is sacred; do not throw your pearls to pigs. If you do, they may trample them under their feet, and then turn and tear you to pieces." The reference to dogs in the first line is matched with the reference to tearing to pieces in the fourth line. Throwing pearls to pigs in the second line is paralleled by the reference to their trampling them under their feet, in line three.

4. *Alternating pattern.* In an alternating pattern, points one and three in a verse or passage are parallel, and points two and four are parallel.[15] In Psalm 31:20, the first line begins with the words "In the shelter of Your presence" and line three begins with the words "in Your dwelling." Then parts two and four are similar: "You hide them" and "You keep them safe." In the four calamities Job experienced (Job 1:13-19), the first two attacks by Satan alternate between human and natural means. The first and third catastrophes were caused by humans (the Sabeans, vv. 13-15, and the Chaldeans, v. 17), and calamities two and four by natural means ("the fire of God," probably lightning, v. 16, and a windstorm, vv. 18-19).

5. *Inversion pattern.* An inversion is similar to a chiasm except that it includes more than four elements and therefore has additional contrasting or comparative points. Items one and six are parallel, items two and five are parallel, and items three and four are parallel. Isaiah 6:10 contains this pattern. Lines one and six refer to the heart, lines two and five refer to the ears, and lines three and four refer to the eyes.

In the Flood narrative, the Flood began seven days after God had commanded Noah to enter the ark (Gen. 7:10). The rains came on the earth for 40 days (vv. 12, 17). The waters flooded the earth for 150 days (v. 24; 8:3). Noah opened the window of the ark 40 days after the tops of the mountains had become visible (v. 6). Noah waited seven days (twice) until he sent the dove out again (vv. 10, 12). This gives the following scheme of periods of time as an inversion:[16]

    7 days

        40 days

            150 days

        40 days

    7 days

The following is another pattern of introversion seen in the Flood narrative.[17]

1. God's covenant with Noah (Gen. 6:11-22)
  2. Noah brought in clean animals (7:1-5)
    3. Noah brought in unclean animals (7:6-10)
      4. Noah entered the ark (7:11-16)
        5. The Flood rose (7:17-24)
          6. The Flood crested, the ark rested, and God remembered Noah (8:1-5)
        7. The Flood abated (8:6-12)
      8. Noah exited the ark (8:13-19)
    9. Noah sacrificed some animals (8:20-22)
  10. Noah's diet (9:1-7)
11. God's covenant with Noah (9:8-17)

In inversions the center portion(s) is usually emphasized. Note the inversion pattern in Matthew 13:15.[18]

6. *Inclusio pattern.* An inclusio is a pattern in which a paragraph or longer portion ends in much the same way in which it began. In the Flood narrative man's wickedness is referred to in Genesis 6:1-8, and at the end of the narrative man's wickedness is again seen (9:20-27).

In Isaiah 1:21 Isaiah referred to Jerusalem as "the faithful city," and in verse 26 the paragraph concludes with another reference to the "faithful city." Proverbs 31:10-30 begins by referring to "the wife of noble character" (v. 10) and near the end again uses the word "noble" (v. 29). In Proverbs 1 "wisdom and discipline" are mentioned in verse 2, and again in verse 7, thus tying together all that is said about the purposes of the Proverbs.

7. *Trilogy pattern.* In this pattern three related things are mentioned, as in Jude 11: "the way of Cain," "Balaam's error," and "Korah's rebellion." Three things are also said about the false teachers against whom Jude wrote in Jude 8: they "pollute their own bodies," "reject authority," and "slander celestial beings."

8. *Acrostic pattern.* In an acrostic each verse begins in succession with a separate letter of the alphabet. Proverbs 31:10-31 is a well-known acrostic, as is Psalm 119. In that psalm, however, every eighth verse begins with a different letter of the 22-letter Hebrew alphabet. Verses 1-8 each begin with the first letter, verses 9-16 each begin with the second letter, verses 17-24 each begin with the third letter, and so forth. In Lamentations 1 each of the 22 verses begins with a different letter of the Hebrew alphabet. The same is true of

Lamentations 2 and 4. Chapter 3, however, is slightly different in that three verses in sequence each begin with the first letter of the alphabet, followed by the next three verses each beginning with the second letter of the alphabet, and so forth. Chapter 5 has 22 verses, but the verses are not in the form of an acrostic. Other psalms also are acrostics, including Psalms 9–10, 25, 34, 37, and 111. The acrostics probably served as memory devices. In addition the acrostics in the Book of Lamentations may also have served as a kind of literary control over Jeremiah's emotion of deep grief.

ASCENDING STRUCTURE IN 1 JOHN

You have several witnesses / therefore you know Him	5:13-21
You have faith in Him / therefore you have several witnesses	5:6-12
You believe that Jesus is the Christ / therefore your faith overcomes the world	5:4-5
You have the Spirit of God / therefore love the brethren and believe that Jesus is the Christ	4:7–5:3
You love others born of Him / therefore test the prophets to see if they are spirits of God	4:1-6
You are born of Him / therefore love others born of Him	3:11-24
You remain in Him / therefore you should practice righteousness because you are born of Him	2:29–3:10
You love the brethren / therefore you remain in Him and heretics don't (they depart, deny, deceive)	2:18-28
We walk in the light / therefore we should love the brethren	2:7-17
We have fellowship with Him / therefore we should walk in the light	1:5–2:6
We witnessed the Word of life / therefore we have fellowship with Him	1:1-4

9. *Ascending or descending pattern*. First John may be viewed as having an ascending structure. As the chart on page 141 illustrates, each section leads to the next.

Bar-efrat suggests the following descending pattern in 2 Samuel 13:3-20.[19]

> Jonadab-Amnon (vv. 3-5)
> > Amnon-David (v. 6)
> > > David-Tamar (v. 7)
> > > > Tamar-Amnon (vv. 8-16)
> > > > > Amnon-servant (v. 17)
> > > > > > Servant-Tamar (v. 18)
> > > > > > > Tamar-Absalom (vv. 19-20)

10. *Repetition pattern*. Repetition is often used for the sake of emotional impact. Isaiah pointed up the ignorance of his readers by repeating the questions, "Do you not know? Have you not heard?" in Isaiah 40:21 and 28. His effective use of the word "who" at the beginning of a good number of questions in that chapter also points rhetorically to the ignorance of the people. (Note the word "who" in verses 12 [twice], 13-14, and 26.)

As Bar-efrat points out, in three instances in 2 Samuel, sexual offense is followed by murder.[20] David's involvement with Bathsheba is followed by his having Uriah killed (2 Sam. 11). Amnon's involvement with Tamar is followed by the killing of Amnon (chap. 13), and Absalom's involvement with David's concubines is followed by the killing of Absalom (chaps. 15–19).

One of the recurring subjects of the Gospel of Mark is the growing opposition to Jesus. Mark 2 includes reference to a number of opponents, each of whom asked the question "Why?" (vv. 7, 16, 18, 24) This is seen in verses 7, 16, 18, and 24. Opposition came because Jesus forgave sins (v. 7), ate with sinners (v. 16), neglected the tradition of fasting (v. 18 – "How" in the NIV can also be translated "Why?"), and He "broke" the Sabbath (v. 24).[21]

Summary

As stated at the beginning of this chapter, attention to the literary quality of the Bible helps points up its artistic beauty, and helps give the Bible interpreter a more accurate picture of the Scriptures and the way in which the content is being communicated.

CHAPTER SEVEN

Figures of Speech

In 1937 W. MacNeile Dixon, professor of English literature at the University of Glasgow, wrote,

> If I were asked what has been the most powerful force in the making of history . . . I should have answered . . . figurative expression. It is by imagination that men have lived; imagination rules all our lives. The human mind is not, as philosophers would have you think, a debating hall, but a picture gallery. . . . Remove the metaphors [i.e., figurative expressions] from the Bible and its living spirit vanishes. . . . The prophets, the poets, the leaders of men are all of them masters of imagery, and by imagery they capture the human soul.[1]

The Bible contains hundreds of figures of speech. E.W. Bullinger grouped the Bible's figures of speech into more than 200 categories, giving 8,000 illustrations from the Scriptures, with the table of contents taking 28 pages to list the 200 categories![2]

What Is a Figure of Speech?

The laws of grammar describe how words normally function. In some cases, however, the speaker or writer purposely sets aside those laws to use new forms, forms we call figures of speech. As Bullinger wrote, "A figure is simply a word or a sentence thrown into a peculiar form, different from its original or simplest meaning or use."[3] If we say, "It is raining hard," we are using a normal, plain statement. But if we say, "It is raining cats and dogs," we have used a sentence that means the same thing but is an unusual, more colorful way of expressing the same thought. Or when we say, "The teakettle is boiling," we mean not the kettle but the water in it.

According to Sterrett, "A figure of speech is a word or phrase that is used to communicate something other than its literal, natural meaning."[4] He then gives these examples of figurative expressions in modern-day English: "That argument doesn't hold water." "Stand up for the Word of God." "I was tickled to death." In the first example the argument has nothing to do with literal water. The point is that the argument is as useless as a bucket with holes. In the second example we are not being encouraged to stand up physically next to a Bible, but rather to defend the truths of Scripture, living in such a way that our convictions are clear. And in the third example the person was instead speaking of being extremely pleased.

When John the Baptist said, "Look, the Lamb of God" (John 1:29), he was not pointing to an animal, but to Jesus, who was being compared by John to a lamb. The individuals hearing those words and readers today reading those words are challenged to think of how Jesus was like a lamb. Since the Jews frequently sacrificed lambs, John no doubt had in mind Jesus' forthcoming sacrificial death on behalf of others and in their place.

In each of these examples certain aspects of the statements are not true in their normal sense, but yet the sentences are conveying truth. The argument is inadequate ("it doesn't hold water"), we are to defend and live in accord with the Bible ("stand up for the Bible"), we are pleased ("tickled to death"), Jesus is a substitutionary sacrifice ("the Lamb of God"). Figures of speech express truths in vivid and interesting ways.

Since the Bible has so many figures of speech, it is important to recognize them and determine what they are communicating.

Why Are Figures of Speech Used?

Figures of Speech Add Color or Vividness

To say, "The Lord is my rock" (Ps. 18:2) is a colorful, vivid way of saying the Lord is the One on whom I can depend because He is strong and unmovable.

Figures of Speech Attract Attention

A listener or reader immediately perks up because of the uniqueness of figures of speech. This is evident when Paul wrote, "Watch out for those dogs" (Phil. 3:2), or when James wrote, "The tongue also is a fire" (James 3:6). When a comparison is made between two things that are normally not alike or normally not compared, then surprise occurs. Similes and metaphors, for example, often have this element of unexpectedness.

Figures of Speech Make Abstract or Intellectual Ideas More Concrete

"Underneath are the everlasting arms" (Deut. 33:27) is certainly more concrete than the statement, "The Lord will take care of you and support you."

Figures of Speech Aid in Retention

Hosea's statement, "The Israelites are . . . like a stubborn heifer" (Hosea 4:16), is more easily remembered than if Hosea had written, "Israel is terribly stubborn." The scribes and Pharisees could hardly forget Jesus' words, "You are like whitewashed tombs, which look beautiful on the outside but on the inside are full of dead men's bones and everything unclean" (Matt. 23:27). Figures of speech are used in many languages because they are easily remembered and make indelible impressions.

Figures of Speech Abbreviate an Idea

They capture and convey the idea in a brief way. Because they are graphic, they eliminate the need for elaborate description. They say a lot in a little. The well-known metaphor, "The Lord is my Shepherd" (Ps. 23:1), conveys briefly many ideas about the Lord's relationship to His own.

Figures of Speech Encourage Reflection

Their resplendence makes the reader pause and think. When you read Psalm 52:8, "But I am like an olive tree flourishing in the house of God," you are challenged to reflect on points of similarities suggested in that simile. The same is true of Isaiah 1:8, "The Daughter of Zion is left like a shelter in a vineyard, like a hut in a field of melons, like a city under siege."

How Do You Know If an Expression Is Figurative or Literal?

Generally an expression is figurative when it is out of character with the subject discussed, or is contrary to fact, experience, or observation. If we hear a sports announcer say, "The Falcons beat the Lions," we understand him to be referring to two football teams, and not to be suggesting that birds of prey are attacking literal lions. The following guidelines may be helpful in noting figurative language.

1. Always take a passage in its literal sense unless there is good reason for doing otherwise. For example, when John wrote that 144,000 will be sealed, with 12,000 from each of the 12 tribes of Israel, there is no reason not to take those numbers in their normal, literal sense (Rev. 7:4-8). And yet in the following verse John referred to "the Lamb" (v. 9), clearly a reference to Jesus Christ, not an animal, as indicated by John 1:29.

2. The figurative sense is intended if the literal would involve an impossibility. The Lord told Jeremiah that He had made him "an iron pillar and a bronze wall" (Jer. 1:18). And John wrote that Jesus held seven stars in His right hand (Rev. 1:16). The Lord does not have wings (Ps. 57:1) nor does the earth have ears ("Listen, O earth," Micah 1:2).

3. The figurative is intended if the literal meaning is an absurdity, as in trees clapping their hands (Isa. 55:12).

4. Take the figurative sense if the literal would demand immoral action. Since it would be cannibalistic to eat the flesh of Jesus and to drink His blood, He obviously was speaking figuratively (John 6:53-58).

5. Note whether a figurative expression is followed by an explanatory literal statement. Those who "fall asleep" (1 Thes. 4:13-15) are then spoken of as those who have died (v. 16). When Paul wrote that the Ephesians "were dead" (Eph. 2:1), he did not mean that they had physically died. He immediately explained that they were dead in "transgressions and sins."

6. Sometimes a figure is marked by a qualifying adjective, as in "Heavenly Father" (Matt. 6:14), "the true Bread" (John 6:32), "living Stone" (1 Peter 2:4).[5] Or sometimes a prepositional phrase hints that the preceding noun is not to be understood literally. In the words "the sword of the Spirit" (Eph. 6:17), the phrase "of the Spirit" shows that the sword is to be understood figuratively, not literally. A similar example is "the good fight of the faith" (1 Tim. 6:12).

Is Figurative Language the Opposite of Literal Interpretation?

In the preceding section in this chapter the word *figurative* may seem to be used in a way that opposes the word *literal*. In point 2 above

I wrote, "The figurative sense is intended if the literal would involve an impossibility." However, this and similar statements should not be understood as suggesting that figurative language does not convey literal truth. Figurative speech, as already discussed, is a picturesque, out-of-the-ordinary way of presenting literal facts that might otherwise be stated in a normal, plain, ordinary way. Saying that "the argument does not hold water" is an unusual way of saying the more ordinary sentence, "The argument is weak." Both sentences convey a *literal* fact. One conveys it in a figurative fashion, the other in a nonfigurative way. In other words, as Radmacher put it, "Behind every figure of speech is a literal meaning, and by means of the historical-grammatical exegesis of the text, these literal meanings are to be sought out."[6] If I say, "He jumped out of his skin," I do not mean this in the way the words "jumped" and "skin" would normally be used in their plain sense. Instead I am using a figurative expression (obviously no one can actually jump out of his skin) that communicates a literal fact, namely, that the person was very frightened.

The figurative is a colorful vehicle for presenting literal truth. As Mounce explains, "A writer may convey his thought either by the use of words in their directly denotative sense or he may choose the more pleasing path of figurative expression. But one thing must be kept clear: In either case the literal meaning is the same.... An interpretation is literal only when it corresponds to what the author intends to convey with his statement."[7]

Figurative language then is not antithetical to literal interpretation; it is a part of it. Perhaps it is better not to speak of "figurative versus literal" interpretation, but of "ordinary-literal" versus "figurative-literal" interpretation.[8] Therefore in this book *figurative* means figurative-literal, and *literal* means ordinary-literal. Both are part of what is normally meant by "literal interpretation." Rather than saying, "Figurative is the opposite of literal," it may be preferable to say, "Ordinary-literal is the antithesis of figurative-literal," while understanding that both are legitimate means of communicating literal truths—truths to be interpreted in their normal, historical, grammatical sense without making them say something not intended by the words. This concept is illustrated in the chart on page 148.

Any figure of speech depends on ordinary-literal language. When Peter wrote, "The devil prowls around like a roaring lion" (1 Peter 5:8), the legitimacy of that figurative comparison is based on our understanding something about actual lions. The same is true of types, symbols, parables, allegories, and fables.[9]

Ordinary-Literal	Figurative-Literal
● Normal, plain, ordinary usage	● Picturesque, out-of-the-ordinary usage
● Plainly expressed literal facts	● Figuratively expressed literal facts
"Literal" (historical, grammatical) interpretation	

Paul Tan uses the words *normal* and *customary* in reference to literal interpretation, "Literal interpretation of the Bible simply means explaining the original sense of the Bible according to the normal and customary usages of its language."[10]

The true antithesis is between what the Reformers called literal (historical, grammatical) interpretation and allegorical interpretation, which was so common for centuries throughout the Middle Ages and which regarded portions of Scripture as having secret, mystical meanings. For more on this distinction and the problems with allegorizing, see chapter 2.

What Are Some Figures of Speech?

Figures of Speech Involving Comparison

Many figures of speech involving comparison are from nature (e.g., rain, water, fire, soil, flowers, trees, animals). Others involve human objects (pottery, tombs, clothing), and others refer to human experiences (birth, death, war, music).

1. *Simile.* A simile is a comparison in which one thing explicitly (by using *like* or *as*) resembles another. Peter used a simile when he wrote, "All men are like grass" (1 Peter 1:24). The Lord's words in Luke 10:3 are a simile: "I am sending you out like lambs among wolves." Similes are also included in Psalm 1: "He is like a tree planted by streams of water" (v. 3) and "they are like chaff" (v. 4). The challenge of similes is to determine the ways in which the two objects are similar. How are men like grass? In what way were Jesus' disciples like lambs? In what sense is the believer like a tree, and the wicked like chaff?

2. *Metaphor.* A metaphor is a comparison in which one thing is, acts like, or represents another (in which the two are basically unlike).[11] In a metaphor the comparison is implicit, whereas in a simile it is explicit. A clue to identifying a metaphor is that the verb

will always be in the form of "to be" ("is," "are," "was," "were," "have been"). An example is Isaiah 40:6, "All flesh is grass" (KJV). Note that this differs from the statement in 1 Peter 1:24, "All men are like grass." (A simile always uses the word *like* or *as*.) The Lord said through Jeremiah, "My people have been lost sheep" (Jer. 50:6). The Lord compared His followers to salt: "You are the salt of the earth" (Matt. 5:13). They were not literally salt; they were being compared to salt. When Jesus affirmed, "I am the gate" (John 10:7, 9), "I am the Good Shepherd" (vv. 11, 14), or "I am the Bread of Life" (6:48), He was implying some comparisons. In certain ways He is like a gate, a shepherd, and bread. The reader is challenged to think of ways Jesus resembles those objects.

3. *Hypocatastasis.* This lesser-known figure of speech is a comparison in which the likeness is implied by a direct naming. When David wrote, "Dogs have surrounded me" (Ps. 22:16), he was referring to his enemies, calling them dogs. False teachers are also referred to as dogs in Philippians 3:2 and as savage wolves in Acts 20:29. The differences between a simile, metaphor, and hypocatastasis may be seen in the following sentences:

Simile: "You wicked people are like dogs."
Metaphor: "You wicked people are dogs."
Hypocatastasis: "You dogs."

In John 1:29 John the Baptist used a hypocatastasis: "Look, the Lamb of God." If he had said, "Jesus is like a Lamb," he would have been using a simile. Or a metaphor would have been used if he had said, "Jesus is a lamb." When Jesus told Peter, "Take care of My sheep" (21:17), He called His followers sheep, using a hypocatastasis.

The context needs to be considered in determining the referent of a hypocatastasis. For example Jeremiah wrote, "A lion has come out of his lair" (Jer. 4:7). The context makes it clear that the lion refers to Babylon.

Each of the seven following verses is either a simile, metaphor, or hypocatastasis. In the line following each verse write the kind of figure of speech.

Isaiah 53:6, "We all, like sheep, have gone astray." _____S_____

Psalm 84:11, "For the Lord God is a sun and shield." _____M_____

2 Peter 2:17, "These men are springs without water and mists driven by a storm." _____ _M_

John 2:19, "Destroy this temple, and I will raise it again in three days." _____ H

Isaiah 57:20, "But the wicked are like the tossing sea." S

Psalm 23:1, "The Lord is my Shepherd." _____ M

Psalm 1:3, "He is like a tree planted by streams of water."
_____ S

Figures of Speech Involving Substitution

4. *Metonymy.* A metonymy is the substituting of one word for another. When we refer to a decision being made by the White House, we mean the President of the United States. We have substituted the residence of the President for the President himself. In the statement, "The pen is mightier than the sword" we mean what is written (the pen) has greater impact than military power (the sword).

In the Bible at least three kinds of metonymy are used.

a. The cause is used for the effect. People who opposed Jeremiah said, "Let's attack him with our tongues" (Jer. 18:18). Since a lashing at him literally with their tongues would be an absurdity, it is obvious they were referring to their words. The tongue was the cause, and the words were the effect. Also note Proverbs 12:18: "The tongue of the wise brings healing." Barnabas "witnessed the grace of God" (Acts 11:23, NASB), which probably means he witnessed the effect of the grace of God, namely, the change of life in the believers in Antioch.

b. The effect is used for the cause. David wrote, "I love you, O Lord, my strength" (Ps. 18:1). Strength, the effect, is used for the cause, the Lord.

c. The object is used for something next to it or associated with it. In Paul's words, "You cannot drink the cup of the Lord" (1 Cor. 10:21), he was referring to the contents in the cup, not the drinking of the cup itself. When the Lord said to Hosea that "the land is guilty of the vilest adultery in departing from the Lord" (Hosea 1:2), his reference to land means the people living on the land. The words "Jerusalem was going out to Him" (Matt. 3:5, NASB) point to the fact that the people of Jerusalem were going to Him; the place was substituted for the residents themselves. Some translations, such as the NIV, seek to clarify this by the rendering, "People went out to Him from Jerusalem." The word *eyes* is closely related to the way a person sees things or his mental perspective, as in "The way of a fool is right in his own eyes" (Prov. 15:12, NASB).

When Jesus said, "If a house is divided against itself, that house cannot stand" (Mark 3:25), He obviously did not mean a literal house. He implied a family living in a house. The "marriage bed" (Heb. 13:4) is a metonymy for marital relations. In Matthew 15:8 what does the metonymy "lips" represent?

5. *Synecdoche.* A synecdoche is the substituting of a part of something for the whole or the whole for the part. Caesar Augustus issued a decree that a census should be taken of "all the world" (Luke 2:1, KJV). He was speaking of the whole, but he meant only the part, namely, the Roman world. Proverbs 1:16, "their feet rush into sin," obviously does not mean that only their feet run. Their feet, the part, represent the whole, namely, themselves.

The word *Greek* (NASB) in Romans 1:16 represents all Gentiles. The Lord said, "I am summoning a sword against all the inhabitants of the earth" (Jer. 25:29, NASB). The sword is the part which stands for the whole, that is, disaster, as translated in the NIV. Priscilla and Aquila "risked their own necks" (Rom. 16:4, NASB) for Paul. In this synecdoche the part, "their necks," represents the whole, their lives.

6. *Merism.* A merism is a form of synecdoche in which the totality or whole is substituted by two contrasting or opposite parts. When the psalmist wrote, "You know when I sit and when I rise" (Ps. 139:2), he was not limiting the Lord's knowledge to times when he sat down and when he got up. Instead he was saying the Lord knew all his actions.

7. *Hendiadys.* A hendiadys is the substituting of two coordinate terms (joined by "and") for a single concept in which one of the elements defines the other. The word *hendiadys* comes from three Greek words: *hen,* "one"; *dia,* "by means of"; and *dis,* "twice." The Hebrew for "pain and childbearing" in Genesis 3:16 probably means "pain in childbearing." "The sacrifice and service" in Philippians 2:17 probably means "the sacrificial service." Similarly when the apostles referred to "this ministry and apostleship" (NASB) they meant "this apostolic ministry" (Acts 1:25).

8. *Personification.* This is the ascribing of human characteristics or actions to inanimate objects or ideas or to animals. The emotion of gladness is assigned to the desert in Isaiah 35:1: "The desert and the parched land will be glad." Isaiah 55:12 refers to mountains and hills singing and to trees clapping their hands. Death is personified in Romans 6:9 and 1 Corinthians 15:55.

9. *Anthropomorphism.* An anthropomorphism is the ascribing

of human characteristics or actions to God, as in the references to God's fingers (Ps. 8:3), ear (31:2), and eyes (2 Chron. 16:9).

10. *Anthropopathism.* This figure of speech ascribes human emotions to God, as seen in Zechariah 8:1, "I am very jealous for Zion."

11. *Zoomorphism.* Whereas an anthropomorphism ascribes human characteristics to God, a zoomorphism ascribes animal characteristics to God (or to others). These are expressive ways of pointing up certain actions and attributes of the Lord in a picturesque way. The psalmist wrote, God "will cover you with His feathers, and under His wings you will find refuge" (Ps. 91:4). The readers would think of young chicks or birds being protected under the wings of the mother hen or bird. Job depicted what he considered to be the furious anger of God lashing out at him when he wrote that God "gnashes His teeth at me" (Job 16:9).

12. *Apostrophe.* This is a direct address to an object as if it were a person, or to an absent or imaginary person as if he were present. In personification the writer speaks about some object as if it were a person, whereas in an apostrophe the writer speaks to the object as if it were a person. When the psalmist addressed the sea directly in his words, "Why was it, O sea, that you fled?" (Ps. 114:5) he used an apostrophe. But in an earlier verse, when he spoke about the sea ("The sea looked and fled," v. 3), he used personification. The prophets sometimes called on the earth to serve as a witness to the sinful condition of Israel or other nations. The earth is addressed directly by Micah in Micah 1:2: "Listen, O earth, and all who are in it." In Psalm 6:8 the psalmist spoke as if his enemies were present: "Away from me, all you who do evil."

13. *Euphemism.* This is the substituting of an inoffensive or mild expression for an offensive or personal one. In English we speak euphemistically of death by saying that a person "passed on," "kicked the bucket," or "went home." The Bible speaks of the death of Christians as falling asleep (Acts 7:60; 1 Thes. 4:13-15).

Figures of Speech Involving Omission or Suppression

14. *Ellipsis.* An ellipsis is an omission of a word or words that must be supplied to complete the sentence grammatically. Sometimes an adjective associated with a noun comes to stand for both the adjective and the noun. In English, "private" represents the two words "private soldier." "The Twelve" represents "the 12 Apostles" (1 Cor. 15:5). Second Timothy 4:18 reads literally, "The Lord . . .

will save me to His heavenly kingdom." The thought seems to be that the Lord would save Paul and bring him to His heavenly kingdom. The words "and bring me" need to be supplied by the reader after the words "save me" in order to complete the sentence grammatically.

15. *Zeugma*. A zeugma is the joining of two nouns to one verb when logically only one of the nouns goes with the verb. Literally Luke 1:64 reads, "His mouth was opened and his tongue." The NIV has supplied the words "was loosed" after the word "tongue" in order to render the sentence in good English.

16. *Aposiopesis*. This is a sudden break in the sentence as if the speaker were not able to finish. As Moses confessed the sins of his people, he said, "If Thou wilt forgive their sin—; and if not, blot me, I pray Thee, out of Thy book which Thou hast written" (Ex. 32:32, KJV). He did not finish the thought in the first part of the sentence ("if Thou wilt forgive their sin"), probably because of the emotion of the moment. Paul did not finish the thought in Ephesians 3:1-2: "For this reason I, Paul, the prisoner of Christ Jesus for the sake of you Gentiles—surely you have heard about the administration of God's grace." The Lord also made a break in a sentence as He wept over Jerusalem (Luke 19:42). Again the emotion of the moment probably caused Him to turn from completing this sentence.

17. *Rhetorical question*. A question is asked rhetorically if it does not require a verbal response and is given to force the reader to answer in his mind and to consider the implications of the answer. Quentilian (A.D. 35–100), a Roman rhetorician, said rhetorical questions increase the force and cogency of proof. When God asked Abraham, "Is anything too hard for the Lord?" (Gen. 18:14) He was not expecting a verbal response. He was facing Abraham with a question to answer in his mind. The same is true when the Lord asked Jeremiah, "Is anything too hard for Me?" (Jer. 32:27) Paul asked a rhetorical question in Romans 8:31, "If God is for us, who can be against us?" These rhetorical questions are ways of conveying information. The first two questions indicate that nothing is impossible with God and Paul's question in Romans 8:31 affirms that no one can successfully oppose the believer in view of God's defense of him.

Sometimes a rhetorical question is directed to oneself as in Luke 12:17, in which the rich man thought to himself, "What shall I do? I have no place to store my crops." When Jesus asked the crowd, "Am I leading a rebellion, that you have come out with swords and clubs to capture Me?" (Matt. 26:55) His question was to get them to realize He was *not* leading a rebellion. A negative response is implied in His questions, "Which of you fathers, if your son asks for a fish, will give him a snake instead? Or if he asks for an egg, will give him a scorpion?" (Luke 11:11-12) Some rhetorical questions rebuke or admonish, others express surprise, some are spoken to get attention.

What is the affirmation suggested by each of the following rhetorical questions?

"How can Satan drive out Satan?" (Mark 3:23) ———— *Get attention*

"Do you bring in a lamp to put it under a bowl or a bed?" (4:21) ———— *attention*

"Do you have eyes but fail to see, and ears but fail to hear?" (8:18) ———— *Admonish*

"What can a man give in exchange for his soul?" (v. 37) ———— *attention*

"If the whole body were an eye, where would the sense of hearing be?" (1 Cor. 12:17) ———— *attention*

Sometimes questions are used to rebuke. They too lead the hearers/readers to think. For example Jesus asked His disciples, "Why are you so afraid? Do you still have no faith?" (Mark 4:40) By these questions He was rebuking them for being afraid and not having faith. Jesus' words to His sleeping disciples in Gethsemane, "Are you still sleeping and resting?" (14:41) rebuked them for sleeping. In interpreting the Bible it is important to be alert to rhetorical questions and to note how they are being used and the thoughts being suggested by them.

Figures of Speech Involving
Overstatement or Understatement

18. *Hyperbole*. A hyperbole is a deliberate exaggeration, in which more is said than is literally meant, in order to add emphasis. When 10 of the Israelite spies reported on their exploration of the land of Canaan, they said, "The cities are large and fortified to heaven" (Deut. 1:28, NASB). Obviously they were not saying the walls of the Canaanite cities reached literally to heaven; they were simply stating that the walls were unusually high.

The psalmist used hyperbole for emphasis when he wrote, "Every night I make my bed swim, I dissolve my couch with my tears" (Ps. 6:6, NASB). The NIV seeks to express the thought of the hyperbole in slightly more literal language by the words, "All night

long I flood my bed with weeping and drench my couch with tears."
Even this softer wording, however, is hyperbolic. David was shed-
ding many tears, but certainly not so many that his bed was swim-
ming or flooded or his couch dissolved or was drenched. Psalm
119:136 is a similar example: "My eyes shed streams of water"
(NASB); the NIV has, "Streams of tears flow from my eyes." Certainly
rivers did not flow from his eyes. He was deeply grieved to the point
of extensive weeping.

Speaking for the sinful nation Israel, Micah the prophet
asked, "Will the Lord be pleased with thousands of rams, with ten
thousand rivers of oil?" (Micah 6:7) Micah's point in using this
hyperbole in a rhetorical question was to emphasize that no matter
how much oil the people brought as a sacrifice to God, that would
not atone for their sins. After David had killed Goliath, the women
from the towns of Israel met King Saul, singing, "Saul has slain his
thousands, and David his tens of thousands" (1 Sam. 18:7). Certainly David had not killed 10 times as many people as Saul; David had
killed only one person. And yet David's defeat of Goliath was expressed by hyperbole to point up the great significance of his victory
over the Philistine giant.

In his lament over Saul and Jonathan, David commented that
"they were swifter than eagles, they were stronger than lions"
(2 Sam. 1:23). No man could literally run swifter than an eagle
could fly, nor is any man physically stronger than a lion. Hence it is
obvious that David spoke with hyperboles to emphasize Saul's and
Jonathan's speed and strength in battle. Such picturesque language
has a strong impact on the readers.

Did Jesus mean that the scribes and the Pharisees were literally straining out gnats and could literally swallow a camel? (Matt.
23:24) No. His point was that while the Pharisees were concerning
themselves with minute details of the Law, like meticulously straining out a gnat from a liquid, they were neglecting the much greater,
more important elements of the Law (v. 23), including justice, mercy, and faithfulness, as if they were easily swallowing a camel!

Other examples of hyperboles are these: "This is what Cyrus
king of Persia says: 'The Lord, the God of heaven, has given me all
the kingdoms of the earth'" (2 Chron. 36:23). "What good will it be
for a man if he gains the whole world, yet forfeits his soul?" (Matt.
16:26) The father of the prodigal son said to his elder son, "This
brother of yours was dead and is alive again" (Luke 15:32). "Take
the plank out of your eye" (Luke 6:42). Cyrus obviously did not rule

over all kingdoms, a person cannot gain the entire world, the prodigal son was not actually dead and resurrected, and a plank cannot be taken from a person's eye. These hyperboles, however, do capture one's attention and add emphasis to what is said.

Is hyperbole error? Is the use of hyperbole consistent with the inerrancy of the Scriptures? If writers using hyperbole were saying more than they intended, is this to be understood as error? No. Error is not reflected by hyperbole because as seen in the above examples hyperbole is generally readily understood by the reader as an exaggerated statement given for emphasis or impact. Therefore the readers are not misled.

Hyperboles are literary devices to reflect what the writers intended to convey. In speaking of Saul and Jonathan being "swifter than eagles," David was accurately conveying his thought that the former king of Israel and his son were usually swift in battle. Furthermore the *thought* conveyed by the hyperbole corresponds to fact. Saul and Jonathan were indeed agile and quick-footed.

In anguish and frustration Job responded to his friends, "Ten times now you have reproached me" (Job 19:3). However, the friends had actually spoken only five times—Eliphaz in chapters 4–5 and again in chapter 15, Bildad in chapters 8 and 18, and Zophar in chapter 11. Was Job then wrong, and does the Bible contain error in 19:3? No, error is not involved when it is understood that Job's hyperbole meant that his friends had insulted him numerous times. Four other times the Old Testament uses the words "ten times": Jacob said to or about Laban, "You changed my wages ten times" (Gen. 31:7, 41). The Lord said to Moses that His people "tested Me ten times" (Num. 14:22). Nehemiah reported that the Jews "told us ten times over, 'wherever you turn, they will attack us'" (Neh. 4:12). Nebuchadnezzar found Daniel and his three friends "ten times better than all the magicians and enchanters in his whole kingdom" (Dan. 1:20). These hyperboles, not to be taken literally, do in fact accurately portray the truth intended by the statements. When a mother chides her recalcitrant child, "I've told you 10,000 times to clean up your room," she means numerous times, not the literal number of 1,000 multiplied by 10. She is not speaking in error; she is speaking truth in an exaggerated way to convey her point emphatically.

19. *Litotes.* A litotes is an understatement or a negative statement to express an affirmation. This is the opposite of hyperbole. When we say, "He is not a bad preacher," we mean he is a very good preacher. The understatement is made for emphasis. When Paul

wrote, "I am a Jew . . . a citizen of no insignificant city" (Acts 21:39, NASB), he meant that Tarsus was in fact a rather significant city.

A litotes is at times a belittling statement, as in Numbers 13:33, "We seemed like grasshoppers in our own eyes, and we looked the same to them." Luke used a number of litotes. He spoke of "no small disturbance among the soldiers" (Acts 12:18, NASB), "no little business" (19:24), and "no small storm" (27:20, NASB). When Luke wrote that Paul and Barnabas stayed in Antioch "a long time" (14:28), the Greek has a litotes. It is literally, "they stayed there not a little time." Paul belittled himself with a litotes in 1 Corinthians 15:9, "For I am the least of the apostles." This statement of genuine humility was written to highlight God's grace in his life as an undeserving sinner (see v. 10).

20. *Irony.* Irony is a kind of ridicule expressed indirectly in the form of a compliment. Irony is often conveyed by the speaker's tone of voice so that the hearers know that irony is intended. This sometimes makes it difficult to determine whether a written statement is to be taken as irony. But the context usually helps determine whether irony is being used. Saul's daughter Michal said to David, "How the king of Israel has distinguished himself today" (2 Sam. 6:20). Verse 22 suggests she was conveying an opposite meaning, namely, that he had humiliated himself by acting in what was to her an undignified manner. Humor is sometimes sensed in irony, as in Elijah's taunting the prophets of Baal, "Shout louder! . . . Surely he is a god!" (1 Kings 18:27) Obviously Elijah was not recognizing any reality to the existence of the false god Baal. In irony he was complimenting Baal in order to prod the prophets to pray even louder. This highlighted the fact that this false god, unlike the true God Yahweh, did not always hear his worshipers.

In Job 12:2 Job's words to his three antagonists drip with irony: "Doubtless you are the people, and wisdom will die with you!" On the surface this sounds as if Job were complimenting his three friends for being so wise. Since they possessed all the world's wisdom, when they would die, wisdom would then be gone. However, his other remarks to the friends, in which he was criticizing them for not knowing his situation, indicates that his words in verse 2 were intended not as a compliment but as ridicule.

Job complained that he received no help from his friends. They were totally unsympathetic to his problem. Therefore he obviously spoke with irony in these words to Bildad: "How you have helped the powerless! How you have saved the arm that is feeble!

What advice you have offered to one without wisdom! And what great insight you have displayed!" (26:2-3) (The word *you* in these verses is in the singular form in Hebrew, thus referring back to Bildad who had just spoken in chapter 25. The *you* in 12:2-3, however, is plural, referring to all three friends.)

When Jesus said to the Pharisees and scribes, "You have a fine way" (Mark 7:9), it sounds as if He were beginning to compliment them. The rest of the sentence, however, indicates that He was ridiculing them. Thus the full sentence is irony: "You have a fine way of setting aside the commands of God in order to observe your own traditions!"

Paul used irony as well. In 1 Corinthians 4:8, he wrote, "You have become kings," but then in the next sentence he added, "How I wish that you really had become kings." The first sentence then is certainly a case of irony. He also wrote with irony, "You are so wise in Christ!" (v. 10) Paul again used irony in addressing the Corinthian believers in 2 Corinthians 11:19. What sounded like a compliment—"You gladly put up with fools since you are so wise!"—was actually a form of ridicule and criticism. They assumed themselves to be wise when actually they were not. Their lack of wisdom was revealed in the fact that they "put up with fools," that is, false apostles mentioned in verse 13. The sting of irony is evident in each of these examples.

Read Amos 4:4-5 and think of the question, Why did Amos tell the Israelites to "go to Bethel and sin; go to Gilgal and sin yet more"? Why did he tell them to bring their sacrifices and "to boast about them"? Surely he was not encouraging sin and pride. What was the point of these sentences of irony?

The above cases are examples of verbal irony. Another kind of irony is dramatic irony. This refers to a situation which is the opposite of what is expected or what is appropriate. For example it is a dramatic irony that Elihu, a person younger than Job and his three friends, would seemingly have more insight into Job's situation than Elihu's three elders. This is the opposite of what is expected. Also after reading of Job's godliness (Job 1:1, 8; 2:3) it is alarming to read of the calamities he experienced. This seems to be the opposite of what the reader would expect.

Dramatic irony also means the readers know some facts the participants in the story apparently do not know. This is illustrated in the fact that the reader knows that Satan was behind Job's calamities, whereas Job himself did not realize that fact. Caiaphas, the high priest, said to the Sanhedrin, "You do not realize that it is better for you that one man die for the people than that the whole nation perish" (John 11:50). Readers of the Gospel of John realize that Caiaphas was speaking more than what he himself understood.

Xerxes asked Haman, "What should be done for the man the king delights to honor?" (Es. 6:6) "The question addressed by King Xerxes to Haman is ironical, since its purpose is to make Haman think it applies to himself, whereas in fact it applies to Mordecai (v. 6)."[12]

The terms *irony* and *sarcasm* are often used interchangeably because irony usually includes an element of sarcasm. However, sarcasm is usually heavier in tone. Being more caustic, sarcasm is usually used to wound. It is a biting criticism. Irony, however, is a more subtle form of ridicule.[13]

21. *Pleonasm.* Pleonasm is a repetition of words or the adding of similar words, which in English would seem redundant. Job said to God, "I have heard of Thee by the hearing of the ear" (Job 42:5, NASB). In this figure of speech the words "heard," "hearing," and "ear" are redundant in good English. Therefore the NIV has rendered this verse, "My ears had heard of You." The Greek of Acts 2:30 is literally, "God took an oath with an oath." Since this in English seems needlessly repetitious, the NIV has rendered the sentence, "God had promised him on oath." Another example is Matthew's statement that the wise men "rejoiced . . . with great joy" (Matt. 2:10, NASB). The thought is that "they were overjoyed" (NIV). "He answered and said" is a pleonasm, as is "he lifted up his eyes and saw."

Figures of Speech Involving Inconsistency

22. *Oxymoron.* This is a combining together of terms that are opposite or contradictory. The word *oxymoron* comes from two Greek words—*oxus* ("sharp") and *moros* ("stupid"). Examples in English are "loud silence," "sweet sorrow," "open secret," and "original copy." In the first example, though silence is not in reality loud, it is so evident that it is as if it were loud. Peter spoke of Jesus' "birth pangs of death" (Greek, Acts 2:24; the NASB and the NIV have "the agony of death"). Jesus' death, in other words, was as painful as that of a mother giving birth to a child. Though "birth pangs" and "death" are opposite experiences not normally associated, they are brought together here as a means of vividly depicting Jesus' death.

The "glory" of the enemies of Christ is "in their shame"

(Phil. 3:19). Glory and shame are not normally coupled, but Paul put them together in this sentence to depict graphically that they were priding themselves in things they should have been ashamed of. "Living sacrifices" (Rom. 12:1) is another biblical oxymoron.

23. *Paradox.* A paradox is a statement that is seemingly absurd or contrary to normal opinion. A paradox is not a contradiction; it is simply something that gives the appearance of the opposite of what is normally understood. It seems paradoxical for Jesus to say, "Whoever loses his life for Me and for the Gospel will save it" (Mark 8:35). A person who loses something normally does not also at the same time save it. Of course Jesus spoke in this fashion in order to stress that by making sacrifices for Him an individual would actually have a more complete and satisfying life.

Figures of Speech Involving Sound

24. *Paronomasia.* This is using the same words or similar-sounding words to suggest different meanings. A paronomasia is sometimes called a "play on words," a word play, or a pun.

Jesus told a man, "Follow Me, and let the dead bury their own dead" (Matt. 8:22). Dead is used in two ways in this statement. The first reference to dead refers to those who are spiritually dead, whereas the second use of the word points to those who are physically dead. The word *house* is used in two ways in 2 Samuel 7. David wanted to build a house for the Lord (v. 5, a temple). God told him he would not have that opportunity, but instead God Himself would build a house, that is, a dynasty for David (v. 11).

Micah used a number of word plays in Micah 1:10-15. He told the people of the village of Beth Ophrah to "roll in the dust" (v. 10) in an expression of their grief. Interestingly Ophrah means dust. They were to live out the meaning of the name of their village. Isaiah used similar-sounding words to make a verbal impact on those who heard or read his words in Isaiah 5:7. The Lord looked for "justice" (*mišpoṭ*) but He saw "bloodshed" (*mišpoḥ*), and instead of "righteousness" (*ṣᵉdāqâh*) there was "distress" (*ṣᵉʾāqâh*). These words in each pair are striking not only because they are similar in sound but also because they are exact opposites in meaning.

Sometimes New Testament writers used words that begin with the same letters. This is called alliteration. Luke 21:11 refers to famines (*loimoi*) and pestilences (*limoi*). In Romans 1:29 Paul put together two similar-sounding Greek words: "full of envy" (*phthonou*) and "murder" (*phonou*). Paul also wrote (v. 31) that the unregenerate are "senseless" (*asynētous*) and "faithless" (*asynthētous*).

The words "blameless," "pure," and "without fault" (Phil. 2:15) begin with the same letters in Greek: *amemptoi, akeraioi, amōma*. Alliterated *kopos* ("labor") and *kenos* ("vain") in 1 Corinthians 15:58 ("your labor in the Lord is not in vain") add to the impact of the sentence.

25. *Onomatopoeia.* This is the occurrence of a word which by its very sound suggests its meaning. Many such words exist in English: boom, buzz, click, hiss, pow, roar, ticktock. The word *swoops* in Job 9:26 (NASB) is an example of onomatopoeia in Hebrew. The Hebrew word is *tuś*, which sounds like the motion of the eagle (or peregrine falcon) when it swoops on its prey at an amazing high speed. The Hebrew word for "clay jar" in Jeremiah 19:1, 10 is *baqbuq*, which sounds like water gurgling out of a jar. Jeremiah also used this word as a paronomasia because in verse 7 the word for "ruin" is *bāqaq*, which sounds like the word for clay jar.

Sometimes two figures of speech blend together. When Micah wrote, "Listen, O earth" (1:2), he used an apostrophe, in which he was directly addressing the earth as if it were present, and he was also using personification in which he personified the earth as a human being with ears. The same two figures of speech occur in Psalm 114:5, "Why was it, O sea?"

How Should We Interpret Figures of Speech?

Determine If a Figure of Speech Is Involved

Sometimes a figure of speech is not recognized as such and the statement is therefore misunderstood. When Paul wrote of enduring hardship like a good soldier, competing as an athlete, and receiving a share of the crops like a farmer (2 Tim. 2:3-6), he was not giving instructions to soldiers, athletes, and farmers. The fact that he encouraged Timothy to be a good soldier of Christ Jesus indicates he was speaking figuratively.

When Jesus said, "Do not give dogs what is sacred; do not throw your pearls to pigs" (Matt. 7:6), he was not referring to dogs, pearls, and pigs in the normal sense because no one in that day would give what is sacred or expensive to dogs or pigs anyway. Those animals were considered unclean and were held in low esteem. This statement then should be understood as a figure of speech in which Jesus was saying that a person should not entrust holy things to unholy people. Since stars do not normally sing, the statement in

Job 38:7, "The morning stars sang together," should not be taken literally. It should be understood as expressing the view that Creation rejoiced (a personification) at God's creative work.

Conversely sometimes a normal statement is wrongly taken as a figure of speech. God said to Israel, "Many times I struck your gardens and vineyards, I struck them with blight and mildew. Locusts devoured your fig and olive trees, yet you have not returned to Me" (Amos 4:9). There is no reason for not understanding these words literally. It would be wrong to take them as speaking figuratively of spiritual hardships. The immediate context suggests they be understood literally, since rain, drought, and thirst (vv. 7-8) and the plagues in Egypt (v. 10) were literal events.

Some people wrongly suggest that the wolf living with the lamb, the leopard lying down with a goat, and the calf and the lion lying together with a child leading them (Isa. 11:6) refer figuratively to spiritual blessing and peace. But there is no reason for not taking them in the usual, literal sense.

Discover the Image and the Nonimage in the Figure of Speech

Sometimes both are given in a verse as in Isaiah 8:7: "Therefore the Lord is about to bring against them the mighty floodwaters of the River." At first glance one may wonder if the Lord is speaking of floodwaters literally or figuratively. This is answered in the very next line of the verse in the words "the king of Assyria with all his pomp." The "floodwaters" are the image and the king of Assyria is the nonimage or referent. Sometimes, however, the nonimage is not specified and may even be misunderstood. This was true of Jesus' words in John 2:19, "Destroy this temple." Temple was the image and the hearers thought the nonimage was Herod's temple, whereas Jesus meant His body.

State the Point of Comparison

In the following chart note that Psalm 1:3 uses the image of a tree to refer to a believer. In what sense is the believer "like a tree planted by streams of water"? As suggested in the chart, he, like a tree, is secure, prosperous, and fruitful. Isaiah wrote, "We all, like sheep, have gone astray" (Isa. 53:6). As shown on the chart the image is sheep, the nonimage is all humans, and they are alike in that they are wayward. Much as sheep tend to wander off physically from the flock, so human beings tend to wander off spiritually from God.

	Image	Nonimage (Referent)	Point(s) of Comparison
Simile Psalm 1:3a	Tree	Believer	Secure, prosperous, fruitful
Isaiah 53:6	Sheep	All humans	Wayward spiritually
Isaiah 57:20		Wicked	
Metaphor Psalm 23:1		Lord	
Psalm 84:11		Lord	
2 Peter 2:17a		False teacher	
Hypocatastasis Matthew 16:11		False teaching	
John 2:19		Jesus' body	

Complete the chart by filling in the images indicated in the verses and then stating the point or points of comparison.

The points of comparison are not always immediately evident in similes or metaphors. When Solomon wrote that the hair of his bride was "like a flock of goats descending from Mount Gilead" (Song 4:1), the meaning of that compliment may not be immediately transparent to Westerners. In fact it does not sound at all like a compliment! Goats in Palestine had dark hair, and when seen from a distance in the sunset as goats were descending from a mountain, they were a beautiful scene. Similarly Solomon's bride's black hair was considered beautiful. The similes in the Song of Songs require careful attention to determine what point of similarity would have been understood by people in the Middle East in Bible times. If the point of similarity is not stated, the Bible student needs to be careful he does not assume the wrong similarity. The same holds true in the English statement, "John eats like a pig." Some point of similarity is intended by that sentence between a pig and John. However, does the statement mean that like a pig he eats too much, or eats fast, or eats sloppily? Either an explicit statement giving the point of similarity or an implicit statement found in the context is needed for the interpreter to be sure of the precise meaning.

In 1 Samuel 2:2, Hannah prayed, "There is no Rock like our God." However, she did not explain what she meant by referring to God as a rock. The Bible interpreter then needs to see how references to God as a rock are used elsewhere in the Scriptures to help determine the meaning. Psalm 94:22 hints at the meaning. Apparently the concept of God being a rock meant that God, like a large rock with a cave for hiding, was one in whom His followers could take refuge from their troubles (cf. 18:2; 31:2; 62:7; 71:3; 94:22).

Sometimes the image is stated, but the nonimage or referent, though not given explicitly, is suggested by the context. In Luke 5:34 the "bridegroom" is not said to be Jesus, but the meaning is implicit since Jesus said in the next verse that the bridegroom would be taken from them. "The guests of the Bridegroom" are not specified, though they are most likely Jesus' disciples because the preceding verse refers to Jesus' disciples who are eating and drinking, much like bridegroom guests.

What nonimage is being conveyed by the image "ax" in Matthew 3:10? What topics are being referred to by the images of the plentiful harvest and the few workers in 9:37?

Do Not Assume a Figure Always Means the Same Thing

Dew in Hosea 6:4 describes the short duration of Judah's love, whereas in 14:5 dew speaks of the Lord's blessing on Israel.

Place Legitimate Limits or Controls on the Figures by Means of Logic and Communication

When the Lord told the church in Sardis, "I will come like a thief" (Rev. 3:3), He did not mean He would come to rob. Instead the point of comparison is that He would come suddenly or unexpectedly. When Job referred to the "pillars" of the earth trembling (Job 9:6), he was referring to the mountains of the earth. He was not picturing the earth as resting on pillars.

How Does an Idiom Differ from a Figure of Speech?

An idiom is a figure of speech which is an expression peculiar to a given language or to people in a certain geographical location. According to Larson, an idiom is "a string of words whose meaning is different than the meaning conveyed by the individual words."[14] She illustrates this by pointing out that in English a person might say, "His fever went down," whereas in the Aguaruna language of Peru the sentence would be "He cooled," and in Ilocano of the Philippines, a person would say, "The fever was no more in him." In English, "He has a hard heart," means "he is indifferent to the needs of others." But the same expression, "to have a hard heart," in the Shipibo language of Peru means "he is brave." Shipibo does have an idiom which means a person is indifferent. It is, "His ears have no holes."

English has the idiom "a horse of a different color," but in Spanish the corresponding idiom is translated "flour from a different bag."[15] An idiom is a combination of words that have a meaning as a whole, but in which the meaning of the combination is not the same as the meaning of the individual words. Other examples are "down in the dumps," "in the doghouse," "kick the bucket," "hit the sack," "step on the gas," "head above water," "snowed under," "out of hand."

When Jesus' mother at the wedding at Cana told Him the wine was used up, He said, "Dear woman, why do you involve Me?" (John 2:4) The Greek is literally, "What to Me and to you?" This was an idiom, a unique way of saying, "What do we have in common regarding this problem?" or in other words, "Why involve Me? It is your problem."

When Elijah called Elisha to follow him and become his

protegé, Elisha asked permission to kiss his parents good-bye. Elijah agreed to his request and asked, "What have I done to you?" (1 Kings 19:20) That question seems peculiar until one realizes it is an idiom meaning, "What have I done to stop you?" or in other words, "Please go ahead; you have my permission."

Linguists speak of idioms as "dead" metaphors, by which they mean that they have become such an accepted part of the language that the person who hears or reads the idiom does not think about the primary sense of the words but only the idiomatic sense. When we hear or read of "the foot of the stairs," we do not think of a human foot. We automatically think of the bottom part of the stairs. In this idiom a comparison is made between a human foot and the lower portion of the stairs. And yet the idiom is a "dead metaphor" since the person hearing or reading it does not think about the comparison but thinks directly of the meaning of the idiom. "Foothills," "head table," and "a fork in the road" are other examples of idioms.

Idioms should not be thought of as mistakes in the Scriptures; they are ways in which the thought is conveyed in that native language. The Greek in Mark 6:7 can be translated, "He sent them two by two." The word *by* is not in the Greek because the idiomatic Greek expression did not require it. English, however, does require that the word *by* be included and so it is given in all English translations. German, on the other hand, has a different idiom: "zwei und zwei" ("two and two").

Jesus said He would be "three days and three nights in the heart of the earth" just as Jonah was "three days and three nights in the belly of the huge fish" (Matt. 12:40). "Three days and three nights" was an idiomatic phrase meaning any parts of three days and three nights. Since Jesus was crucified on Friday and resurrected on Sunday, it was impossible for Him to be in the grave three full 24-hour days.

The Greek of Romans 16:4 reads, "They laid down their neck." This idiom is best rendered in English by the words "they risked their own necks," or as in the NIV, "they risked their lives." The idiom "the son of" followed by a quality indicates that the person possesses that quality as in Ephesians 5:6, "the sons of disobedience" (Greek). Christians are "sons of the light" (1 Thes. 5:5) in that they are characterized by light, that is, they do not consistently live in the darkness of sin. A "son of peace" (Greek, Luke 10:6) is one who is characterized by peace.

Matching of Figures of Speech
with Their Definitions

(In each group of five, match the definitions with the figures of speech on the right.)

1. A comparison in which likeness is implied by a direct naming.
2. A substituting of one word for another.
3. A comparison of one thing with another by using the word *like* or *as*.
4. A comparison in which a thing represents another by using the word *is* or *are*.
5. Substituting of a part for the whole or the whole for the part.

a. Metonymy

b. Synecdoche

c. Hypocatastasis

d. Simile

e. Metaphor

* * *

1. Ascribing human characteristics or actions to inanimate objects or ideas or animals.
2. Ascribing animal characteristics to God or others.
3. Ascribing human characteristics or actions to God.
4. Ascribing human emotions to God.
5. Substituting an inoffensive or mild expression for an offensive or personal one.

a. Anthropomorphism

b. Personification

c. Zoomorphism

d. Euphemism

e. Anthropopathism

* * *

1. An exaggeration in which more is said than is literally meant.
2. An understatement in which less is said than is literally meant.
3. A kind of ridicule which sounds like a compliment.
4. A question to which a verbal answer is not expected.
5. A statement that is seemingly absurd.

a. Irony

b. Hyperbole

c. Rhetorical question

d. Paradox

e. Litotes

* * *

Want to see how well you know the figures of speech discussed in this chapter? Look up the following references and write which figure of speech is used in each verse.

Psalm 114:3 ———————————————
John 21:25 ———————————————
Jeremiah 17:6a ———————————————
Matthew 23:33a ———————————————
Isaiah 49:13a ———————————————
2 Thessalonians 3:2b ———————————————
Psalm 105:4b ———————————————
Micah 5:2a ———————————————
Matthew 26:26 ———————————————
Ruth 2:12b ———————————————
2 Corinthians 6:9-10 ———————————————
Genesis 42:38b ———————————————
Exodus 34:14 ———————————————
Mark 15:32 ———————————————
Genesis 4:1a ———————————————
Amos 3:3-4 ———————————————

* * *

For another exercise study Isaiah 40:1-17 looking for all the figures of speech you can find. Some verses have several figures.

CHAPTER EIGHT

Testing the Types and Sensing the Symbols

Most Bible students recognize that the Old Testament includes types that are later specified in some way in the New Testament. The two Testaments are related by types and antitypes, shadows and fulfillments. The New Testament looks back to a number of persons, things, and events in the Old Testament and treats them as foreshadowing then-future persons, things, and events.

However, Bible interpreters differ widely on the extent to which types are to be seen in the Scriptures. Some say types are evident throughout much of the Old Testament. Numerous objects and events are said to be pictures of New Testament truths. For example the hinges in the door to Solomon's temple are said to be a type of the two natures of Christ. Others say types are those that are either explicitly designated in the New Testament or are implicit. Some Bible students suggest that types are only those that are designated as such in the New Testament, that is, those that are explicitly said to be types. Still others suggest no typology is to be seen in the Bible at all.

Several questions must be considered. What is a type? That is, what are its characteristics? What elements in the Old Testament are to be accepted as legitimate types? What guidelines are necessary for interpreting the types?

New Testament Terms Used in Relation to Typology

The word *type* comes from the Greek *typos,* used 15 times in the New Testament. It is translated in various ways as seen in the following verses:

"The nail *marks* in His hands" (John 20:25)

"The *idols* [figures or images] you made to worship" (Acts 7:43)

"The tabernacle . . . according to the *pattern* [Moses] had seen" (v. 44)

"He wrote a letter *as follows* [of this kind or to this effect]" (23:25)

"Adam, who was a *pattern* of the One to come" (Rom. 5:14)

"You wholeheartedly obeyed the *form* of teaching" (6:17)

"Now these things occurred as *examples*" (1 Cor. 10:6)

"Join with others in following my *example*" (Phil. 3:17)

"And so you became a *model* to all the believers in Macedonia and Achaia" (1 Thes. 1:7)

"We did this . . . in order to make ourselves a *model* for you to follow" (2 Thes. 3:9)

"Set an *example* for the believers" (1 Tim. 4:12)

"In everything set them an *example*" (Titus 2:7)

"Make everything according to the *pattern* shown you on the mountain" (Heb. 8:5)

"Being *examples* to the flock" (1 Peter 5:3).

These verses reveal that *typos* is rendered in a variety of ways: mark, form, pattern, model, example. The idea common to all these occurrences is correspondence or resemblance. The person, event, or thing was fashioned to resemble another, to answer to it in some way. One was to match the other.

The lives of the Philippians were to resemble that of Paul (Phil. 3:17). Believers are to resemble the pattern set by Timothy (1 Tim. 4:12). The tabernacle was to resemble the pattern shown to Moses (Heb. 8:5). Even the nail prints in Jesus' hands resembled or reflected the nails themselves. The one corresponds to the other. The idol images reflected or corresponded to the worshipers' ideas or concepts of their fallen gods (Acts 7:43). And when Paul spoke of "the form of teaching" which the Roman believers obeyed (Rom. 6:17), he was referring to his doctrine as a standard or pattern which they were to follow, that is, teachings to which their lives were to correspond.

Obviously the word *typos* is not a technical term in that every time it is used it means the same thing or always suggests a theological type. In fact the only occurrence of *typos* which is related to a prefiguring in the Old Testament of something in the New, is Hebrews 8:5. *Typos* may derive from the verb *typtō*, "to strike." *Typos* then originally carried the idea of the result of a blow or what gives a blow or impression. From that developed the thought of mark, mold, stamp, cast, form, model, outline, sketch.[1]

A related word, *typikōs,* is used in 1 Corinthians 10:11: "These things happened to them as *examples.*" This is to be understood as an adverb, "These things happened to them *typically.*"

The word *antitypos* is used twice in the New Testament. It speaks of something corresponding to a pattern. In 1 Peter 3:21 water baptism is said to be an antitype of the floodwaters in Noah's day. The Flood was a type or figure of baptism in that in both instances the water spoke of judgment; the Flood meant death for the wicked, and water baptism pictures the death of Christ and the identification of the believer with Christ's death. Again the idea of resemblance is present. According to Hebrews 9:24, the sanctuary or holy place of the tabernacle was a copy (*antitypa*) of the true tabernacle in heaven. That is, the one corresponded to the other. The word *antitype* literally means "answering to the type" and means a counterpart.

First Timothy 1:16 uses a similar word, *hypotyposis.* Christ's "unlimited patience" was "an *example* for those who would believe on Him." Paul used the same word in 2 Timothy 1:13: "What you heard from me keep as the *pattern* of sound teaching."

Two words related to *typos* are *deigma* ("Sodom and Gomorrah. . . . serve as an example," Jude 7) and *hypodeigma.* This latter word is used six times, as follows:

"I have set you an *example*" (John 13:15)

"Their *example* of disobedience" (Heb. 4:11)

"They serve at a sanctuary that is a *copy* and shadow of what is in heaven" (8:5)

"It was necessary, then, for the *copies* of the heavenly things to be purified" (Heb. 9:23)

"Brothers, as an *example* of patience in the face of suffering, take the prophets" (James 5:10)

"Sodom and Gomorrah [are] an *example* of what is going to happen to the ungodly" (2 Peter 2:6).

Clearly in each of these cases the word means an example, copy, or pattern to be followed.

Another word is *skia,* a "shadow." Just as a shadow is an image cast by an object, so some objects in the Old Testament were a sketch or shadow of things yet future. This word is used three times in the New Testament in this figurative sense. Hebrews 8:5 reads,

"They serve at a sanctuary that is a copy and shadow [*skia*] of what is in heaven." Interestingly three related words are used in this one verse: "copy" (*hypodeigma*), "shadow" (*skia*), and "pattern" (*typos*). "The Law is only a shadow [*skia*] of the good things that are coming—not the realities themselves" (10:1). And Paul wrote that religious festivals, New Moon celebrations, and the Sabbath "are a shadow of the things that were to come; the reality, however, is found in Christ" (Col. 2:16-17).

A shadow implies something that is dim and transitory, but it also suggests a degree of resemblance. Each of these five words suggests the idea of correspondence or resemblance. However, it should be kept in mind that the word *typos* does not always mean an official type in which something in the Old Testament is foreshadowing or prefiguring something in the New Testament. It often simply means a pattern, example, or model to be followed.

When Is a Type a Type?

Resemblance

The first characteristic of a type is that a resemblance, similarity, or correspondence exists between the type and the antitype. However, this should not be thought of as some superficial relationship, but rather a genuine and substantial counterpart. It should be natural and not forced. As seen in the discussion of the Greek words for types or examples, the idea of substantial correspondence or resemblance is evident.

However, not everything that has correspondence or resemblance is a type, though all types must have the element of correspondence.

Numerous things in the Old Testament are similar to things in the New Testament, but they are not necessarily types. A type has resemblance to that for which it is a type, but it has more than resemblance. The following elements are also necessary in order to have an official type.

Historical Reality

Persons, events, or things in the Old Testament that are types of things in the New Testament had historical reality. A type in the Old Testament is not something without reality. The types were persons who lived, events that happened, things that were seen.

Seeing types in the Old Testament does not mean the Bible

student should look for hidden or deeper meanings in the text. He should stick with the historical facts as recorded in the Old Testament. In other words the type should rise naturally out of the text, and should not be something the interpreter is reading into the text. The tabernacle is a type (Heb. 8:5; 9:23-24), but that does not mean that every small item in the construction of the tabernacle in some way depicted a New Testament truth.

Prefiguring

A type has a predictive or foreshadowing element to it. It looks ahead and anticipates and points to the antitype. A type is a shadow (Col. 2:17) that points ahead to another reality. A type is a form of prophecy. Prophecy is prediction by means of words, whereas typology is prediction by correspondence between two realities, the type and the antitype. Again there are many similarities and resemblances in the Scriptures, but not every correspondence or resemblance is a type. To be an official type, the correspondence or resemblance must have a predictive element, a foreshadowing and anticipation of the antitype. The type, in other words, has a forward focus.

Does this mean that people in the Old Testament knew that various things were types? When the Israelites killed the Passover lambs every year, did they know that the lambs depicted Christ, who John the Baptist said is "the Lamb of God"? (John 1:29) Did Melchizedek know he was a type of Christ? (Ps. 110:4; Heb. 6:20) It seems unlikely that they would be aware of the antitypes. Possibly they had some awareness that these items were typical of forthcoming realities, but it seems unlikely they had any full awareness of the relationships between the types and the antitypes. As Mickelsen explains, "Even though a person, event, or thing in the Old Testament is typical, it does not mean that the contemporaries of the particular person, event, or thing recognized it as typical."[2] More likely these were prophetic from God's standpoint and when the antitypes were revealed, then it was evident that the predictive element was present. What God saw as prospective, man later saw as retrospective. Man sees the resemblance as he looks back and compares the type with the antitype. Types were signposts pointing toward persons, events, or things yet to come.

Heightening

In typology, the antitype is greater than and superior to the type. There is an increase, a heightening, an escalation. Christ is superior to Melchizedek. Christ's redemptive work is greater than that of the Passover, of which He is the antitype answering to the Passover, the type. Many aspects of the Old Testament illustrate truths in the New Testament, but without the heightening (as well as prefiguring) they are not types. The antitypes were on a higher plane than the types.

Divine Design

Types are not mere analogies or illustrations which Bible readers note. Instead they are resemblances planned by God. The type was designed in such a way that it carried a likeness to the antitype, and likewise was planned by God to be the "fulfillment" and heightening of the type. Since centuries separated most of the types from their antitypes, it obviously required God's planning to have the types depict or picture the antitypes.

This fact shows that types have apologetic value, for typology points to the evidence of divine design between the Old and New Testaments.

How do we know which persons, events, and things in the Old Testament were planned by God to serve as types? God must have designed the types but the problem is, How do we determine what He intended? This brings us to the most difficult question in the study of typology. As stated near the beginning of this chapter, some Bible teachers see many more types than do others. And others suggest that types are only those that are explicitly designated in the New Testament. Still others take a position midway between these two views, saying that types may be those that are explicitly designated and also those that are implicit, that is, suggested but not explicitly so stated.

Early church fathers, especially Origen and Jerome, found types in many trivial incidents and events, and extreme typology resulted in allegorizing. Others in more recent days also seek to find numerous types in the Bible. Wilson wrote, "When we read of the 'Red Sea' or 'the Jordan,' we know this to be a type just because it teaches so many interesting and profitable lessons."[3] In fact Wilson discusses 1,163 types which he says he has "discovered" in the Bible. Actually many of his so-called types are figures of speech, including many similes and metaphors. Others are illustrations or analogies. Habershon also sees numerous types in the Bible.[4]

Bible scholars who have seen types as those that are both explicit and implicit include Solomon Glassius, who wrote *Philologia Sacra* (in five volumes, 1623–1636); Johannes Cocceius (1602–

1669), who wrote *Summa Doctrina de Foedere et Testaments Dei;* Joseph Frey (*The Scripture Types,* 1841); Patrick Fairbairn (*Typology of Scripture* [1852; reprint, Grand Rapids: Zondervan Publishing House. n.d.]); and Milton S. Terry (*Biblical Hermeneutics* [Grand Rapids: Zondervan Publishing House, n.d.]).

Some who hold the third view—that types are only those that are so designated in the Scriptures—are Joseph Angus (*The Bible Hand Book,* rev. Samuel G. Green [New York: Fleming H. Revell, 1908]); Sylvester Burnham (*The Elements of Biblical Hermeneutics* [Hamilton, N.Y.: Publican Press, 1916]); Thomas Hartwell Horne (*An Introduction to the Critical Study and Knowledge of the Holy Scriptures,* 2 vols. [Philadelphia: J. Whetham and Son, 1841]); Herbert Marsh (*Lectures on the Criticism and Interpretation of the Bible* [London: J.G. & Rivington, 1838]); and Moses Stuart (*Hints on the Interpretation of Prophecy* [Andover: Allen, Morrill, and Wardwell, 1842]). Marsh stated this view as follows: "Just so much of the Old Testament is to be accounted typical as the New Testament affirms to be so, and no more."[5]

In summary, a type must have at least these five elements: a notable resemblance or correspondence between the type and the antitype, historical reality in both the type and the antitype, a prefiguring or predictive foreshadowing of the antitype by the type, a heightening in which the antitype is greater than the type, and divine design.

Must Types Be Designated as Such in the New Testament?

If we accept the five characteristics of a type discussed earlier, we still are left with the question whether types can be those that are implicit along with those that are explicitly designated, or whether they are only those that are so designated in the New Testament. For example many Bible teachers say Joseph and Moses are types of Christ, based on the many similarities they see between the lives of Joseph and Christ, or Moses and Christ. Granted, there are a number of analogies between Joseph and Christ, but on what basis can we say with assurance that God intended us to see Joseph as a type of Christ?

Looking at the five characteristics or elements, we can say there is resemblance, certainly there is historical reality to the lives of Joseph and Christ, and without question Christ is greater than Joseph. But can we say that Joseph's life was a prophetic foreshadowing of Christ and that his life was intended by divine design to be a type of Christ? Since it is difficult to determine with certainty that Joseph has these last two criteria, we may question whether Joseph is in fact an official, valid type of Christ. Certainly he is an illustration of Christ because of the many analogies between the two individuals, but mere correspondences do not make a type. Habershon lists 131 comparisons between Joseph and Christ (one of which, interestingly, is that both went to the city of Shechem!). She also sees Moses as a type of Christ, based on 69 comparisons. If Joseph is a type of Christ, why do Bible teachers not also say that Isaac, Samuel, Elijah, Jeremiah, and Daniel were types of Christ? Certainly there are similarities between them and Christ as well.

Others suggest Solomon was a type of Christ. But again did God give us the record about Solomon in order to illustrate Christ? One may find some analogies or resemblances and certainly both Solomon and Christ were historical individuals, but does Scripture give any indication that Solomon was a shadow pointing ahead to Christ and that Christ was superior to Solomon and that this was planned by God? Is Aaron's rod that budded a type of the resurrection of Christ, as a number of writers suggest? Where again is the predictive element and the divine design?

How do we keep from making "an evident and manifest analogy," as Glassius put it in 1623, of everything in the Old Testament? Where do we draw the line? What controls do we have? I suggest that for a figure to be a type it must also have a sixth characteristic or element: *It must be designated in the New Testament*. Scripture must in some way indicate that an item is typical. As already seen, that designation need not always be by the word *typos* and related words. Types, then, are designated in the New Testament; illustrations on the other hand, are broader and more numerous. Illustrations or analogies are not called such, but Bible students can sense parallels or analogies between Old Testament and New Testament truths.

A type may be defined as an Old Testament person, event, or thing having historical reality and designed by God to prefigure (foreshadow) in a preparatory way a real person, event, or thing so designated in the New Testament and that corresponds to and fulfills (heightens) the type. An illustration, on the other hand, may be defined as a biblical person, event, or thing having historical reality, that pictures or is analogous to some corresponding spiritual truth in a natural and unforced way and is not explicitly designated in the New Testament as a type.

In this definition an illustration has three of the six elements necessary for a type: correspondence or resemblance, historical reality, and divine design. However, illustrations are not predictive, they do not include a heightening or escalation, nor are they called types.

For example Elijah is an illustration of a man of earnest prayer (James 5:17). An illustration is one of many possibilities. James could also have used Samuel or Daniel as examples of men of prayer. Joseph is an illustration of Christ, since both of them were rejected and were delivered. Moses illustrates Christ as a prophet, and David illustrates Him as a king. The Old Testament priests illustrate the ministry of Christians as priests, and the ark may illustrate Christ as providing safety for believers. In each of these cases there are parallelisms or analogies but a mere parallelism or analogy does not signify the presence of a true type. When Paul spoke of the church as "a holy temple in the Lord" (Eph. 2:21), he was merely drawing an analogy or parallel between Solomon's temple and the church as both being God's spiritual dwelling place. He was not stating that Solomon's temple was a type of the church. Even the parallel Jesus drew between Jonah's being "in the belly of a huge fish" and His own burial (Matt. 12:40) need not be considered a type. Jonah's experience was not necessarily prophetic with a forward focus nor was it designated as a type (though some suggest that the words *as* and *so* in verse 40 point to the type being designated as such). "It is possible that some Old Testament persons and events have been wrongly interpreted as types when they were intended to be understood as no more than illustrations."[6]

A type looks forward to and prefigures the antitype, whereas in an illustration the truth referred to in the New Testament is pointing back to an analogous person or situation in the Old Testament and drawing some parallels. One looks ahead; the other looks back.

How does typology differ from allegorizing? The following chart may help point up differences between types, illustrations, and allegorizing.

As can be seen in the following chart a type and an illustration have correspondence or resemblance, whereas allegorizing has no natural correspondence but instead sees a hidden meaning or meanings behind the text. In types and illustrations historical reality is recognized whereas it is ignored or denied in allegorizing. A type is a prefiguring or foreshadowing of the antitype, whereas an illustration has no prefiguring and allegorizing looks behind the text rather

Typology*	Illustration (Example, Parallel)	Allegorizing**
1. The type and the antitype have a *natural correspondence or resemblance*.	1. The illustration and the truth have a *natural correspondence or resemblance*.	1. There is no natural correspondence. Instead, a *forced* or hidden meaning is sought behind the text.
2. The type has a *historical reality*. (The type/antitype relationship depends on the literal meaning.)	2. The illustration/ truth relationship depends on the *historical reality* of the illustration.	2. The Old Testament historical reality is *ignored or denied*. The literal meaning is unimportant.
3. The type is a *prefiguring or foreshadowing of the antitype. It is predictive; it looks ahead* and points to the antitype.	3. The illustration has *no prefiguring*. It is not predictive; it is only an example. The truth looks *back* to the Old Testament example.	3. The allegorizing is a conjuring up of hidden ideas, foreign to and behind the Old Testament text. It looks *behind*, not ahead.
4. The type is "*fulfilled*" (or completed or *heightened*) by the antitype. The antitype is greater than and superior to the type.	4. The illustration is not "*fulfilled*" (or completed or heightened) by the truth it illustrates.	4. The allegorizing *does not "fulfill"* the Old Testament texts.
5. The type is *divinely designed*. It is planned by God.	5. The illustration is *divinely designed* by God as a picture of a truth.	5. The allegorizing is in the *interpreter's imagination,* not in the design of God.
6. The type and the antitype are *designated as such* in the New Testament.	6. The truth/illustration is *not called a type*.	6. The allegorizing is *not designated* in the Scripture.
*For something in Scripture to be a type, it must meet *all* six criteria.		**The system of allegorizing practiced by the Alexandrian Jews and Alexandrian Church Fathers (Clement and Origen) is not the same as the *analogy* Paul wrote about in Galatians 4.

than ahead. In a type-antitype relationship there is a heightening, whereas this is not true in either an illustration or allegorizing. Divine design is present in both types and illustrations, but not in allegorizing, which is the result of the interpreter's imagination. A type is so designated in the New Testament, whereas this is not true of either an illustration or allegorizing.

Which Types Are Valid?

The discussion thus far has suggested that for something in Scripture to be a type it must meet all six criteria. To determine which types are valid in Scripture, we must ask the following questions:

    1. Is there a definite correspondence or resemblance between the type and the antitype? Does the type exhibit the same truths, principles, and relationships as the corresponding New Testament reality?

    2. Is the antitype in harmony with the historical setting of the type?

    3. Is the type a prefiguring or foreshadowing of the antitype, or is it merely an example or illustration? Is there a forward focus in the type which looks ahead to something in the future?

    4. Does the antitype heighten or "fulfill" the type, with the antitype being superior to the type?

    5. Can divine design be observed in the relationship of the type and the antitype?

    6. Does the New Testament in some way designate the type and the antitype?

    Given these six criteria, which Old Testament persons, events, or things are types? I would suggest the following 17.

Type	Antitype	Scripture
Persons		
1. Melchizedek	Christ's perpetual priesthood	Heb. 7:3, 15-17
2. Aaron	Christ's priestly ministry	Heb. 5:4-5
Events		
3. Passover feast	Christ our sacrifice	1 Cor. 5:7
4. Feast of Unleavened Bread	Believer's holy walk	1 Cor. 5:7-8

5. Feast of First-fruits	Christ's resurrection a pledge of believers' resurrection	1 Cor. 15:20-23
6. Feast of Pentecost	The coming of the Holy Spirit	Joel 2:28; Acts 2:1-47
7. Feast of Trumpets	Israel's regathering	Matt. 24:21-23
8. Day of Atonement	Israel's national conversion by the blood of Christ	Zech. 12:10; Rom. 11:26-27; Heb. 9:19-28
9. Feast of Tabernacles	God's provision for man's need (with Israel in the kingdom)	John 7:2, 37-39
10. Sabbath	The Christian's spiritual rest	Col. 2:17; Heb. 4:3, 9, 11

Things

11. Tabernacle	Christ, the believer's access to God and basis of fellowship with God	Heb. 8:5; 9:23-24
12. Tabernacle curtain	Christ, the believer's access to God	Heb. 10:20
13. Burnt offering	Christ's offering of Himself as the perfect sacrifice	Lev. 1; Heb. 10:5-7; Eph. 5:2
14. Grain offering	Christ's offering of Himself as the perfect sacrifice of the highest quality	Lev. 2; Heb. 10:8
15. Fellowship offering	Christ's offering of Himself as the basis for fellowship with God	Lev. 3; Eph. 2:14; Col. 1:20
16. Sin offering	Christ's death for the sinner in relation to the guilt of sin	Lev. 4:1–5:13; Heb. 13:11-12
17. Guilt offering	Christ's death as an atonement for the injury of sin	Lev. 5:14–6:7; Heb. 10:12

Only one of Israel's seven feasts, the Passover, is specifically pointed up as a type (1 Cor. 5:7), but Colossians 2:16-17 suggests that all the religious festivals were "a shadow of the things that were to come." Based on this the chart on pages 179–180 includes all the feasts as types. Similarly Hebrews 9:9-10 seems to suggest that all five of Israel's sacrificial offerings were types.

What about Adam? Why is he not included as a type of Christ? It is true that Adam was a *typos* of Christ, according to Romans 5:14. But as we have seen earlier, the word *typos* does not always refer to an official type. It is not a technical term to designate types since it often simply means an example, pattern, or analogy. Adam was analogous to Christ in some ways but did not point predictively toward Christ. Adam's life, in view of his fall, hardly predicted or prefigured Christ. Romans 5:14 is simply affirming that Adam was an example or illustration of Christ in that they had one thing in common: both were the head of a race of people—Adam the head of humanity, and Christ the Head of the church. Jonah's three days and three nights in the fish's stomach illustrates Christ's burial. The brass serpent lifted up by Moses in the desert illustrates the need for people today to look to Christ for salvation, but the brass serpent did not predict or foreshadow Christ to that generation.

In other words Adam, Jonah, and the brass serpent are illustrations rather than official types since they do not meet all six criteria for an official type.

Paul wrote that certain events in the nation Israel under Moses' leadership "occurred as examples" (1 Cor. 10:6). The four events referred to in verses 1-4 of that chapter are: the crossing of the Red Sea, the guidance by the cloud, the provision of manna, and the rock. Some Bible students take these as official types. Others, however, suggest that again *typos* in verse 6 points to these events as illustrations, not valid types. Verse 6 states that the purpose of these examples was "to keep us from setting our hearts on evil things as they did." A similar point is made in verse 11: "These things happened to them as examples [*typikōs*] and were written down as warnings for us."

The responses of the Israelites in the wilderness, then, serve as examples for believers not to become involved in idolatry, immorality, testing the Lord, or complaining (vv. 7-10). It seems unlikely that these would be types. It is more fitting to consider them as examples in a negative way for Christians.

What Steps Should Be Followed in Interpreting Types?

1. *Determine the literal sense of the type.* Always basic to accurate interpretation is determining the literal sense of the passage.

2. *Note the specific point or points of correspondence or resemblance between the type and its antitype.* For example Melchizedek was a king and a priest, and he was superior to Aaron. In at least these two ways he typifies Christ, since Christ is a King and a Priest and in His priesthood is superior to Aaron. The major points of similarity should be looked for, not the incidental and trivial.

3. *Note the specific areas of contrast or dissimilarity in order to avoid making those elements aspects of the type.* Melchizedek was human, but Christ was God as well as human. Aaron had to offer sacrifices for his own sins, but Christ did not need to do that because of His sinless nature as God in the flesh. In Israel's Passover feast animals were slain but Christ our Passover was Himself slain. The sacrifices which depict various aspects of Christ were repeated, whereas Christ's death on the cross was a once-for-all event.

4. *Note the direct assertions in the New Testament that verify the typological correspondence.*

Why Be Concerned about Typology?

While scholars differ in their approach to this subject, the study of types and their antitypes does have definite benefits.

For one thing it enables us to see God's design of history, as He chose certain persons, events, and things in Israel to depict and predict aspects of Christ and His relationship to believers today. Seeing these type-antitype relationships helps us see God's hand in history.

Careful attention to criteria for determining types helps give us more tangible controls in interpreting the Old Testament. If the water in the tabernacle laver is a type of the Holy Spirit, why can we not also say that acacia wood is a type of Christ's humanity? Ignoring the six criteria for official types launches us on a sea of uncertainty which may result in our saying, as did Keach, that Samson's defeating a lion in the desert is a type of Christ's overcoming the roaring lion, the devil, in the wilderness.[7]

Keeping in mind the six criteria for determining types, look at the following list of 37 items, all of which have been said by various authors to be types, and check which of them are types, which ones are illustrations, and which ones are allegorizing.

Write a "T" in front of those items you think are types, an "I" in front of those you think are illustrations, and an "A" in front of those you think are allegorizing.

____I____ 1. Adam is a type of Christ.

____I____ 2. Aaron's rod that budded is a type of the resurrection of Christ.

____A____ 3. The inn in the Parable of the Good Samaritan is a type of the church which should be full of Christians who will nourish newborn Christians.

____I____ 4. Solomon in the glory of his kingdom was a type of Christ in His glory.

____I____ 5. David eating the tabernacle showbread was a type of Christ eating grain on the Sabbath.

____A____ 6. The water in the laver in the tabernacle is a type of the Word ministered by the Holy Spirit.

____I____ 7. Jonah being expelled from the fish's stomach is a type of the resurrection of Christ.

____I____ 8. The brass serpent being lifted up in the wilderness is a type of Christ being crucified.

____A____ 9. Jacob's pillow of stone is a type of Christ going from the temple to the cross.

____A____ 10. The wicks on the tabernacle lampstand are a type of the Christian's old sin nature which constantly needs trimming.

____A____ 11. Abraham's servant finding a bride for Isaac is a type of the Holy Spirit finding a bride (the church) for Christ.

____I____ 12. Joseph is a type of Christ.

____A____ 13. Moses praying with his arms held up is a type of Christ being crucified on the cross.

____I____ 14. Abraham is a type of all who believe.

____A____ 15. The priest trimming the wicks on the lampstand is a type of Christ dealing with our sins.

____I____ 16. Melchizedek is a type of Christ's unending and superior priesthood.

____A____ 17. The clothes of Esau which Jacob wore when he deceived his father Isaac are a type of the church dressed in the righteousness of Christ.

____A____ 18. The fine flour in the meal offering is a type of the evenness and balance of Christ's character.

____A____ 19. The cooking of the fine flour in the grain offering is a type of Christ being tested by suffering.

_A_ 20. Samson meeting the lion is a type of Christ meeting Paul on the Damascus Road.

_A_ 21. The acacia wood in the tabernacle is a type of the humanity of Christ.

_A_ 22. The altar of incense in the tabernacle is a type of Christ's intercessory work.

_A_ 23. The rams' skins dyed red (and placed over the tabernacle) were a type of Peter and Paul after they were saved.

_T_ 24. The Passover feast was a type of Christ as our sacrifice.

_T_ 25. Isaac being sacrificed by Abraham is a type of Christ being sacrificed for us.

_A_ 26. The bells and pomegranates on the hem of Aaron's robe are a type of the proclamation of the Gospel.

_A_ 27. The divided hoof in some animals (Lev. 11:3) is a type of the Christian whose spiritual walk is divided.

_T_ 28. The manna in the wilderness is a type of Christ sustaining the believer spiritually.

_T_ 29. Cain is a type of the natural man.

_____ 30. Enoch is a type of the church saints who will be raptured before the Tribulation.

_____ 31. The Feast of Pentecost is a type of the church being formed on the Day of Pentecost.

_A_ 32. The hinges in the doors to the holy place and the most holy place in Solomon's temple are a type of the motives in the life of the Christian.

_____ 33. Abel is a type of the spiritual man whose sacrifice of blood evidenced his acceptance of a substitute for his sin.

_____ 34. Eve is a type of the church as the bride of Christ.

_____ 35. The two loaves in the Feast of Pentecost are a type of Jews and Gentiles.

_T_ 36. The rest on the Sabbath is a type of the Christian's spiritual rest and peace in Christ.

_T_ 37. The goats' hair covering over the tabernacle is a type of serviceableness.

Sensing the Symbols

What Constitutes a Symbol?

The English word *symbol* comes from the Greek word *symballē*, which means "a throwing together." A symbol is some object (real or imagined) or action which is assigned a meaning for the purpose of depicting rather than stating the qualities of something else.

Symbols and types are both representative of something else. However, a type represents something to come, but a symbol has no time reference. A type is fulfilled at a specific time by its antitype. The tabernacle in the wilderness was a type of Christ; as a type, no other tabernacle resembled and pointed forward to Christ. On the other hand in speaking of Christ as a lion, any lion can be thought of as depicting a certain characteristic of Christ.

A symbol "does not have its symbolic meaning because of what it is in itself. This meaning is assigned to it, and belongs to it only in its use as a symbol."[8] Melchizedek was a type of Christ because both he and Christ are priests. This is a normal association, in which the type has its typical meaning because of what it is in and of itself. In a symbol, however, the meaning is assigned. A person would not normally associate a symbol with that which it symbolizes. For example nothing inherent in the nature of good figs would normally suggest Jewish captives in Babylon, and yet that is what they symbolized in Jeremiah 24:3-5.

What Are Some Principles for Interpreting Symbols?

1. *Note the three elements in symbolic interpretation: the object (which is the symbol), the referent (what the symbol refers to), and the meaning (the resemblance between the symbol and the referent).* In John 1:29 a lamb (object) pictures Christ (referent), and the meaning or resemblance is that Christ is a sacrifice just as many lambs were sacrifices. Or as in Isaiah 53:6, sheep (object) picture human beings (referent), and the meaning or resemblance is that humans spiritually go astray from God just as sheep physically stray from their flock.

2. *Remember that symbols have their base in reality.* Symbols are based on literal objects or actions, such as a lion, a bear, a boiling pot, shaking dust off one's feet, etc. When Christ is said to be a lamb or a lion, He is not Himself literally a lamb or a lion, but those animals do exist in reality so that a meaningful resemblance can be drawn between the object and the referent. In prophetic passages symbols are sometimes based on imagination rather than actuality. No beast known today has seven heads and ten horns (Rev. 17:3), nor has any leopard ever had four heads and four wings (Dan. 7:6), nor is a woman normally transported in a basket (Zech. 5:5-11). Yet those symbols contain elements of reality, such as heads, horns, a leopard, wings, a woman, a basket.

3. *Determine what meaning or resemblance, if any, is explicitly*

assigned by the text to the referent. In prophecy if an object or action is intended as a symbol, the text usually designates it as such. For example in Revelation 9:1 the star that fell from heaven is referred to in verse 2 as "he" to whom was given a key. This indicates the star symbolizes a person. Comparing this passage with 20:1, it seems clear that the one referred to is an angel. The dragon in verse 2 is identified in the same verse as Satan. Sodom and Egypt in 11:8 are symbols that are said to refer to Jerusalem. The ten horns on the fourth beast in Daniel 7 are said to be, that is, to symbolize or resemble, "ten kings who will come" (v. 24).

4. *If the verse does not give the meaning or resemblance of the symbol, then check other passages, check the nature of the symbol, and check which major characteristic the referent and the object have in common.* When John referred to Christ as "the Lamb of God, who takes away the sin of the world" (John 1:29), he was using a lamb as a symbol of Christ, but without explicitly stating the resemblance.

5. *Be careful not to assign the wrong characteristic of the symbol to the referent.* A lion is both ferocious and strong, but only its furious nature points to Satan (1 Peter 5:8) and only its strong nature refers to Christ (Rev. 5:5). Doves are docile and flighty, but in Matthew 10:16 only their docile nature is indicated as the point of reference to believers, whereas in Hosea 7:11 only their flighty nature is indicated as the point of reference to Israel.

6. *Look for the one major point of resemblance.* Resist the temptation to draw many parallels between the symbol and that which it symbolizes.

When . . . water represents the Word of God, it is because both things cleanse; not because they are clear, refreshing, inexpensive, or healthful. When oil symbolizes the Holy Spirit, it is because the individual is anointed with both. Oil is not symbolic of the Spirit because it gives light when it burns, nor because it is used to soften the scab on the wound, nor because it is extracted from the fruit only when it is pressed. Searching for several points of similarity is faulty handling of the symbol.[9]

7. *Realize that one referent may be depicted by several objects.* Christ, for example, is said to resemble a lamb, a lion, a branch, a root, and others. The Holy Spirit is symbolized by water, oil, wind, and a dove.

8. *In prophetic literature do not assume that because a prophecy*

contains some symbols everything else in that prophecy is symbolic. In
Revelation 19:19 the "beast" is a symbol, but that does not mean
that "the kings of the earth and their armies" in the same verse are to
be taken as symbols. In verse 15 the sword from Christ's mouth is a
symbol (of His judging by His words), but that does not mean that
the nations referred to in the same verse are a symbol of something
else.

9. *In prophetic literature do not symbolize (make into a symbol)
descriptions of the future that are possible or plausible.* Revelation 8:12
states that a third of the sun, moon, and stars will be struck and will
not give light. It is plausible that this will actually take place, therefore the sun, moon, and stars in this verse need not be thought of as
symbolizing something else. In Revelation 9 the locusts from the
Abyss are a reasonable possibility as either literal locusts or locust-
like creatures and therefore are not to be taken as symbols of the
Turks, as some have done in the past. The prophecy of the 144,000
in 7:4-8 need not be considered a symbolic number. The number is
to be taken in its normal, literal sense because 12,000 people are said
to be sealed from each of the 12 tribes of Israel. Since the tribal
names are literal and not symbolic, there is no reason to take the
numbers symbolically.

What Are Some of the Symbols in the Bible?
The following are some though not all of the symbols in the Bible,
given in six categories.

Object or Action (Symbol)	Meaning
Divine Symbols	
Sword at the east of Eden (Gen. 3:24)	Breach of fellowship between man and God
Burning bush (Ex. 3:2)	God's holiness
Pillar of cloud (Ex. 13:21-22)	God's presence and guidance
Symbols Seen in Visions	
Boiling pot (Jer. 1:13)	Judgment from the North
Good figs (Jer. 24:3-5)	Jewish captives in Babylon
Bad figs (Jer. 24:3, 8)	Remnant of Jews who stayed in Judah
Dry bones given new flesh (Ezek. 37)	Israel restored
Four beasts (Dan. 7)	Babylon, Medo-Persia, Greece, Rome

Object or Action (Symbol)	Meaning
Ram and goat (Dan. 8)	Persia and Greece
Basket of summer fruit (Amos 8:1-12)	Judgment is coming (just as fruit indicates the end of summer)
Gold lampstand (Zech. 4:2)	Israel as God's witness to the world
Two olive trees (Zech. 4:3, 11-14)	Zerubbabel and Joshua
Oil (Zech. 4:1-6)	The Holy Spirit
Woman in a basket (Zech. 5:5-11)	Sinful Israel
Seven golden lampstands (Rev. 1:12-20)	Seven churches
Seven stars (Rev. 1:12-20)	Angels (or ministers) of the seven churches

Material symbols

Blood (Deut. 12:23-25; Lev. 17:11; Heb. 1:3; 7:16; 9:14; 13:20)	Life
Bread and wine (Luke 22:19-20)	Christ's body and blood
Carved cherub (Ex. 25:18-22)	God's holiness
Dove (Matt. 10:16)	Docile believers
Dove (Hosea 7:11)	Flighty Israel
Dragon (Rev. 12:3-17; 13:2, 4, 11; 20:2)	Satan
Horn (1 Sam. 2:1; Ps. 112:9; Lam. 2:3)	Strength and defense
Incense (Rev. 8:3-4)	Prayer
Keys (Matt. 16:19)	Authority
Lamb (Isa. 53:6)	Human waywardness
Lamb (John 1:29)	Christ as a substitutionary sacrifice
Lion (1 Peter 5:8)	Satan as a ferocious being
Lion (Rev. 5:5)	Christ as King
Rainbow (Gen. 9:13-16; Ezek. 1:28; Rev. 4:3)	God's faithfulness
Serpent (Gen. 3:1; 2 Cor. 11:3; Rev. 12:9, 14-15; 20:2)	Satan

Object or Action (Symbol)	Meaning
Stone (Dan. 2:44-45; Isa. 28:16)	Christ
Water (John 7:38-39)	Holy Spirit
Water (Eph. 5:26)	The Word of God
Water (Titus 3:5)	Regeneration

Symbolic gestures

Placing one's hands on another person (Gen. 48:13-14, 17; Matt. 19:15)	Imparting a blessing
Beating one's breast (Luke 18:13)	Expressing remorse
Sitting in dust and ashes (Job 42:6) or in sackcloth and ashes (Luke 10:13)	Expressing repentance
Tearing one's clothes (Job 1:20)	Symbolizing grief
Tearing one's clothes (Mark 14:63)	Expressing anger
Shaking dust off one's feet when leaving a city that rejected Christ (Matt. 10:14; Acts 13:51)	Symbolizing that the city was so despised by the disciples that it was as if its very dust was unwanted
Washing one's hands (Matt. 27:24)	Expressing innocence and removal of responsibility

Symbolic actions

A seraph (angel) placed a live coal on Isaiah's lips (Isa. 6:5-6)	Isaiah was cleansed inwardly (Isa. 6:7)
Jeremiah buried a linen belt in a rock crevice and later, when it had rotted, dug it up (Jer. 13:1-8)	False gods worshiped by Judah were useless like the rotten belt (Jer. 13:10)
Jeremiah watched a potter making a clay pot (Jer. 18:1-4)	God is sovereign over His people (Jer. 18:5-6)
Jeremiah broke a clay jar (Jer. 19:10)	Judah would be ruined like a broken jar (Jer. 19:11)
Jeremiah wore a yoke (Jer. 27:1-2)	Zedekiah was to surrender to the authority of Babylon (Jer. 27:12)

Object or Action (Symbol)	*Meaning*
Jeremiah buried stones in clay in the brick pavement at the palace in Egypt (Jer. 43:8-9)	Babylon would conquer Egypt (Jer. 43:10-13)
Ezekiel ate a scroll with words of lament and mourning and woe (Ezek. 2:8–3:3)	Ezekiel was to give a message of lament and woe to Israel (Ezek. 2:10)
Ezekiel drew an outline of Jerusalem on a clay tablet, and built siege works and a ramp against it (Ezek. 4:1-3)	Jerusalem would be attacked by Babylon (Ezek. 4:3)
Ezekiel lay 390 days on his left side and 40 days on his right side, weighed out his food, and cooked it, using cow manure for fuel (Ezek. 4:4-6, 9-15)	The people of Jerusalem would eat ceremonially defiled food in nations that would capture them (Ezek. 4:13)
Ezekiel shaved his head and beard, and burned one third of the hair, cut one third of it and threw it to the wind and tucked some in his garment (Ezek. 5:1-4)	One third of the people of Jerusalem would die by plague or famine, one third by the sword, and one third be scattered (Ezek. 5:12)
Hosea married an adulterous woman, who left him, and then he bought her back and loved her again (Hosea 1:2-3; 3:2)	God will restore Israel even though she has sinned against God (Hosea 3:5)
John ate a scroll (Rev. 10:9-10)	John was to appropriate the message God would give him (Rev. 10:11)

Even the ordinances of the church—baptism and the Lord's Supper—are symbolic actions. Water baptism symbolizes the believer's identification with Christ in His burial, death, and resurrection. In taking the elements in the Lord's Supper, believers symbolically proclaim the Lord's death, with the bread picturing Jesus' body which was broken in His crucifixion, and the cup picturing His blood which was shed on the cross for the remission of sins.

Symbolic Numbers

Some numbers seem to suggest certain concepts because they are frequently used in association with those ideas. Seven is often associated with perfection (Gen. 2:2-3; Rev. 1:12; 4:5; 5:1; 8:1; 15:1; 16:1). Forty is often associated with testing, as in Moses' 40 years in Midian (Acts 7:29-30), Israel's 40 years in the wilderness (Num. 32:13), Jesus' 40 days of temptation (Luke 4:2).

However, though some numbers have symbolic connotations because of their associations, this is no basis for making the numbers mean something other than their normal, literal meaning. Though the length of Jesus' temptation is associated with the concept of testing, He was in fact tempted for 40 literal days. While the seven golden lampstands symbolized seven churches (Rev. 1:12, 20), with the number seven symbolizing completeness, this does not give us liberty to disregard the literal nature of seven and to imagine fewer or more than seven lampstands.

Symbolic Names

Names of some people and places in the Bible take on significance symbolically. No attempt, however, should be made by Bible students to see symbolism in names, unless they are so designated in the Scriptures. The name Eve was given to Adam's wife "because she would become the mother of all the living" (Gen. 3:20). The word *Eve* in Hebrew means "living." Apparently this was an expression of Adam's faith as he looked to the future, even though God had just pronounced that they would be subject to death (v. 19). God changed Abram's name to Abraham to signify that he would be the ancestor of many people. Abram means "exalted father," and Abraham means "father of many" (17:5). God also changed the name of his wife Sarai to Sarah, which means "princess" (v. 15).

Sometimes mothers gave their children names that related to the circumstances of their births or to characteristics they anticipated their children would acquire. Jacob's wife Leah was not loved by Jacob, and yet when the Lord gave her a child she named him Reuben, saying that the Lord had seen her misery. The word *Reuben* sounds like the Hebrew "He has seen my misery." The name of her second son Simeon probably means "one who hears." Levi sounds like the Hebrew word for "attached," and so Leah named her third son Levi for she said, "Now at last my husband will become attached to me, because I have borne him three sons." When her fourth son Judah was born she praised the Lord, for the word *Judah* sounds like the Hebrew word for praise (29:31-35). The children of Jacob's other wife Rachel also were given names relating to the circumstances of their births (see 30:1-24, and the NIV footnotes).

Pharaoh's daughter named the baby boy found in the Nile River Moses "saying, 'I drew him out of the water'" (Ex. 2:10). The word *Moses* sounds like the Hebrew for "draw out." In Hebrew, Moses is *mōšeh* and the Hebrew verb *māšâh* means "to draw out."

Hannah named her son Samuel for she said, "Because I asked the Lord for him" (1 Sam. 1:20). However, the name Samuel is not related to the Hebrew word for "asked" *(šā'al),* but to the word "heard" *(šāma').* By her statement Hannah was suggesting that God had heard what she asked. "Samuel" is from the Hebrew words that mean "heard of God."

Daniel's name means "God has judged" or "God is my Judge." Nebuchadnezzar changed Daniel's name to Belteshazzar, which means "Lady, protect the king." Nebuchadnezzar wanted Daniel to forget the name of God, included in the name given to Daniel by his parents. Similar changes were made in the names of Daniel's three friends (Dan. 1:6-7).

The three children of Gomer, Hosea's wife, take on significance as messages for the nation Israel. Jezreel, the name of the first son, suggests that God will break Israel's bow in the Valley of Jezreel (Hosea 1:5); the daughter's name Lo-Ruhamah means "she is not loved" and indicates that God's love for Israel would be cut off for a time (v. 6); and the second son Lo-Ammi, which means "not my people," conveyed the message to Israel that God was not considering sinful Israel as His people.

Jesus changed Simon's name to Cephas (Aramaic) and Peter (Greek), which mean rock (John 1:42; cf. Matt. 16:18). His new name pointed ahead to his new role in the founding of the church (Acts 2).

The names of places sometimes took on significance in relation to events that occurred at those spots or in relation to the characteristics of people at those places. When the Angel of the Lord appeared to Hagar, she named the well Beer Lahai Roi because, as she explained, "I have now seen the One who sees me" (Gen. 16:13-14). The Hebrew words mean "well of the living One who sees me." Jacob changed the name of the town Luz to Bethel, which means "house of God" because he had said, "This is none other than the house of God" (28:17, 19).

Occasionally a city or nation is given another name. For instance God referred to Jerusalem's leaders as the "rulers of Sodom" and the inhabitants of Jerusalem as the "people of Gomorrah" (Isa. 1:10) because they had become as sinful as those ancient cities. Ezekiel gave the name Sodom to the nation Judah (Ezek. 16:46), and Jerusalem is figuratively called Sodom and Egypt in Revelation 11:8. Scholars differ on whether Peter's reference to Babylon in 1 Peter 5:13 should be understood as referring to the literal city of Babylon on the Euphrates River or symbolically to Rome. Those holding the latter view suggest that Babylon may have been disguised as a reference to Rome to protect the believers there from persecution under Nero. According to historical evidence, Peter was in Rome during the final years of his life and his "son" Mark, who is referred to in the same verse, may be John Mark, whom Paul said was in Rome (Col. 4:10).

Symbolic Colors

Sometimes colors take on emblematic significance, but again caution should be used here to avoid going beyond the clear designations of Scripture. Purple seemed to be a color used in fabrics to depict royalty (Jud. 8:26; Es. 1:6; 8:15; Song 3:10; Dan. 5:7, 16, 29; Mark 15:17, 20) or wealth (Prov. 31:22; Luke 16:19; Rev. 17:4; 18:16).

White is often associated with purity (Isa. 1:18; Dan. 7:9; Matt. 17:2; 28:3; Acts 1:10; Rev. 1:14; 3:4-5; 4:4; 6:11; 7:9, 13-14; 19:11, 14; 20:11).

We should avoid drawing meanings for other colors, such as blue, red, scarlet, black, or yellow, since the Scriptures do not seem to point clearly to their meanings by associations. Again, students of the Bible should avoid reading into the Scriptures something that is not there.

CHAPTER NINE

Probing the Parables and Analyzing the Allegories

Parables, allegories, and fables require special attention in Bible study. A parable is a form of figurative language involving comparisons. But rather than using a single word or phrase to make the comparison or analogy, as in a simile, metaphor, or hypocatastasis, a parable is an extended analogy in story form. A parable is a true-to-life story to illustrate or illuminate a truth. It is true to life though it may not have actually occurred in all details as the story is presented. Historic events may serve as illustrations; but parables are special stories, not necessarily historic events, that are told to teach a particular truth. Since parables are true to life, they differ from allegories and fables, which will be discussed later in this chapter.

The word *parable* comes from the Greek *para* ("beside or alongside") and *ballein* ("to throw"). Thus the story is thrown alongside the truth to illustrate the truth. Hearers and readers, by sensing the comparison or analogy between the story and their own situation, are prodded to think. In interpreting parables we need to ask, What is the point of the story? What spiritual truth is being illustrated? What analogy is being made? Parables are sometimes unusual and startling, but never unlifelike or fictitious.

Besides referring to stories the Greek word *parabolē* also refers to short statements (sometimes called similitudes) and to proverbs. Similitudes normally refer to customary habits, stated in the present tense, whereas the story parable records a specific instance, using the past tense (e.g., "A farmer went out to sow his seed," Matt. 13:3).

Five of the following six similitudes are referred to as parables, in which the writer used the Greek word *parabolē*.

Jesus' Similitudes

A paradoxical statement

"It is what comes out of a man that makes him 'unclean.' . . . His disciples asked Him about this parable" (Mark 7:16-17). Meaning: Evil deeds come from the heart (vv. 21-23).

An admonition

"He told them this parable: 'When someone invites you to a wedding feast, do not take the place of honor . . . but when you are invited, take the lowest place, so that when your host comes, he will say to you, "Friend, move up to a better place"'" (Luke 14:7-8, 10). Meaning: Everyone who exalts himself will be humbled and vice versa (v. 11).

A question

"Can you make the guests of the bridegroom fast while he is with them?" (Luke 5:34) Meaning: Jesus' disciples were not fasting because He was with them. (Though this question by Jesus is not called a *parabolē*, it is similar to the others.)

A maxim about life

"'If a blind man leads a blind man, both will fall into a pit.' Peter said, 'Explain the parable to us'" (Matt. 15:14-15). Meaning: The Pharisees, being blind spiritually, are leading others astray spiritually (v. 12; cf. Matt. 23:16-17, 19, 24, 26).

Observations from nature

"He told them this parable: 'Look at . . . all the trees. When they sprout leaves, you . . . know that summer is near'" (Luke 21:30). Meaning: Certain events will indicate that "the kingdom of God is near" (v. 31).

"People do not pick figs from thornbushes, or grapes from briers" (Luke 6:44). Meaning: Good actions stem from a good heart, not from a bad heart.

In the New Testament the word *parabolē* is used once of a proverb. This is in Luke 4:23 ("Physician, heal yourself!") in which the Greek word is in fact translated "proverb" in the NIV. Other proverbs Jesus spoke are seen in the following box:

Jesus' Proverbs

Statements

"A city on a hill cannot be hidden" (Matt. 5:14).

"No one can serve two masters" (Matt. 6:24).

"It is not the healthy who need a doctor, but the sick" (Matt. 9:12).

"Only in his hometown and in his own house is a prophet without honor" (Matt. 13:57).

"If a blind man leads a blind man, both will fall into a pit" (Matt. 15:14).

"A student is not above his teacher" (Luke 6:40).

"The worker deserves his wages" (Luke 10:7).

"A person who has had a bath needs only to wash his feet" (John 13:10).

"No servant is greater than his master" (John 13:16).

"Wherever there is a carcass, there the vultures will gather" (Matt. 24:28).

Questions

"You are the salt of the earth. But if the salt loses its saltiness, how can it be made salty again?" (Matt. 5:13)

"Do you bring in a lamp to put it under a bowl or a bed?" (Mark 4:21)

Command

"Physician, heal yourself!" (Luke 4:23)

Some parables also occur in the Old Testament. Like *parabolē* in the New Testament, the Hebrew word *māšāl* in the Old Testament refers to short stories but has other meanings as well. *Māšāl* probably comes from the verb meaning "to be like" and thus suggests a likeness or comparison. It is used of short sayings: "Is Saul also among the prophets?" (1 Sam. 10:12) "From evildoers come evil deeds" (24:13). In these sayings the question or statement in the form of a popular proverb points to a likeness between the statement and reality. The maxims or wise sayings in the Book of Proverbs compare those observations with realities in daily life (Prov. 1:1, 6; 10:1; 25:1). *Māšāl* is also used of oracles (e.g., Num. 24:20-23), taunts (Isa. 14:4), bywords in which a person is seen as an undesirable example to others (Job 17:6; 30:9; Ps. 44:14), and of lengthy discourses (Job 27:1; 29:1). *Māšāl* is also used to refer to dark sayings or riddles, as in Psalms 49:4 and 78:2. Some consider Isaiah's words in Isaiah 5:1-7 about the Lord's vineyard a parable, but others call it an allegory.

Though not called a parable, Nathan's story of a lamb (2 Sam. 12:1-13) has the characteristics of a true parable.

Most of the parables in the Bible were told by Jesus. The following chart lists His parables. As seen in the chart Matthew and Luke record most of the parables. Matthew has 18, with 11 of them unique to him. Luke has 22, with 7 of them in common with Matthew, and 15 others unique to Luke. Mark has only 5, with only 2 of them unique to his Gospel and both of them are short (Mark 4:26-29; 13:34-37).

Why Did Jesus Speak in Parables?

When the disciples asked Jesus why He spoke to the people in parables (Matt. 13:10; Mark 4:10), He said that His parables had two purposes. One was to reveal truths to His followers and the other was to conceal truth from "those on the outside" (Mark 4:11). While these purposes may seem contradictory, the answer to this dilemma may lay in the nature of the hearers. Since the teachers of the Law (3:22) had already demonstrated their unbelief and rejection of Jesus, they revealed the hardened condition of their hearts. This made them unable to comprehend the meaning of His parables. Blinded by unbelief, they rejected Him, and so as He spoke in parables they normally would not comprehend their meaning. On the other hand His followers, open to Him and His truths, would understand the parables.

Parables were an effective form of communication because, as stories, they immediately sparked interest in the hearers. As the people heard Jesus' stories, all of which were true-to-life, they were immediately drawn into the stories with Him. Their curiosity was aroused as they wondered how the stories would develop and conclude.

Parables encouraged people to think. By drawing analogies Jesus wanted His hearers "to pass a judgment on things on which they were well-acquainted, and then to compel them to transfer that judgment to something whose significance they had been blind."[1] Jesus did not narrate the parables simply to entertain audiences with stories. He relayed the parables so that those for whom they were intended would "apply them, even if resentfully or reluctantly, to themselves."[2] His parables were thus often disarming.

The Parables of Jesus

1.	The Two Houses	Matthew 7:24-27
		(Luke 6:47-49)
2.	The New Cloth and New Wineskins	Matthew 9:16-17
3.	The Sower	Matthew 13:3-8
		(Mark 4:3-8; Luke 8:5-8)
4.	The Weeds	Matthew 13:24-30
5.	The Mustard Seed	Matthew 13:31-32
		(Mark 4:30-32; Luke 13:18-19)
6.	The Yeast	Matthew 13:33
		(Luke 13:20-21)
7.	The Hidden Treasure	Matthew 13:44
8.	The Pearl of Great Price	Matthew 13:45-46
9.	The Fishing Net	Matthew 13:47-50
10.	The Unforgiving Servant	Matthew 18:23-35
11.	The Workers in the Vineyard	Matthew 20:1-16
12.	The Two Sons	Matthew 21:28-32
13.	The Wicked Vinegrowers	Matthew 21:33-46
		(Mark 12:1-12; Luke 20:9-19)
14.	The Wedding Banquet	Matthew 22:1-14
15.	The Two Servants	Matthew 24:45-51
		(Luke 12:42-48)
16.	The Ten Virgins	Matthew 25:1-13
17.	The Talents	Matthew 25:14-30
18.	The Seed Growing Secretly	Mark 4:26-29
19.	The Doorkeeper	Mark 13:34-37
20.	The Rude Children	Luke 7:31-35
21.	The Two Debtors	Luke 7:41-43
22.	The Good Samaritan	Luke 10:25-37
23.	The Friend at Midnight	Luke 11:5-8
24.	The Rich Fool	Luke 12:16-21
25.	The Barren Fig Tree	Luke 13:6-9
26.	The Great Banquet	Luke 14:15-24
27.	The Unfinished Tower and the King's Rash War	Luke 14:28-33
28.	The Lost Sheep	Matthew 18:12-14
		(Luke 15:4-7)
29.	The Lost Coin	Luke 15:8-10
30.	The Prodigal Son	Luke 15:11-32
31.	The Shrewd Manager	Luke 16:1-9
32.	The Servant's Reward	Luke 17:7-10
33.	The Unjust Judge	Luke 18:1-8
34.	The Pharisee and the Tax Collector	Luke 18:9-14
35.	The Pounds (or Minas)	Luke 19:11-27

From *The Bible Knowledge Commentary*, New Testament (Wheaton, Ill., Victor Books, 1983), p. 35, used by permission.

What Features Characterize Jesus' Parables?

Jesus' parables have appeal because they deal with common everyday elements. *Commercial* items include a fisherman, builder, merchant, money, interest, debts, treasure, employer, master, servants, creditor, debtors, tax collector, traveler, pearl, steward. *Farming* elements Jesus referred to include a farmer, shepherd, sheep, soil, seeds, trees, birds, thorns, harvest, pigpen, vineyard, vinegrowers, watchtower, barns, and fig tree.

Domestic items include houses, cooking (leaven and meal), sewing, coins, sweeping, sleeping, eating, children playing, widow, wineskins, doorkeeper. Jesus also referred to *social* events in His parables, including a wedding, a banquet, bridesmaids, father and son, a friend at midnight, a host, and guests. *Religious* individuals include a priest, a Levite, a Samaritan, and a Pharisee; and *civil* elements include a judge, king, and war.[3]

Jesus' parables included suspense, simple plot conflicts, heightened contrasts, and in some cases exaggeration.[4] The reader is held in suspense wondering how the merciful master will treat his unmerciful servant (Matt. 18:21-35). What will happen to the landowner's tenants who killed his servants and his son? (21:33-46) What will the king do to the guest not wearing wedding clothes? (22:1-14) What will the master do to his wicked servant when the master returns? (24:45-51) When the prodigal son left home, how will things turn out for him? When he returns to his father, will the son be accepted? (Luke 15:11-32) If two men refuse to help a man wounded by the highway, what will the third bypasser do? (10:25-37)

Numerous contrasts abound in Jesus' parables, heightening the hearers' and readers' interest. The chart on page 200 lists these many contrasts. Also note the many times two persons are contrasted to a single character as with the two servants who invested their pounds or mina and the one servant who did not invest even one mina; the merciful creditor in relation to the two debtors who were unable to pay; and the two passersby and the good Samaritan.

Many parables have three major characters or groups of characters, as seen in the following list.

The Unforgiving Servant (Matt. 18:23-35): King, forgiven servant, unforgiven servant

The Workers in the Vineyard (Matt. 20:1-16): Landowner, workers hired during the day, workers hired at the 11th hour

Contrasts in the Parables

House built on a rock	House built on sand
New cloth	Old garment
New wine	Old wineskins
Seed on good soil	Seed on poor soil
Sower sowed wheat	Enemy sowed tares
Small mustard seed	Huge tree
Small amount of leaven	Huge amount of meal
Treasure, and pearl	All one's possessions of less value
Good fish	Bad fish
A servant forgiven a huge debt	He refused to forgive another a small debt
Vineyard workers worked all day for a denarius	Other workers worked one hour for the same wage
A son refused to work but later did	A son promised to work but didn't
Those invited to a wedding feast refused to attend	Those compelled to attend a wedding feast attended
Faithful servant	Evil servant
Five foolish virgins	Five wise virgins
Two servants invested their mina	One servant did not invest one mina
Creditor	Two debtors unable to pay
Priest and Levite pass by the wounded man	Good Samaritan cares for the wounded man
Friend at midnight	Sleeping friend
Rich man acquiring more wealth	Rich man losing his soul
Fig tree owner anxious to cut down the tree	Vineyard-keeper anxious to wait one more year
Prodigal son whose return is celebrated	Older brother who is not celebrated

The Two Sons (Matt. 21:28-32): Man, first son, second son
The Wicked Vinegrowers (Matt. 21:33-46): Landowner, tenants, son
The Wedding Banquet (Matt. 22:1-14): King, those who refused to come, those who did come

The Two Servants (Matt. 24:45-51): Master, wise servant, wicked servant
The 10 Virgins (Matt. 25:1-13): Bridegroom, 5 wise virgins, 5 foolish virgins
The Talents (Matt. 25:14-30): Master, servants who invested their talents, servant who did not invest his one talent
The Two Debtors (Luke 7:41-43): Moneylender, debtor owing a large debt, debtor owing a small debt
The Good Samaritan (Luke 10:25-37): Injured Jew, negligent religious leaders, Samaritan
The Friend at Midnight (Luke 11:5-8): Man who is asked to help, guest who asks for help, the friend in need
The Great Banquet (Luke 14:15-24): Invitees with three excuses
The Lost Sheep (Luke 15:4-7): Shepherd, 99 sheep, 1 lost sheep
The Prodigal Son (Luke 15:11-32): Father, prodigal son, older brother
The Unjust Judge (Luke 18:1-8): Judge, widow, her opponent
The Pounds (Luke 19:11-27): Servant with 10 pounds, servant with 5, servant with 1.

Conflicts abound in the parables. Examples include the men who worked one hour and those who worked all day (Matt. 20:1-16), the wise virgins who refused to give oil to the foolish virgins (25:1-13), the persistent man in conflict with his friend who had already gone to bed (Luke 11:5-8), the persistent widow and the judge (18:1-8), and the conflict between the prodigal son and his father and between the prodigal son and his older brother (15:11-32).

Unexpected turns are sometimes seen in the parables. One is surprised to read that a person who worked only one hour received the same wages as those who worked all day (Matt. 20:1-16), or that a king was so enraged he sent his army to destroy some murderers and to burn their city (22:6-7). It is also remarkable that the prodigal's father ran to meet his son (Luke 15:20), or that a Samaritan expressed more compassion and kindness than religious leaders, since no Samaritan was considered by the Jews to be good (10:25-37). Again it is remarkable that everyone invited to a banquet would refuse the invitation (Matt. 22:3), or that a man to whom another owed a small debt would refuse to cancel the debt when he himself had been forgiven a large debt (18:23-35).

The effect of some of the parables is increased by their unusual departure from normal procedure.

A king does not normally allow a servant to incur a debt running into millions (Matt. 18:24). It is unusual for a whole
room full of guests to go back on their initial acceptance of an
invitation (Luke 14:18-20). Workmen do not commonly expect to be paid at the same rate for one hour as for the whole
day; like the early workers in the parable, they insist on their
differentials (Matt. 20:9).[5]

Exaggerations, hyperboles, reversals, and atypical circumstances increase the impact of many of the parables.[6]

Ryken speaks of "end stress," in which the last element in a
parable is the most important.[7] In the Parable of the Sower the fertile
soil is mentioned last. The last servant, who did not invest his mina,
is judged harshly, the last traveler in the Parable of the Good Samaritan is generous, and those who are last invited to the banquet accept
the invitation.

Another interesting feature of Jesus' parables is the inclusion
of direct discourse, in which He gave the actual words spoken by the
characters in the stories. This too adds to their appeal as story-
parables. Related to this is the kind of speech called soliloquy in
which a character talks to himself, thus revealing to the hearers and
readers something of his thinking, plans, and concerns. Perhaps the
best-known soliloquy in the parables is that of the prodigal son, who
said, "How many of my father's hired men have food to spare, and
here I am starving to death! I will set out and go back to my father
and say to him: 'Father, I have sinned against heaven and against
you. I am no longer worthy to be called your son; make me like one
of your hired men'" (Luke 15:17-19). In another parable the shrewd
"manager said to himself, 'What shall I do now? My master is taking
away my job. I'm not strong enough to dig, and I'm ashamed to
beg—I know what I'll do so that, when I lose my job here, people
will welcome me into their houses'" (16:3-4). The rich fool
"thought to himself, 'What shall I do? I have no place to store my
crops.' Then he said, 'This is what I'll do. I will tear down my barns
and build bigger ones, and there I will store all my grain and my
goods. And I'll say to myself, "You have plenty of good things laid
up for many years. Take life easy; eat, drink and be merry"'" (12:17-
19).

On hearing the persistent pleas of a widow, the judge said to
himself, "Even though I don't fear God or care about men, yet
because this widow keeps bothering me, I will see that she gets

justice, so that she won't eventually wear me out with her coming!" (18:5)

A sinful woman wet Jesus' feet with her tears, kissed His feet, and poured perfume on them. The Pharisee who invited Jesus to dinner said to himself, "If this Man were a prophet, He would know who is touching Him" (7:39). In still another parable a wicked servant said to himself, "My master is staying away a long time" (Matt. 24:48).

Still another interesting aspect of the literary feature of the parables is the occurrence of rhetorical questions. These encourage the reader to respond in his mind to the challenges Jesus gave. For example after Jesus spoke of a shepherd losing 1 of his 100 sheep He asked, "Does he not leave the ninety-nine in the open country and go after the lost sheep until he finds it?" (Luke 15:4) He asked a similar question after mentioning the example of a woman who lost 1 of 10 coins: "Does she not light a lamp, sweep the house and search carefully until she finds it?" (v. 8) In speaking to one of the vineyard workers, a landowner asked, "Don't I have the right to do what I want with my own money? Or are you envious because I am generous?" (Matt. 20:15)

In speaking of the two servants, Jesus introduced the subject by the question, "Who then is the faithful and wise servant, whom the master has put in charge of the servants in his household to give them their food at the proper time?" (24:44-45) And in introducing the subject of the rude children, Jesus asked, "To what, then, can I compare the people of this generation? What are they like?" (Luke 7:31)

Three of the five sentences in Jesus' Parable of the Servant's Reward are rhetorical questions (Luke 17:7-10). In His parable about the persistent widow Jesus asked the rhetorical question, "When the Son of man comes, will He find faith on the earth?" (18:8)

Other times Jesus asked questions to which He expected His hearers to respond. After telling Simon Peter about the two debtors, Jesus asked him, "Now which of them will love him more?" (7:42) After telling the Parable of the Good Samaritan to the expert in the Law, Jesus asked him, "Which of these three do you think was a neighbor to the man who fell into the hands of robbers?" (10:36) In speaking of the two sons, Jesus asked the chief priests and elders, "Which of the two did what his father wanted?" (Matt. 21:31)

These many literary features of the parables—suspense, contrast, characterization, conflict, surprise, hyperbole, reversal, end stress, direct discourse, and rhetorical questioning — demonstrate the unusual impact Jesus' stories would have had on His hearers.

What Kinds of Parables Did Jesus Tell?

As you read Jesus' 35 parables, you note that some of them are similar to others. They have a common subject or theme, such as the "seed" parables, or a common character, such as the "servant parables," "landowner" parables, the parables with a father, and those with a king. Other parables share an emotional element such as rejoicing or compassion. In some something offered is received, whereas in other parables something offered is refused. In a number of parables reward and punishment are meted. All the parables teach something about Jesus, or His kingdom, or His followers. The chart on pages 205–208 illustrates these groupings.

In interpreting the parables it is important to keep in mind that they all refer in some way to the kingdom of God. Many Bible scholars, including some nondispensationalists as well as most dispensationalists, recognize this fact. The chart on page 209 on the kingdom in the parables lists them under seven headings: progress in the kingdom, conflict between Jesus' concept of the kingdom and that of the Pharisees, grace and sinners in the kingdom, characteristics of those in the kingdom, rejection of the King and His kingdom, judgment on those who reject the King and/or reward for those who accept Him, and alertness to and preparedness for the King's coming.

The Gospels give ample basis for seeing the parables in relationship to God's kingdom or rule. First, in introducing 11 of his parables, Matthew wrote, "The kingdom of heaven is like" (13:24, 31, 33, 44-45, 47; 18:23; 20:1; 22:2), or "The kingdom of heaven will be like" (25:1), or "It will be like" (v. 14). In addition Mark recorded that Jesus said, "This is what the kingdom of God is like" (Mark 4:26). All seven parables in Matthew 13 relate to the kingdom. The Parable of the Sower is not introduced with the words "The kingdom of heaven is like," but when Jesus explained the parable He related it to the kingdom by His words, "When anyone hears the message about the kingdom" (v. 19). Further reference is made to the kingdom in verses 38, 41, 43, and 52. In that same chapter Jesus said, "The knowledge of the secrets of the kingdom of heaven has been given to you" (v. 11).

Second, two parables in Luke follow immediately after a

Classifications of the Parables

Seed parables

1. The Sower (Matt. 13:3-8)
2. The Weeds (Matt. 13:24-30)
3. The Mustard Seed (Matt. 13:31-32)
4. Yeast (Matt. 13:33)
5. The Seed Growing Secretly (Mark 4:26-29)

Nature parables

1-5. All the seed parables listed above
6. The Two Houses—on rock and sand (Matt. 7:24-27)
7. The New Cloth and New Wineskins (Matt. 9:16-17)
8. The Hidden Treasures—in a field (Matt. 13:44)
9. The Pearl of Great Price (Matt. 13:45-46)
10. The Fishing Net—with good and bad fish (Matt. 13:47-50)
11. The Workers in the Vineyard (Matt. 20:1-16)
12. The Wicked Vinegrowers (Matt. 21:33-46)
13. The Barren Fig Tree (Luke 13:6-9)
14. The Lost Sheep (Luke 15:4-7)

Servant parables

A. Parables in which the master departs, leaving the servants on their own. When he returns, the good servants are rewarded and/or the bad ones are punished.
   1. The Two Servants (Matt. 24:45-51)
   2. The Talents (Matt. 25:14-30)
   3. The Doorkeeper (Mark 13:34-37)
   4. The Pounds—or Minas (Luke 19:11-27)
B. The servant departs or is away and then returns to report to his master. The reckoning received is unexpected.
   1. The Unforgiving Servant (Matt. 18:23-35)
   2. The Workers in the Vineyard (Matt. 20:1-16)
   3. The Wicked Vinegrowers (Matt. 21:33-46)
   4. The Shrewd Manager (Luke 16:1-9)
   5. The Servant's Reward (Luke 17:7-10)

Father parables

1. The Two Sons (Matt. 21:28-32)

Classifications of the Parables (Continued)

2.   The Wicked Vinegrowers (Matt. 21:33-46)
3.   The Wedding Banquet (Matt. 22:1-14)
4.   The Prodigal Son (Luke 15:11-32)

King parables
1.   The Unforgiving Servant (Matt. 18:23-35)
2.   The Wedding Banquet (Matt. 22:1-14)
3.   The King's Rash War (Luke 14:31-33)
4.   The Pounds—or Minas (Luke 19:11-27)

Money (or treasure) parables
1.   The Hidden Treasure (Matt. 13:44)
2.   The Pearl of Great Price (Matt. 13:45-46)
3.   The Unforgiving Servant (Matt. 18:23-35)
4.   The Workers in the Vineyard (Matt. 20:1-16)
5.   The Talents (Matt. 25:14-30)
6.   The Two Debtors (Luke 7:41-43)
7.   The Good Samaritan (Luke 10:25-37)
8.   The Rich Fool (Luke 12:16-21)
9.   The Shrewd Manager (Luke 16:1-9)
10. The Pharisee and the Tax Collector (Luke 18:9-14)
11. The Pounds—or Minas (Luke 19:11-27)

Harvest parables
1.   The Weeds (Matt. 13:24-30; see vv. 30, 39)
2.   The Wicked Vinegrowers (Matt. 21:33-46; see v. 41)
3.   The Talents (Matt. 25:14-30; see vv. 24, 26)
4.   The Seed Growing Secretly (Mark 4:26-29)

Women parables
1.   The Yeast (Matt. 13:33)
2.   The Virgins (Matt. 25:1-13)
3.   The Lost Coin (Luke 15:8-10)
4.   The Unjust Judge (Luke 18:1-8)

Social or domestic parables
1.   The Wedding Banquet (Matt. 22:1-14)
2.   The Ten Virgins (Matt. 25:1-13)

Classifications of the Parables (Continued)

3. The Doorkeeper (Mark 13:34-37)
4. The Rude Children (Luke 7:31-35)
5. The Good Samaritan (Luke 10:25-37)
6. The Friend at Midnight (Luke 11:5-8)
7. The Great Banquet (Luke 14:15-24)
8. The Lost Coin (Luke 15:8-10)
9. The Prodigal Son (Luke 15:11-32)
10. The Servant's Reward (Luke 17:7-10)
11. The Unjust Judge (Luke 18:1-8)
12. The Pharisee and the Tax Collector (Luke 18:9-14)

Compassion parables
1. The Good Samaritan (Luke 10:25-37; see v. 33)
2. The Great Banquet (Luke 14:15-24; see v. 21)
3. The Lost Sheep (Luke 15:4-7; see v. 4)
4. The Prodigal Son (Luke 15:11-32; see v. 20)

Rejoicing parables
1. The Hidden Treasure (Matt. 13:44)
2. The Lost Sheep (Luke 15:4-7)
3. The Lost Coin (Luke 15:8-10)
4. The Prodigal Son (Luke 15:11-32)

Feast parables
1. The Wedding Banquet (Matt. 22:1-14)
2. The Ten Virgins (Matt. 25:1-13)
3. The Great Banquet (Luke 14:15-24)
4. The Prodigal Son (Luke 15:11-32)

Refusal parables
1. The Unforgiving Servant (Matt. 18:23-35). The servant whose debts were canceled refused to cancel a debt someone owed him, and so the king put him in jail and refused to cancel his debt after all.
2. The Wicked Vinegrowers (Matt. 21:33-46). The tenants refused to treat the landowner's servants and his son kindly, and so the landowner refused to leave his vineyard in those tenants' hands.

Classifications of the Parables (Continued)

3. The Wedding Banquet (Matt. 22:1-14). Those invited to the wedding banquet refused to come, and so the king refused to let them live.
4. The Talents (Matt. 25:14-30). The man with one talent refused to invest it, and so the master refused to let him keep even the one talent.
5. The Rich Fool (Luke 12:16-21). The rich fool refused to honor God, and so God refused to allow him to live.
6. The Barren Fig Tree (Luke 13:6-9). The owner of a fig tree refused to let it grow.
7. The Great Banquet (Luke 14:15-24). Those invited to the banquet made excuses for not attending and refused to come.

---

reference to the kingdom. Jesus told the Parable of the Great Banquet immediately after He said, "Blessed is the man who will eat at the feast in the kingdom of God" (Luke 14:15), thus obviously relating the banquet parable to feasting in His kingdom. Since "the people thought that the kingdom of God was going to appear at once" (19:11), Jesus told the Parable of the Pounds or Minas. After Jesus gave the Parable of the Unjust Judge which recorded the story of the persistent widow, He concluded, "However, when the Son of man comes, will He find faith on the earth?" (18:8)

Third, the several parables that refer to a king or landowner being away and then returning clearly point to the present age when Jesus is away and in which we anticipate His return. These parables, along with the others just referred to in relation to the kingdom, suggest that a form of the kingdom exists today but with the King not present on the earth. (See the chart on page 210 on the meanings of the parables of the kingdom in Matt. 13.) At the conclusion of Jesus' Parable of the Two Sons, He associated that parable with the kingdom of God by saying, "I tell you the truth, the tax collectors and the prostitutes are entering the kingdom of God ahead of you" (21:31). In the Parable of the Two Servants, reference is made to the return of the master (24:46) who will find his servant faithful, and to the wicked servant who said, "My master is staying away a long time" (v. 48). In this same parable Jesus referred to the master who "will come on a day when he [his servant] does not expect him" (v. 50).

The Kingdom in the Parables

Progress in the kingdom
The Weeds, The Mustard Seed, The Yeast, The Seed Growing Secretly

Conflict between Jesus' concept of the kingdom and that of the Pharisees
The New Cloth and New Wineskins, The Rude Children

Grace and sinners in the kingdom
The Hidden Treasure (Israel), The Pearl of Great Price (Church), The Workers in the Vineyard, The Two Sons, The Rude Children, The Two Debtors, The Barren Fig Tree, The Great Banquet, The Lost Sheep, The Lost Coin, The Prodigal Son, The Pharisee and the Tax Collector

Characteristics of those in the kingdom
Compassion: The Good Samaritan
Humility: The Servant's Reward
Faithfulness: The Two Servants, The Talents, The Pounds—or Minas
Persistent prayer: The Friend at Midnight, The Unjust Judge
Attitude toward wealth: The Rich Fool, The Shrewd Manager
Forgiveness: The Unforgiving Servant
Willingness to sacrifice: The Unfinished Tower and The King's Rash War

Rejection of the King and His kingdom
The Sower, The Two Sons, The Wicked Vinegrowers, The Wedding Banquet, The Rude Children, The Great Banquet, The Pounds—or Minas

Judgment on those who reject the King and/or reward for those who accept Him
The Two Houses, The Weeds, The Fishing Net, The Worker in the Vineyard, The Wicked Vinegrowers, The Wedding Banquet, The Two Servants, The 10 Virgins, The Talents, The Doorkeeper, The Two Debtors, The Barren Fig Tree, The Great Banquet, The Pounds—or Minas

Alertness at and preparedness for the King's coming
The 10 Virgins, The Doorkeeper

Parables of the Kingdom in Matthew 13

Parables	References	Meanings
1. The Sower	13:13-23	The good news of the Gospel will be rejected by most people.
2. The Wheat and the Weeds	13:24-30, 36-43	People with genuine faith and people with a false profession of faith will exist together between Christ's two Advents.
3. The Mustard Seed	13:31-32	Christendom, including believers and unbelievers, will grow rapidly from a small beginning.
4. The Yeast	13:33-35	People who profess to belong to God will grow in numbers without being stopped.
5. The Hidden Treasure	13:44	Christ came to purchase (redeem) Israel, God's treasured possession.
6. The Pearl	13:45-46	Christ gave His life to provide redemption for the church.
7. The Net	13:47-52	Angels will separate the wicked from the righteous when Christ comes.

From *The Bible Knowledge Commentary*, New Testament (Wheaton, Ill., Victor Books, 1983), p. 52, used by permission.

In the Parable of the Ten Virgins, they go out with lamps "to meet the bridegroom" (Matt. 25:1). Jesus' words at the close of this parable also point to the need for watchfulness during the time of His absence since no one knows when He will return (v. 13).

In the Parable of the Talents, the kingdom of heaven is compared to "a man going on a journey" (v. 14) who "after a long time . . . returned" and had the worthless servant thrown "into the darkness" (v. 30).

The Parable of the Doorkeeper, in which Jesus urged His followers to be alert (Mark 13:33) follows soon after He referred to "the Son of man coming in clouds with great power and glory" (v. 26). In that same parable Jesus said the situation is "like a man going away" who "leaves his house in charge of his servants" (v. 34). The doorkeeper is urged to keep watch because he does not know when the owner of the house will return. Again this calls for alertness (vv. 35-37).

The Parable of the Pounds or Minas also refers to a man going away to "a distant country" and returning (Luke 19:12, 15). This same parable refers to the "man of noble birth" going away to be "appointed king" (v. 12; cf. v. 15).

If Bible students do not recognize the emphasis on the kingdom in the parables, they overlook an important key to understanding those stories and why Jesus told them.[8]

What Are Some Guidelines for Interpreting the Parables?

Note the Story's Natural Meaning

This relates to what has been said in earlier chapters about first understanding a passage in its normal, grammatical sense, without reading something into the passage.

As already stated, a parable is a story that seeks to illustrate a truth by analogy. Two things, then, are being brought together in a parable—a true-to-life incident and the spiritual truth it is illustrating or illuminating. Therefore to understand the spiritual truth properly, it is essential first to comprehend fully the true-to-life incident. Picture a house built on a foundation of rock, which withstands the storms, and a house built on sand which collapses in a storm of rain and wind. Understand all you can about the mustard seed that grows to great heights in a short period of time from an unusually small seed. (See the explanation of the mustard seed in chap. 4, pp. 85–86.) As you understand the true-to-life incident of the parable in its full cultural setting, you are better prepared to understand the message of the parable. A fishing net, a vineyard, a wedding banquet, oil lamps, talents of money, a fig tree still barren after three years, the value of a single coin to a housewife, the people's despicable attitude toward tax collectors, the meaning of pounds or minas— understanding these elements sheds light on the significance of the parables and helps make the right transition to the spiritual truth.

Determine the Problem, Question, or Situation That Prompted the Parable

Seeing why Jesus told certain parables when He did helps point up the proper analogy between the life incident He related and the spiritual truth He was making in the parable.

The parables may be grouped under the following nine occasions or purposes. As you study a given parable, look to this list to find the occasion or setting.

Parables in answer to questions. John's disciples asked Jesus, "How is it that we and the Pharisees fast, but Your disciples do not fast?" (Matt. 9:14) Jesus then told the Parable of the New Cloth and the New Wineskins to say that His ways were new. An expert in the Law asked Jesus, "Teacher . . . what must I do to inherit eternal life?" (Luke 10:25; cf. Matt. 19:16) and "Who is my neighbor?" (Luke 10:29) Jesus then told the Parable of the Good Samaritan (vv. 30-37) and the Parable of the Workers in the Vineyard (Matt. 20:1-16).

Peter asked Jesus, "Lord, how many times shall I forgive my brother when he sins against me? Up to seven times?" (18:21) This question prompted Jesus to give the Parable of the Unforgiving Servant. When the chief priests and the elders asked, "By what authority are You doing these things?" and "Who gave You this authority?" Jesus responded by giving the Parables of the Two Sons and of the Wicked Vinegrowers.

Parables in answer to requests. The Parable of the Friend at Midnight (Luke 11:5-8), in which Jesus was obviously emphasizing persistence in prayer, follows soon after one of His disciples requested, "Lord, teach us to pray, just as John taught his disciples" (v. 1). The Parable of the Rich Fool (12:16-21) followed the request made by someone in the crowd that Jesus tell the man's brother to divide their father's inheritance with him (v. 13). Jesus declined to be an arbitrator in that situation and, urging people to be on guard against greed (vv. 14-15), He then told the Parable of the Rich Fool.

Parables in answer to complaints. When a Pharisee invited Jesus to dinner, he thought, "If this Man were a Prophet, He would know who is touching Him and what kind of woman she is—that she is a sinner" (7:39). Knowing this, Jesus spoke of the two debtors (vv. 41-43). When the Pharisees and the teachers of the Law complained, "This Man welcomes sinners and eats with them" (15:2), Jesus gave the Parables of the Lost Sheep, the Lost Coin, and the Lost or Prodigal Son. By these stories Jesus indicated that He ate with sinners because they, like the three lost elements, were in need of being "found" spiritually.

Parables given with a stated purpose. Jesus told the Parable of the Unjust Judge to show His disciples "that they should always pray and not give up" (18:1). Since some Pharisees "were confident of their own righteousness and looked down on everybody else" (v. 9), Jesus gave the Parable of the Pharisee and the Tax Collector. And since "the people thought that the kingdom of God was going to appear at once" (19:11) Jesus related His Parable of the Pounds or Minas.

Parables of the kingdom given because of Israel's rejection of Jesus as Messiah. Matthew 12 records the height of the rejection of Jesus by the Pharisees, in which they accused Him of performing healing miracles by demonic power (v. 24). Since many were rejecting Him (and only those who did His will were His spiritual relatives, vv. 48-50), Jesus told the seven parables of the kingdom in Matthew 13. See the chart on page 210 on the parables of the kingdom in Matthew 13 for the meaning of each of these in light of Israel's rejection of Jesus as Messiah.

Parables following an exhortation or principle. Several times Jesus gave an exhortation or principle and then followed it with a parable to illustrate or illumine the point just made. For example Mark 13:33 records that Jesus said, "Be on guard! Be alert! You do not know when the time will come." Then He gave the Parable of the Doorkeeper (vv. 34-37).

Jesus may have told the story of the lost sheep on more than one occasion. In Luke 15:4-7, the Parable of the Lost Sheep follows the complaint of the Pharisees and the teachers of the Law that He was welcoming and eating with sinners. In Matthew 18 the Parable of the Lost Sheep (vv. 12-14) follows His exhortation that the disciples "not look down on" children (v. 10).

Jesus followed His announcement of blessing on those who would "eat at the feast in the kingdom of God" (Luke 14:15) with His Parable of the Great Banquet (vv. 16-24). After urging His disciples to "be ready because the Son of man will come at an hour when you do not expect Him" (Matt. 24:44), He then told the Parable of the Two Servants (vv. 45-51).

Parables followed by an exhortation or principle. Sometimes Jesus gave a parable and then followed it with an exhortation or principle. For example the Parable of the Friend at Midnight (Luke 11:5-8) is followed by His exhortation for them to persist in prayer (vv. 9-10).

The Parable of the Workers in the Vineyard (Matt. 20:1-15) is followed by the principle, "So the last will be first, and the first will be last" (v. 16). Interestingly almost identical words precede the parable as well, for Jesus said in 19:30, "But many who are first will be last, and many who are last will be first."

The fact that discipleship involves sacrifice is illustrated by the Parable of the Unfinished Tower and the King's Rash War (Luke 14:28-32), and the principle is then stated in verse 33.

The unusual Parable of the Shrewd Manager (Luke 16:1-8) is followed by Jesus' statement in verse 9 which gives the point of His parable: "I tell you, use worldly wealth to gain friends for yourselves, so that when it is gone, you will be welcomed into eternal dwellings." That is, they were to be wise in using their money for eternal purposes.

After telling about the servant who was to be faithful in doing his duty even when not thanked, Jesus said that His followers should obey without any ulterior motive for reward. "So you also, when you have done everything you were told to do, should say, 'We are unworthy servants; we have only done our duty'" (17:10).

Jesus' Parable of the Pharisee and the Tax Collector was given, as stated earlier, to respond to the Pharisees who felt confident in their own righteousness. That observation about their pride preceded the parable (18:9), but then after the parable Jesus explained, "For everyone who exalts himself will be humbled, and he who humbles himself will be exalted" (v. 14).

The Parable of the Marriage of the King's Son (Matt. 22:1-14) concludes with the principle, "For many are invited, but few are chosen." Similarly the Parable of the Ten Virgins (25:1-13) concludes with the Lord's exhortation, "Therefore keep watch" (v. 13).

Parables to illustrate a situation. Jesus introduced the Parable of the Two Houses by pointing up that anyone who heard His words and put them into practice was like the man building a house on a rock (7:24). Then He added that those who do not put into practice what He said are like those who build houses on sand (v. 26).

What was the occasion for Jesus' comparing the people of His day with children playing in the marketplace? Those words in Luke 7:31-35 follow the setting in which the Pharisees obviously were rejecting Jesus' words (vv. 29-30). Another situation illustrated by a parable is seen in Luke 13. After explaining that failure to repent would lead to eternal judgment (vv. 1-5), Jesus gave the Parable of the Barren Fig Tree (vv. 6-8) in which He was obviously pointing up the imminence of judgment.

Parables with the purpose implied but not stated. The Parable of the Talents (Matt. 25:14-30) does not have a purpose statement nor is it preceded or followed by an exhortation or principle, nor does it occur in response to a question, request, or complaint. The parable does, however, seem to point up what is expected of Jesus' followers while He is away (see v. 14) and to indicate that He expects His followers to serve Him faithfully while He is absent.

Also the purpose of the Parable of the Seed Growing Secretly (Mark 4:26-29) is not stated, but it seems to suggest rapid numerical growth of believers during the present age. This seems to be suggested because it speaks of the coming harvest or judgment (v. 29) and because it is immediately followed by the Parable of the Mustard Seed (vv. 30-32).

Ascertain the Main Truth Being Illustrated by the Parable

Usually a parable, like a sermon illustration, is teaching a single truth. When Jesus explained a number of His parables, He usually, though not always, stated one spiritual truth. For example when the man found his one lost sheep, he rejoiced, and Jesus said this illustrates the truth that there is rejoicing in heaven when a sinner repents (Luke 15:7). Verse 10 records the same interpretation of the Parable of the Lost Coin. In the Parable of the Unjust Judge, in which the judge finally exercised justice on behalf of the persistent woman, Jesus' interpretation of the parable was that God would bring about justice for those who come to Him (18:7). Jesus' purpose in telling the story of the Vineyard Workers was to indicate that "the last will be first, and the first will be last" (Matt. 20:16). He gave one simple spiritual lesson, and made no attempt to see any spiritual significance to the vineyard, the denarius, the sixth hour, the ninth hour, or the eleventh hour, nor the vineyard foreman.

However, in support of the major point, some details in the parables are analogous to certain spiritual facts. Sometimes this is necessary for the major point of the parable to be fully drawn. In the Parable of the Lost Sheep, the shepherd obviously represents Jesus, the 1 sheep represents a lost sinner, as Jesus explained in Luke 15:7, and the remaining 99 sheep represent "righteous persons who do not need to repent." And yet other details such as the open country, the shepherd's shoulders, and his home and friends and neighbors should not be made analogous to some spiritual elements. They simply are parts needed to make the story lifelike and to add local color.

In the Parable of the Good Samaritan, Jesus did not give any interpretation of the robbers, the man's clothes, the man's wounds, the oil and wine, the donkey, the two silver coins, or the innkeeper. These were elements needed to complete the story and to put it in its proper cultural setting.

Sometimes Jesus did explain a number of the details of a parable, as in the Parable of the Sower in which He explained the meaning of each of the four places where the seed fell (Matt. 13:18-23). He also interpreted several details in the Parable of the Weeds, including the sower, the field, the good seed, the weeds, the enemy, the harvest, and the harvesters (vv. 37-39).

Since Jesus did not normally point up analogies in all parts of His parables, these examples in Matthew 13 should be seen as exceptions. The purpose of the story about the 10 virgins is to encourage Jesus' followers to keep watch for His return, not to draw parallels for every element including the oil, jars, and lamps. Nor should truths be drawn from the parables for which there is no scriptural warrant in the story. Some people say the Ten Virgins parable is speaking against selfishness, since the wise virgins refused to share their oil. But the passage gives no clue that this is the parable's purpose.

To hunt for meanings in every detail in the parables is to turn them into allegories. An allegory, as discussed later in this chapter, is a story in which every element or almost every element has some meaning. A well-known example is Augustine's allegorizing of the Parable of the Good Samaritan. The man who fell into the hands of robbers is Adam. Jerusalem is heaven, and Jericho signifies man's mortality. The robbers are the devil and his angels who stripped man of his immortality. In beating him they persuaded him to sin, and in leaving him half dead the devil and his angels have left man in a condition in which he has some knowledge of God but is yet oppressed by sin. The priest represents the Law, and the Levite represents the Prophets. The Good Samaritan is Christ who, in bandaging the man's wounds, seeks to restrain sin. Oil is hope and wine is a fervent spirit. The man's donkey is Jesus' incarnation, and the man being placed on a donkey pictures his belief in the incarnation of Christ. The inn is the church. The next day pictures the Lord's resurrection, the two coins represent either the two precepts of love or this life and the life to come. The innkeeper is the Apostle Paul.[9]

Obviously this is a clear case of eisegesis—reading into the Scriptures something that is not there. Nowhere does the passage hint that all these elements are to be given any interpretation at all and it is clear that Augustine's interpretations are purely arbitrary. Other examples of eisegesis in parabolic interpretation are these: the shrewd manager pictures Satan, and the three measures of flour in the Parable of the Yeast represent the sanctification of the body, mind, and spirit or salvation of the human race.

Another example of allegorical eisegesis is Origen's interpretation of the Parable of the Ten Virgins. He said the five lamps of the wise represent five natural senses, all trimmed by proper use. The oil is the teaching of the Word, the sellers of oil are the teachers, and the price for the oil is perseverance. Again, this kind of interpretation is arbitrary because there is no indication in either this passage or other passages in Scripture that the parable is to be understood in this way.

Validate the Main Truth of the Parable with Direct Teaching of Scripture

Are we correct in assuming that the Bridegroom in the Parable of the Ten Virgins refers to Christ? Yes, because Jesus' words in Matthew 9:15 clearly indicate that He identified Himself as the Bridegroom. John's disciples wondered why Jesus' disciples did not fast and Jesus responded that the guests of a bridegroom fast not when he is present but when he is gone. He then is the Bridegroom and His disciples were the Bridegroom's guests. Also John the Baptist referred to the friend who attends the Bridegroom, clearly pointing to the fact that he was a servant of Christ, the Bridegroom (John 3:27-30). Immediately before giving the Parable of the Ten Virgins, Jesus spoke of His return and of the importance of being ready since the date of His return is unknown (Matt. 24:36, 42, 44). Since the same admonition to "keep watch" occurs at the end of the parable Jesus obviously was intending that He be understood as the Bridegroom.

However, some elements in the parables need not always mean the same everywhere in Scripture. Yeast often represents evil (e.g., Ex. 12:15; Lev. 2:11; 6:17; 10:12; Matt. 16:6, 11-12; Mark 8:15; Luke 12:1; 1 Cor. 5:7-8; Gal. 5:8-9). However, if the yeast in the parable in Matthew 13:33 stands for evil, this seems redundant because of the weeds, which already are seen to represent evil (vv. 24-30). Since yeast causes the process of leavening, Jesus may have been implying that "those who profess to belong to the kingdom would grow in numbers and that nothing would be able to stop their advance."[10]

Note the Actual or Intended Response of the Hearers

The hearers' response often gives a clue to the meaning of the parable. After giving the story of the Good Samaritan, Jesus asked a question of the expert in the Law: "Which of these three do you think was a neighbor to the man who fell into the hands of robbers?" By this question Jesus was seeking to explain that being "neighborly" meant having compassion for a person in need. The punch line, or call for action, then came in Jesus' next words, "Go and do likewise" (Luke 10:37). To follow the example of a Samaritan, whom the expert in the Law hated, would have jolted the lawyer! This unexpected conclusion would have caused him to broaden his concept of loving his neighbor (v. 27) beyond anything he had ever previously considered.

In the Parable of the Rich Fool (12:16-21) Jesus was warning against greed and materialism (v. 15). Jesus' concluding sentence in verse 21 draws the parallel between the rich fool who met an untimely death and those who store up things for themselves but are not rich toward God. The point of the parable, then, is that spiritual wealth far exceeds material wealth in value. The point of the parable is not that death may come at any time but rather that centering one's life on possessions and pleasures is not to be the focus of one's life. To allegorize the parts of the parable, including the crops, barns, and goods, is to go beyond the clear purpose of the parable.

When Jesus told the Parable of the Unforgiving Servant, He concluded, "This is how My Heavenly Father will treat each of you unless you forgive your brother from your heart" (Matt. 18:35). Before giving the Parable of the Two Sons, Jesus challenged His hearers with the question, "What do you think?" (21:28) Then by asking, "Which of the two did what his father wanted?" (v. 31) He got them to interact. When they answered "the first," He then stated the point of the parable in the second half of verse 31.

Want an interesting study project? Note the way each parable is introduced and how it is concluded or the response expected. The chart on pages 219–221 may be useful in making such a study. The first three are already filled in to help get you started. This will be helpful in ascertaining the points Jesus made by means of His parables.

Give attention to the cultural and historical setting, consider the plain statements of the Scriptures, let the passage speak for itself without reading something into it, and note the rhetorical-literary quality and structure of the passage.

In interpreting the parables follow the same steps you use in interpreting any portion of Scripture.[11]

Parable	Way It Was Introduced	Hearer(s)	Action Commanded or Response Expected
1. The Two Houses (Matt. 7:24-27)	(Part of the Sermon on the Mount)	Jesus' disciples	Amazement
2. The New Cloth and New Wine-skins (Matt. 9:16-17)	Question about fasting	John's disciples	(Not stated)
3. The Sower (Matt. 13:3-8)	(Not stated)	Crowds	Disciples asked why Jesus spoke in parables (v. 10)
4. The Weeds			
5. The Mustard Seed			
6. The Yeast			
7. The Hidden Treasure			
8. The Pearl of Great Price			
9. The Fishing Net			
10. The Unforgiving Servant			
11. The Workers in the Vineyard			
12. The Two Sons			
13. The Wicked Vinegrowers			
14. The Wedding Banquet			
15. The Two Servants			

Parable	Way It Was Introduced	Hearer(s)	Action Commanded or Response Expected
16. The Ten Virgins			
17. The Talents			
18. The Seed Growing Secretly			
19. The Doorkeeper			
20. The Rude Children			
21. The Two Debtors			
22. The Good Samaritan			
23. The Friend at Midnight			
24. The Rich Fool			
25. The Barren Fig Tree			
26. The Great Banquet			
27. The Unfinished Tower and the King's Rash War			
28. The Lost Sheep			
29. The Lost Coin			
30. The Prodigal Son			
31. The Shrewd Manager			
32. The Servant's Reward			

Parable	Way It Was Introduced	Hearer(s)	Action Commanded or Response Expected
33. The Unjust Judge			
34. The Pharisee and the Tax Collector			
35. The Pounds			

Analyzing Allegories

An allegory is a narrative or word picture which may or may not be true-to-life, with many parts pointing symbolically to spiritual realities. A parable usually has one major point of comparison, whereas an allegory has several points of comparison. A parable records an incident that is true-to-life, whereas an allegory may be either true to life or fictitious. As we have seen, not all parables include an explicitly stated interpretation, but if an interpretation is given it usually occurs after the story. In an allegory, however, the interpretations of the points of analogy are made throughout the story. Whereas a parable is an extended simile, an allegory is an extended metaphor. Like parables, allegories are designed to teach spiritual truths by comparison. The following summarizes these points:

Parable	Allegory
Has one major point of comparison	Has many points of comparison
True to life	May be true to life or fictitious
Interpretation, if given, usually occurs after the story (or sometimes at the beginning)	The interpretations of the points are intertwined in the story
Is an extended simile	Is an extended metaphor

Sometimes more than one element in a parable may be explained, as in Jesus' interpretation of the Parable of the Sower and the Parable of the Weeds. However, even though several parts are interpreted, each parable has one *major* point.[12] The point of the sower is that many people reject the message of the Gospel, and the point of the weeds is that some people falsely profess faith in Christ, but they will not be separated from true believers till the end of the age.

A fable, on the other hand, is a fictitious story in which animals or inanimate objects are personified to teach a moral lesson. Jotham told the Shechemites a fable about some trees that encouraged first an olive tree, then a fig tree, a vine, and a thornbush to be their king (Jud. 9:7-15). Jotham then applied the fable in verses 16-20, in which he rebuked the people for accepting Abimelech as their king, much as the trees accepted a mere thornbush as their king. Another biblical fable is King Jehoash's story about a thistle that sent a message to a cedar demanding that the cedar give its daughter in marriage to the thistle's son. But a wild beast trampled the thistle (2 Kings 14:9). By hinting that the thistle was Amaziah, king of Judah, Jehoash was indicating that Amaziah could easily be defeated, much as a wild beast could easily squash a thistle, even though Amaziah was arrogant (v. 10).

The following chart lists 14 passages that are generally considered allegories.

	Allegories in the Bible	
1.	Psalm 23:1-4	The Lord as the believer's Shepherd
2.	Psalm 80:8-16	Israel as a destroyed vine
3.	Proverbs 5:15-20	Marital fidelity as a cistern
4.	Proverbs 9:1-6	Wisdom as a housewife
5.	Isaiah 5:1-7	Israel as an unproductive vine
6.	Ezekiel 13:8-16	Israel's prophets as a collapsed wall
7.	Ezekiel 16	Jerusalemites as a baby who grew and then became a prostitute
8.	Ezekiel 17	Nebuchadnezzar and Egypt as two eagles, and Judah as a vine
9.	Ezekiel 23	Samaria and Jerusalem as two prostitutes
10.	John 10:1-16	Jesus as a Shepherd
11.	John 15:1-6	Jesus as a Vine
12.	1 Corinthians 3:10-15	Christian workers as builders
13.	Galatians 4:21-31	Hagar and Sarah as two covenants
14.	Ephesians 6:11-17	The Christian's spiritual defense as armor

Some Bible teachers view the Song of Songs as an extended allegory to depict God's relationship to Israel or Christ's relationship to the church. However, since there is no indication in the book that this is the case, it is preferable to view the book as extolling human love and marriage. Some see Ecclesiastes 12:3-7 as an allegory, though instead of explaining this passage as either the decline of an estate or the gloom of the household after the death of its head it seems better that Solomon used various figures to depict the declining physical and psychological abilities of old age.

In interpreting allegories three guidelines should be followed.

Note the Points of Comparison That Are Explained or Interpreted in the Passage

In John 10:1-16 the Shepherd is Jesus for He calls Himself the Good Shepherd (vv. 11, 14), and though He never says the sheep are believers it is clear that they are intended by the analogy because Jesus said the good shepherd "lays down His life for the sheep" and His sheep know Him. The thieves and robbers, who steal sheep, are not explicitly identified but they are referred to as "all who ever came before Me" (v. 8) and thus may be false religious leaders. Other elements in the allegory are not explained, including the watchman (v. 3), the stranger (v. 5), the hired hand and the wolf (v. 12), the sheep pen and the flock (v. 16).

In 15:1 the Vine is obviously Jesus for He said, "I am the true Vine" and He identified God the Father as the Gardener. The branches are believers ("you are the branches," v. 5).

Look up the passages following and answer the questions to help you identify the elements in the allegories that are interpreted.

Psalm 80:8-16

Who is the vine brought "out of Egypt"? _____

Proverbs 5:15-20

What is pictured by the cistern or well mentioned in verse 15? (See v. 18.) _____

In the context of marital fidelity what is meant by springs that "overflow in the streets" mentioned in verse 16? (See v. 17.)

_____

Proverbs 9:1-6

What is the meaning of the woman inviting the simple to "eat her food," mentioned in verse 5? (See v. 6.) _____

_____

Isaiah 5:1-7

What does the vineyard in verse 1 represent? (See v. 7.) __

_____

What is the good fruit mentioned in verses 2 and 4? (See v. 7.) _____

Ezekiel 13:8-16

What do the wind, hail, and rain depict? (See v. 15.) ____

_____

Who are those who whitewashed the wall, as mentioned in verse 14? (See vv. 15-16.) _____

Ezekiel 16

Who is the abandoned baby who was found and cared for by the Lord? (See v. 2.) _____

What is the meaning of her beauty, mentioned in verse 13? (See v. 14.) _____

On whom were the Jerusalemites depending as a prostitute depends on her lovers? (See vv. 26, 28-29.) _____

Ezekiel 17

Who is identified as the first eagle in verses 3-4? (See v. 12.)

_____

What is possibly suggested by the top shoot of the vine taken to a land of merchants, as stated in verses 3-4? (See vv. 12-13.)

_____

_____

Who is the second eagle referred to in verses 7-8? (See vv. 15, 17.) _____

_____

Ezekiel 23

What are the identities of the two prostitutes Oholah and Oholibah? (See v. 4.) _____

What is the explanation of the Babylonians defiling the two women? (See vv. 23-24.) _____

_____

John 10:1-16

Who is the Shepherd? (See vv. 11, 14.) _____
Who are the sheep? (See v. 14.) _____

John 15:1-6

Who is the Vine? _____
Who is the Gardener? _____
Who are the branches? _____

1 Corinthians 3:10-15

   Who is the Master-builder? _____

   Who is the Foundation? _____

   Who are the builders? _____

   What are the materials? _____

   Who do Hagar and her son Ishmael represent? _____

Galatians 4:21-31

   Who do Sarah and her son Isaac represent? (See vv. 26-28, 31.) _____

Ephesians 6:11-17

   What is the belt? _____

   What is the breastplate? _____

   With what are the Christian's feet to be shod? _____

   What is the shield? _____

   What is the helmet? _____

   What is the sword? _____

As is evident in these passages each allegory has a number of points of comparison, though not every element (person, object, or action) is interpreted. This leads to the second principle.

Do Not Attempt to Interpret Details in Allegories That Are Not Explained

Some suggest that the hired hand in John 10:12 refers to religious leaders in Jesus' day, but since the hired hand is not interpreted in the passage, we cannot be sure. This may simply be a detail that completes the picture of the allegory. In the Parable of the Vine in Psalm 80:8-16 the "boars from the forest" that are said to have ravaged the vine are not identified, though other passages of Scripture would suggest this may be a subtle reference to the Assyrians and the Babylonians who attacked Israel and Judah.

   In the allegory of the house built by wisdom (Prov. 9:1-6), we need not ask what the meat, wine, table, or maids resemble. They simply add local color to complete the idea of a sumptuous meal being prepared, which, of course, is likened to wisdom in verse 6.

   Nor should each point in the allegory in the vineyard in Isaiah 5:1-7 be compared to some spiritual truth. The fertile hillside, stones, watchtower, winepress (vv. 1-2) and the hedge and the wall (v. 5) are not explained in the text and therefore we ought not search for parallels. The same is true of the water, blood, ointments, clothing, jewelry, and food mentioned in the allegory in Ezekiel 16:9-13. These details simply adorn the narrative to give the reader an impression of the extensive care of the Lord for the nation Israel which had a lowly beginning.

Determine the Main Point of the Teaching

As in parables, so in allegories the interpreter should look for the major point of analogy or resemblance. Though there are many points of *comparison,* the reader should ask, what is the major *truth* being taught by this allegory? The truth being taught in Psalm 80:8-16 is indicated at the end of that passage in which the psalmist prayed that God would watch over the vine (vv. 14-15). The point of Proverbs 9:1-6 is that people would heed the "invitation" of wisdom and, by partaking in her banquet, become wise. The main point of the lengthy allegory in Ezekiel 16 is indicated in the closing verses: God will punish the Jerusalemites for their sin (v. 59), but He will also restore them (vv. 62-63).

The point of the allegory in John 15:1-6 is clearly stated, namely, that the branches (believers) are to abide with Christ in order to bear fruit (v. 4).

The interpretation of allegories should not be confused with "allegorizing" or the allegorical method of interpretation. Allegorizing is an approach that searches for deeper meanings than are apparent in the text, ideas that differ from those clearly indicated in the Bible passages. An example of allegorizing is Augustine's attempt to draw analogies from almost every element in the Parable of the Good Samaritan (see p. 216). This is allegorizing since the biblical text gives no basis for those farfetched explanations. Allegorizing is discussed in more detail in chapter 2 on the history of interpretation. Also discussed there is the question of whether Paul used allegorizing in Galatians 4:21-31.

CHAPTER TEN

Interpreting Prophecy

Most people are instinctively curious about the future. We have a forward bent. Tomorrow somehow holds more intrigue and fascination than yesterday.

People use many ways to seek what lies ahead, to decipher the future. They hire someone to "read" the lines in the palms of their hands. They confer with crystal ball interpreters, and they "read" tea leaves, interpret tarot cards, consult Ouija boards, attend witches' covens. Millions faithfully follow the advice of astrologers whose counsel is based on the positions of the stars and planets.

On a less esoteric note many businessmen watch Wall Street trends to determine the direction of their financial investments. Others consult friends and counselors for guidance on decisions that will affect their future. In ancient times people even consulted the lines in the livers of sacrificed animals or "divined" the future based on the flights of birds. The Pharaohs of Egypt and Nebuchadnezzar of Babylon had their astrologers and prognosticators. Obviously the unknown future brings anxiety to many individuals. They scramble for some sense of assurance regarding what lies ahead.

The only voice of certainty about the future is God Himself. He planned the future and therefore He knows it. Prophecy is unique in that only God can declare the future. As Isaiah wrote, "Who foretold this long ago, who declared it from the distant past? Was it not I, the Lord? And there is no God apart from Me" (Isa. 45:21). The word *prophecy* comes from two Greek words meaning "to speak for or before." Thus prophecy is the speaking and writing of events before they occurred. They could not have been foreseen by human ingenuity. For this reason it is erroneous for some scholars to say that Bible writers wrote of events after they occurred, but recorded them *as if* they were prophecies of events yet to come.

The prophecies of the Bible came from God Himself. "No prophecy of Scripture came about by the prophet's own interpretation" (2 Peter 1:20). The Greek word translated "interpretation" in this verse is *epilyseōs*, which literally is "unloosing." The thought is that no prophecy of Scripture has come about by a prophet's own origin. That is, the prophetic Scriptures did not stem from the prophets themselves. As a divine book, the Bible contains predictions of the future, which only God could provide. Many of the Bible's predictions of the future have been fulfilled, especially in the life of Christ. And yet numerous prophecies, some of them in startling detail, await fulfillment in connection with and following His return.

The range of prophetic subject matter in the Bible is wide. The Scriptures include predictions about Gentile nations, the nation Israel, individuals, the Messiah, Planet Earth, the Tribulation, the Millennium, life after death, and the eternal state. Some predictions pertain to events that were soon fulfilled, whereas others pertain to events that were or will be fulfilled dozens or even hundreds of years after the predictions. The former are sometimes called "near" prophecies and the others are referred to as "far" prophecies. Examples of "near" prophecies are these: Samuel prophesied the death of Saul (1 Sam. 28:16-19), Jeremiah prophesied the 70-year Captivity in Babylon (Jer. 25:11), Daniel predicted that Belshazzar's kingdom would be taken over by the Medes and Persians (Dan. 5:25-30), Jesus predicted that Peter would deny Him (Matt. 26:34) and that Judas would betray Him (vv. 23-25), Agabus prophesied that Paul would be arrested (Acts 21:10-11).

Perhaps in no other area of Bible interpretation do evangelicals differ so widely as in eschatology, the study of future events (from the Greek word *eschatos*, "last").

Why Study Prophecy?

Though differences of opinion have prevailed for many years on how to interpret the Bible's prophetic statements, the Bible does give a number of reasons for studying its prophetic literature.

Prophecy Comforts

After assuring the Thessalonian believers that their believing loved ones who had already died would precede the Rapture of the living saints, Paul wrote, "Therefore encourage [*parakaleō*] each other with these words" (1 Thes. 4:18). This news provided comfort and encouragement (the Greek word *parakaleō* has both shades of meaning).

In the Upper Room Discourse, Jesus introduced His comments about returning to heaven with the words, "Do not let your hearts be troubled" (John 14:1). No doubt the disciples were calmed when hearing Jesus say He would return to "take you to be with Me that you may also be where I am" (v. 3; cf. 17:24).

Prophecy Calms

Our age is characterized by immorality, violence, insecurity, hatred, and increased disregard for spiritual things. And terrible days are yet to come (2 Tim. 3:1-5). Even so, Christians rest in the fact that God knows and controls the future. For this reason the second coming of Christ is called a "blessed hope" (Titus 2:13), an event that will bring blessing to His own.

Prophecy Converts

In the Book of Acts several sermons given by the apostles include God's plans for the future, and as a result a number of people became believers in Christ. Much of Peter's message in 3:12-26 spells out how Jesus fulfilled a number of Old Testament prophecies. "Many who heard the message believed" (4:4). In Athens Paul concluded his message on Mars Hill (Areopagus) by affirming that God "has set a day when He will judge the world with justice by the Man He has appointed" (17:31). As a result of Paul's message a few people believed in Christ (v. 34).

When Paul was under house arrest (28:30), he preached the kingdom of God and taught about the Lord Jesus Christ (v. 31). And in this century many people have come to Christ as a result of hearing sermons on prophetic events.

Prophecy Cleanses

Knowing that the Lord may come at any moment influences believers to lead lives pleasing to the Lord. Immediately after referring to the "blessed hope" Paul referred to the Lord's desire "to purify for Himself a people that are His very own, eager to do what is good" (Titus 2:14). As believers look forward to the new heaven and the new earth, they should "make every effort to be found spotless, blameless and at peace with Him" (2 Peter 3:14). John affirmed that when Christ "appears, we shall be like Him," and then he added, "Everyone who has this hope in Him purifies himself, just as He is pure" (1 John 3:2-3).

Prophecy Compels

In view of the brevity of life and the soon return of the Lord, which Paul said would occur "in a flash, in the twinkling of an eye" (1 Cor. 15:52), believers should "stand firm," letting nothing move them and always giving themselves "fully to the work of the Lord" (v. 58). Since each believer must "appear before the Judgment Seat of Christ" (2 Cor. 5:10), we should "try to persuade men" to come to Christ for salvation (v. 11). "Christ's love compels us" or motivates us to action (v. 14).

Prophecy Clarifies

Bible prophecy presents many details about what God will do in the future. These facts, given in many parts of the Bible, present a harmonized pattern of God's future program for the church, the world, unbelievers, nations, and Satan.

What Are the Differences between the Millennial Views?

Interpreting Bible prophecy involves the serious Bible student in many prophetic details. However, two issues are basic to the study of eschatology. They are the millennial issue (does the Bible teach a future millennial reign of Christ on the earth?), and the dispensational issue (does the Bible teach different dispensations?).

What Is Premillennialism?

The word *millennium* comes from the Latin words *mille* ("thousand") and *annus* ("year"). The prefix "pre" before the word "millennialism" means "before." So the term "premillennialism" means that the Millennium or a 1,000-year period will be preceded by Christ's return to the earth. Sometimes premillenarians are referred to as chiliasts, from the Greek word *chilioi*, which means "one thousand."

The basic tenets of premillennialism are these:

1. Christ will return in the Rapture at the end of this age and will reign with His saints on the earth for 1,000 years as King. (Premillenarians differ in their views on the relationship of the Rapture to the Tribulation. See the footnote on p. 236.)

2. In the Millennium the nation Israel will experience the

blessings of God promised to Abraham and David pertaining to Israel's land, nationality ("seed"), and king ("throne").

3. Therefore the church today is not fulfilling these promises made to Israel as a nation.

What Is Amillennialism?

The prefix "a" means "no" or "none," and thus amillennialism is the view that there will be no literal reign of Christ on earth for 1,000 years.

The basic teachings in amillennialism are these:

1. The kingdom is in existence now between Christ's two advents. Since Christ is ruling now from heaven, He will not reign on the earth for 1,000 years. "We are in the Millennium now."[1]

2. The kingdom is either the church on earth (Augustine's view now perpetuated by the Roman Catholic Church) or the saints in heaven (the view of Benjamin Warfield). Thus there will be no future reign of Christ on the earth, and 1,000 is a symbolic number indicating a long period of time.

3. The promises to Israel about a land, nationality, and throne are being fulfilled now in a spiritual way among believers in the church.

4. God's promises to Israel were conditional and have been transferred to the church because the nation did not meet the condition of obedience to God.

5. Christ is ruling now in heaven where He is seated on the throne of David, and Satan is now bound between Christ's two advents.

What Is Postmillennialism?

Since the prefix "post" means "after," postmillennialism means that Christ's coming will occur after the Millennium. This view includes the following points.

1. The church is not the kingdom but it will bring the kingdom (a utopian, Christianized condition) to the earth by preaching the Gospel. Or, as a number of liberal theologians believe, the Millennium will come about through human effort and natural processes.

2. Christ will not be on the earth during the kingdom. He will rule in the hearts of people, and He will return to the earth after the Millennium.

3. The Millennium will not last for a literal 1,000 years.

4. The church, not Israel, will receive the fulfillment of the promises to Abraham and David in a spiritual sense.

The view one should hold on the millennial question is not settled by appeals to historical references. But it is noteworthy that a good number of leaders in the first several centuries of the early church were clearly premillennial (see the following chart "Premillennialism in the Early Church").

Amillennialism has its beginnings with Clement of Alexandria (A.D. 155–216) and Origen (ca. 185–254). For more details on their views see chapter 2 on the history of interpretation. Origen "spiritualized" much of Scripture and taught that the present age between the two advents of Christ is the Millennium. The Emperor Constantine (272–337) helped pave the way for the development of amillennialism by uniting the church and the state. This led the theologian Augustine (354–430) to teach that the church is the kingdom on earth. Though he spiritualized much of biblical prophecy, he taught that Christ would return around A.D. 1000. In the Middle Ages the papacy taught that the Roman Catholic Church is the kingdom of God on earth. It is easy to see why the church then denied a future reign of Christ on the earth.

A number of the Reformers were amillennial. These included John Wycliffe, Martin Luther, Philip Melancthon, John Calvin, and Ulrich Zwingli. However, William Tyndale and many of the Anabaptists were premillennial. The Moravians and the Huguenots were generally premillennial.

Postmillennialism was first taught by Daniel Whitby (1638–1725) and was held by Jonathan Edwards, Charles Wesley, Charles Hodge, A.A. Hodge, Augustus H. Strong, James Snowden, and Lorraine Boettner.

Postmillennialism virtually died out a number of years ago. The impact of two world wars led many to renounce postmillennialism because of its optimistic view that the world is getting better. But in recent years postmillennialism has been revived.

Present-day "dominion theology" is postmillennial. Dominion theologians maintain that Christians should "take over" (have dominion or leadership) in every aspect of society, including government. In this sense they teach that the church should Christianize society and thus "bring in the kingdom." Proponents of this view include Greg L. Bahnsen, David Chilton, Kenneth L. Gentry, Jr., James B. Jordan, Gary North, Rousas J. Rushdoony, and Douglas Wilson.

Premillennialism in the Early Church

1. *Clement of Rome* (ca. 30–95)

   "Of a truth, soon and suddenly shall His will be accomplished, as the Scriptures also bear witness, saying, 'Speedily will He come, and will not tarry,' and the Lord shall suddenly come to His temple, even the Holy one, for whom ye look" *(First Letter to the Corinthians,* chap. 23).

   "Let us then wait for the kingdom of God from hour to hour in love and righteousness, seeing that we know not the day of the appearing of God" *(Second Letter to the Corinthians,* chap. 12).

2. *The Didache* (ca. 105)

   "And then shall appear the signs of the truth; first, the sign of an outspreading in heaven; then the sign of the sound of the trumpet; and the third, the resurrection of the dead; yet not of all" (16:6-7).

3. *The Shepherd of Hermas* (ca. 140–150)

   "You have escaped from great tribulation on account of your faith, and because you did not doubt the presence of such a beast. Go, therefore, and tell the elect of the Lord His mighty deeds, and say to them that this beast is a type of the great tribulation that is coming" *(Visions,* 1. 4. 2).

4. *Barnabas*

   Barnabas believed that after 6,000 years of history, Christ would return to destroy the Antichrist and set up His kingdom on the earth for the seventh "day" of a thousand years *(Epistle of Barnabas,* chap. 15).

5. *Polycarp* (70–155)

   "If we please Him in this present age, we shall receive also the age to come, according as He promised to us that He will raise us from the dead, and that if we live worthily of Him, 'we shall also reign with Him.' "

6. *Ignatius* (ca. 35–107)

   He refers in his writings to the last times and emphasized the attitude of expectancy for Christ's return.

Premillennialism in the Early Church (Continued)

7. *Papias* (80–163)

   He wrote that after the resurrection of the dead will come the Millennium "when the personal reign of Christ will be established on the earth" (fragment VI, quoted by Irenaeus and Eusebius).

8. *Justin Martyr* (ca. 100–164)

   "But I and whoever are on all points right-minded Christians know that there will be resurrection of the dead and a thousand years in Jerusalem, which will then be built, adorned, and enlarged as the prophets Ezekiel and Isaiah and the others declare. . . . And John, one of the Apostles . . . predicted by a revelation that was made to him that those who believed in our Christ would spend a thousand years in Jerusalem, and thereafter the general . . . the eternal resurrection and judgment of all men would likewise take place" (*Dialogue with Trypho,* chaps. 80–81).

9. *Irenaeus* (ca. 130–202)

   "But when this Antichrist shall have devastated all things in this world, he will reign for three years and six months, and sit in the temple at Jerusalem; and then the Lord will come from heaven in the clouds, in the glory of the Father, sending this man and those who followed him into the lake of fire; but bringing in for the righteous the times of the kingdom, that is, the rest, the hallowed seventh day; and restoring to Abraham the promised inheritance, in which kingdom the Lord declared, that many coming from the east and from the west would sit down with Abraham, Isaac, and Jacob. . . . The predicted blessing, therefore, belongs unquestionably to the times of the kingdom, when the righteous shall bear rule upon their rising from the dead" (*Against Heresies,* 5, 30-33).

10. *Tertullian* (ca. 160–220)

    Tertullian referred to Christ in His second advent as the stone of Daniel 2, who would smash the Gentile kingdoms and establish His everlasting reign (*The Resurrection of the Flesh,* chap. 22).

Premillennialism in the Early Church (Continued)

"We do confess that a kingdom is promised to us upon the earth . . . it will be after the resurrection for a thousand years in the divinely built city of Jerusalem" *(Against Marcion,* 3. 25).

11. *Hippolytus* (d. 236)
He expounded Daniel 2, 7, and 8 as teaching a literal reign of Christ on the earth *(A Treatise on Christ and Antichrist).*

12. *Cyprian* (195–258)
"Why with frequently repeated prayers do we entreat and beg that the day of His kingdom may hasten, if our greater desires and stronger wishes are to obey the devil here, rather than to reign with Christ?" *(On Morality,* chap. 18)

13. *Commodianus* (third century)
"They shall come also who overcame cruel martyrdom under Antichrist, and they themselves live for the whole time. But from the thousand years God will destroy all those evils" *(Instructions for the Christian Life,* chap. 44).

14. *Nepos* (third century)
He wrote *A Compilation of the Allegorists* in defense of premillennialism after Origen had attacked it and sought to explain it figuratively.

15. *Lactantius* (240–330)
"About the same time also the prince of the devils, who is the contriver of all evils, shall be bound with chains, and shall be imprisoned during the thousand years of the heavenly rule in which righteousness shall reign in the world, so that he may contrive no evil against the people of God" *(Epitome of the Divine Institutes,* 7, 24).

The three millennial systems may be illustrated as follows:

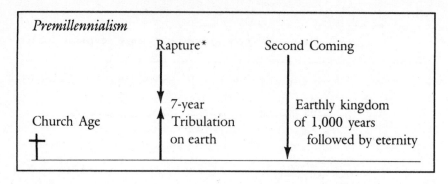

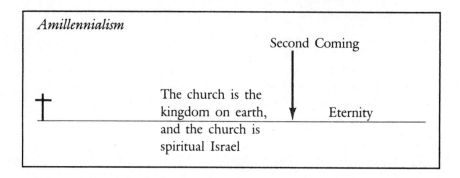

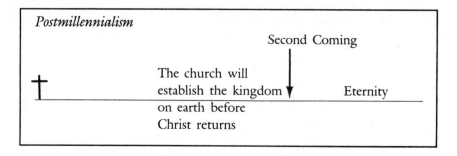

Hermeneutical Bases of Amillennialism

1. *The kingdom in the church.* The interpretive system of amillennialism begins with the assumption that God's kingdom is being manifested today in the church, as first advocated by Augustine.

*This chart presents the premillennial pretribulational view. Other premillenarians hold a posttribulational view, in which they say the Rapture will occur after the Tribulation in conjunction with the Second Coming. Others hold to a mid-tribulational Rapture, the view that the Rapture will occur in the middle of the seven-year Tribulation period.

2. *The unity of the people of God.* Since God has always ruled in His kingdom and since His kingdom is now evident in the church, amillennialists conclude that God has a single overall program in all ages. That program is to provide salvation for the people of God whether they were in the days of Moses or earlier or are in the present age. This program is worked out in three covenants: the covenant of works, an agreement between God and Adam in which God promised him life if he obeyed and death if he disobeyed; the covenant of redemption, an agreement among the Persons of the Trinity in which They decided to provide redemption; and the covenant of grace, an agreement between God and the elect sinner in which God provides grace for salvation.

3. *Israel and the church.* Since there is one "program," namely, salvation, for a single "people of God" throughout all ages, Israel and the church do not have distinct "programs" in God's economy. They share in one continuous program. Thus the promises to Israel are applicable to the church. As Allis wrote, "The millennium is to be interpreted spiritually as fulfilled in the Christian Church."[2]

4. *"Spiritualizing" of prophecy.* How can promises to Israel (about a land, a nation, and a king—Gen. 12:2; 15:18-20; 2 Sam. 7:12-16) and promises about God's kingdom be relevant to the church? Amillenarians "spiritualize" these prophecies. By this they mean seeing a so-called "spiritual sense" in those passages. They state that the promise in Isaiah 11:6-9 that ferocious animals will be tame refers to a spiritual transformation as in Saul of Tarsus, who was changed from a vicious wolflike persecutor to a lamblike follower of Christ.[3] However, seeing a "spiritual," church-related sense in prophetic passages is viewing those passages in a way that is other than the normal sense. "Spiritualizing" becomes almost synonymous with allegorizing. Amillennialists argue, though, that the New Testament takes Old Testament passages nonliterally, but prophecy can be spiritualized because it contains much figurative and symbolic language, and that the great teachings of the Bible are spiritual, not earthly.[4] The first of these arguments, how the New Testament takes Old Testament passages, is discussed in the following chapter. The other points will be discussed later in this chapter.

Hermeneutical Bases of Premillennialism

1. *Normal, grammatical interpretation of Scripture.* According to premillenarians the normal approach to Scripture means that the promises about Christ returning to establish His millennial reign on earth

of 1,000 years are to be taken literally. His kingdom is now in existence in heaven (Acts 28:31; Rom. 14:17; 1 Cor. 4:20; Col. 1:13) but will be present on the earth during the Millennium following the return of Christ to the earth. Believers are part of God's present kingdom or rule (John 3:3, 5).

2. *Israel in the land with the King.* Since the promises to Israel—about being a nation and being regathered to and having possession of the land with their Messiah-King ruling over them—are unconditional and have not yet been fulfilled, they therefore yet remain to be fulfilled. This is seen in the nature of the three biblical covenants—the Abrahamic, Davidic, and New.

Ryrie spells out the significance of this hermeneutical point:

(1) Does the Abrahamic Covenant promise Israel a permanent existence as a nation? If it does, then the church is not fulfilling Israel's promises, but rather Israel as a nation has a future yet in prospect; and (2) Does the Abrahamic Covenant promise Israel permanent possession of the promised land? If it does, then Israel must yet come into possession of that land for she has never fully possessed it in her history.[5]

3. *Israel and the church.* Since Israel is yet to possess the land under her Messiah-King, the promises to the nation have not been transferred to the church. Since the church began on the Day of Pentecost, the church is separate from the nation Israel and therefore is not inheriting Israel's promises. Grammatical interpretation thus makes a warranted distinction between Israel and the church. The church does not now possess the land of Palestine, promised to Israel. And in the New Testament Age, since the church began, there is still a distinction between unsaved Jews, unsaved Gentiles, and the church (1 Cor. 10:32).

4. *Consistency in interpretation.* Premillennialism maintains that its hermeneutic is consistent, for it does not approach nonprophetic Scripture in the normal sense and approach prophetic passages in a spiritualized, nonliteral sense.

What Are the Basic Differences between Covenant Theology and Dispensational Theology?

Covenant theology is a theological system that centers on the so-called covenant of grace, an arrangement between God and the elect sinner in which God provides grace for salvation. Most covenant theologians are also amillenarian, though some covenant theologians are premillennial. The three major tenets of covenant theology are these: (1) The "church" consists of God's redeemed people of all ages, not just those in the present age between the Day of Pentecost and the Rapture. (2) The Abrahamic, Davidic, and New Covenants are fulfilled in the present age. (Premillenarian theologians hold that though there may be fulfillment in the present age of some aspects of these three covenants, there will also be a future fulfillment. Amillenarians, as covenant theologians, deny any future fulfillment of these covenants.) (3) The purpose of God's program is soteriological, that is, for the purpose of bringing people to salvation.

Dispensational theology includes essentially two concepts: (1) the church is distinct from Israel, and (2) the purpose of God's program is doxological, that is, to bring glory to Himself (Eph. 1:6, 12, 14). As for the first of these, the church is seen as distinct from the nation Israel because the church has a distinct character. Paul wrote of a dispensation in which God is making believing Jews and Gentiles equal members of the body of Christ. This was unknown in Old Testament times (3:5-6). In the Old Testament, since the days of Moses, God was dealing mainly with the nation Israel, but today the church consists of believing Jews and Gentiles in one body of Christ, the church. First Corinthians 12:13 speaks of believers being baptized into the body of Christ, and 10:32 speaks of the nation Israel as distinct from the church. A future dispensation or administration is the coming millennial kingdom (Eph. 1:10). Romans 10:1 also speaks of national Israel as a distinct entity.

The church is seen as distinct from Israel not only because of its distinct character, but also because of its distinct time. The Church Age began after Christ's resurrection (Eph. 1:20-22) and ascension (4:7-12). Since all believers in this age are baptized into the body of Christ (1 Cor. 12:13), the beginning of the Church Age is to be identified with the event when the Holy Spirit began that baptizing ministry. Gentile believers at Cornelius' house "received the Holy Spirit just as we have," Peter said (Acts 10:47), and "the Holy Spirit came on them as He had come on us at the beginning" (11:15). Peter's reference to the Jews' already having received the Holy Spirit and his reference to the Holy Spirit coming on them "as He had come on us at the beginning" points back to the event on the Day of Pentecost, recorded in Acts 2. This is clearly the event indicated because just before that, as the Lord was ascending to heaven,

He said they would receive the Holy Spirit (1:8).*50 days after Passover*

The church, begun on the Day of Pentecost, is a unique program, which distinguishes the present age from the arrangement introduced by the giving of the Law to the nation Israel. Special promises were given to the nation Israel, and separate promises have been given to the church, the body of Christ. Of course in each dispensation, individuals are saved by faith, apart from works.

In addition, before the Mosaic Law God was dealing with the world in a way that differed from His dealings after the giving of the Law. And a different arrangement was in existence before the fall of man in Genesis 3. Thus at least five dispensations are distinguished in the Scriptures.

Dispensationalists begin with a consistent approach to hermeneutics, in which they see normal, grammatical interpretation as the essential foundation to their system of hermeneutics. This base then leads to the dispensational distinction between Israel and the church. As Radmacher wrote, "Literal interpretation . . . is the 'bottom-line' of dispensationalism. . . . Undoubtedly, the most significant of these [tenets] is the maintaining of the distinction between Israel and the church."[6] Ryrie also speaks to this point: "If plain or normal interpretation is the only valid hermeneutical principle and if it is consistently applied, it will cause one to be a dispensationalist. As basic as one believes normal interpretation to be, to that extent he will of necessity become a dispensationalist."[7] Accepting the terms *Israel* and the *church* in their normal, literal sense results in keeping them distinct entities. *Israel* always means ethnic Israel and is never switched with the term *church,* nor is the term *church* ever used in Scripture interchangeably with or as a synonym of *Israel.*

As stated earlier, a second concept of dispensational theology is God's doxological program. While covenant theologians do not deny that God's program is to bring glory to Himself (through the present covenant of grace), they seem to give more emphasis to the Lord's soteriological purpose. For example Hoekema wrote that the purpose of the kingdom of God "is to redeem God's people from sin."[8] Dispensationalists also emphasize that God's plan of salvation through faith unifies all the dispensations, while at the same time elevating the glory of God as the *primary* principle that unifies all the dispensations. In other words God's program in each dispensation or divine stewardship is designed to bring glory to Himself. While both covenant theologians and dispensationalists stress the glory of God (doxology) and salvation (soteriology), dispensationlists teach that the overriding purpose of God in each dispensation is to glorify Himself. One major *way* He does this is through salvation by faith (in every age), but the ultimate *goal* is His glory.

What Guidelines Should Be Followed in Interpreting Prophecy?

As suggested in chapter 3, two axioms form the basis for a number of interpretive corollaries. Those same two axioms—the Bible is a book, and the Bible is a divine book—give a framework for principles to follow in interpreting prophecy. The first three principles build on the axiom that the Bible is a book, and the next five principles build on the axiom that the Bible is a divine book.

Follow the Normal Principles of the Hermeneutical System Known as Historical, Grammatical, Literary Interpretation

Considering the historical element in prophetic interpretation means that the cultural background and circumstances of the prophets are considered. The prophets spoke on behalf of another, namely, God. They were responsible to communicate the messages they received from God. The prophets often spoke of circumstances contemporary with their generation, sometimes pointing up what God was doing in the immediate future and other times projecting events to be fulfilled in the distant future. God's words, in other words, were not isolated from the stream of history. Even the words of Paul regarding the Rapture of the church (1 Thes. 4:13-18) were addressed to a problem the Thessalonian believers faced. The Apostle John wrote the Book of Revelation to believers when they were undergoing persecution in the reign of the Roman Emperor Domitian (A.D. 51–96). Reading that God's program would include the establishing of Christ's reign on earth with the accompanying destruction of His enemies, would have given the first-century Christians great comfort, just as it has done for every generation of believers since that time.

Moses, Samuel, Isaiah, Jeremiah, Ezekiel, Daniel, and each of the 12 prophets from Hosea through Malachi, as well as New Testament prophets, spoke God's prophetic word in their cultural settings.

Take Words of Prophecy in Their Normal, Grammatical Sense

Nowhere does Scripture indicate that when we come to prophetic portions of Scripture we should ignore the normal sense of the words and overlook the meanings of words and sentences. The norms of grammatical interpretation should be applied to prophetic as well as to nonprophetic literature.

Fulfillment should be seen in accord with the words of the prediction. In speaking of the Millennium, Isaiah wrote that many people will live well beyond 100 years of age (Isa. 65:20). There is no reason to take this in any sense other than its normal, grammatical meaning. The following verse (v. 21) states, "They will build houses and dwell in them; they will plant vineyards and eat their fruit." Again no hint is given in this passage that the building of houses is to be taken figuratively.

Of course figurative language and symbolic language is used extensively in prophetic passages, but this does not mean that *all* prophecy is figurative or symbolic. We should begin with the assumption that the words are to be taken in their normal sense unless a figure of speech or symbol is indicated. (See chap. 7 for more discussion on this subject.) Deeper and mystical senses should not be sought.

While it is true that some prophecies are conditioned on the response of the persons addressed, other prophecies are unconditional. When God made His covenant with Abraham in Genesis 15, He alone contracted the obligation, passing between the pieces of the animals He had cut in two (vv. 12-20). No condition was attached to the Lord's words that He would give Abraham's descendants that land. Reaffirmations of this Abrahamic Covenant indicate that it was "an everlasting covenant" in which "the whole land of Canaan" would be theirs "as an everlasting possession" (17:7-8). Also note the references to the everlasting nature of the covenant in verses 13, 19; 26:2-4; 28:13-15; 1 Chronicles 16:16-17; Psalm 105:9-10.

Therefore since Israel has not yet possessed the land to the boundaries specified in Genesis 15:18-21, we should take the promise of the Abrahamic Covenant pertaining to Israel's land as being unconditional and yet future.

Consider the Literary Element, Which Recognizes
the Place of Figurative and Symbolic Language

As discussed in chapter 7, language includes the use of figures of speech. The first prophecy in the Bible, Genesis 3:15, includes figurative language. The prediction, "You will strike His heel," indicates that Satan would cripple the offspring of Eve, which would include humanity at large and then Christ in His crucifixion. Then Christ as *the* Seed would "crush your [Satan's] head," that is, defeat him. This latter statement may be a synecdoche, in which the part, Satan's "head," represents him completely. Christ will accomplish this at His second coming.

John's description of the glorified Christ, recorded in Revelation 1:13-16, uses several similes, each introduced by the word *like*. Numerous other figures of speech occur in Revelation, including metaphors, metonymies, personifications, hyperboles, and rhetorical questions. An example of a hyperbole is in 18:5, "For her sins are piled up to heaven." Revelation 13:4 includes the rhetorical question, "Who is like the beast?" Another rhetorical question is seen in 18:18: "Was there ever a city like this great city?"

A large portion of the prophetic literature of the Bible records what the prophets saw in visions. These portions are often referred to as "apocalyptic." Portions of Ezekiel, Daniel, Zechariah, and much of Revelation are apocalyptic. (*Apocalyptic* comes from the Greek word *apokalypsis* translated "revelation" in Revelation 1:1. An apocalypse then is a disclosure from God.) Most apocalyptic literature was written by prophets when they were out of the land of Israel. Ezekiel and Daniel were in Babylon, and the Apostle John was on the Island of Patmos. Though Zechariah was in Jerusalem, having returned from Babylon, he was still writing in a time when Israel was under Gentile domination. He gave the prophecies in his first six chapters in the second year of Darius, which was 520 B.C. He gave his later prophecies (Zech. 7–14) in the fourth year of King Darius, 518 B.C. The apocalyptic writings would have challenged and encouraged God's oppressed people.[9]

Besides being given in times of exile or Gentile oppression, apocalyptic literature has four other characteristics: (1) It consists of prophecies given in elaborate visions, (2) it includes many symbols, (3) an angel was often seen in the visions and frequently gave interpretations, and (4) it includes messages regarding the distant future.

The heavy symbolic content of much of prophetic literature makes interpreting prophecy difficult. It also has caused many Bible students to assume that because some things in prophecy are symbolic, everything in prophetic passages is to be taken symbolically. This, however, is an error. If we follow the basic hermeneutical principle of normal, grammatical interpretation, then we should understand prophetic literature, as well as other forms of biblical literature, in their normal, ordinary-literal sense, unless there is reason for taking the material figuratively or symbolically.

For example no reason exists for not taking literally the reference to silence in heaven "for about half an hour" (Rev. 8:1), nor is there any reason for not taking literally the references to "hail and fire mixed with blood" (v. 7). And when John wrote in that same verse that "a third of the earth was burned up, a third of the trees were burned up, and all the green grass was burned up," again there is nothing in the immediate context to indicate that those words should not be taken in their ordinary sense. However, in verse 8 of that same chapter we read that "something like a huge mountain, all ablaze, was thrown into the sea." The wording suggests that John was not referring to a literal mountain.

Figurative language is present if the statement taken in its normal sense would be impossible or illogical (see the discussion in chap. 7). Therefore the star referred to in verse 10 which "fell from the sky on a third of the rivers," probably was not a literal star, since it is known that all stars are larger than the earth. Some have suggested that this "star" will be a meteor. Again verse 12 speaks of a literal angel sounding a literal trumpet and there seems to be no reason for not understanding that a third of the sun was literally struck, as well as a third of the moon, and a third of the stars. And yet the very next verse (v. 13) speaks of an eagle that called out in a loud voice. Since eagles do not speak, obviously this is to be understood symbolically. A prostitute obviously cannot sit on seven hills at once (17:9) and so we conclude that the hills are symbols. In fact in that same verse the interpretation is given: the seven hills are (represent) seven kings. This suggests that she will dominate seven kings. According to verse 14, 10 kings "will make war against the Lamb." From other Scripture we note that the Lamb refers to Jesus Christ (John 1:29; Rev. 5:6-13) and thus is a figure of speech, and yet war (17:14) is to be understood literally.

What about numbers in prophetic literature? One writer suggests, "in a book where almost all the numbers seem to have symbolic value (7 seals, trumpets, bowls, etc.; 144,000 Israelites; 42 months/1,260 days/3 1/2 years) should not 1,000 years indicate a long period of time rather than a number of calendar years?"[10] But are all the numbers he mentions to be taken as symbols? Do they not have meaning as ordinary, literal numbers? If 7, 42, 1,260 are not to be taken literally, then what about the reference to the 2 witnesses in 11:3? And if 1,000 means simply a large number, then what about the reference to 7,000 people in verse 13? On what basis do we say that 7,000 does not mean a literal 7,000? And if 1,000 is a large indefinite number, do the references to 4 angels (7:1) and 7 angels

(8:6) mean simply small numbers? If these numbers in the Book of Revelation have no normal, literal numerical value, then what has happened to the principle of normal, grammatical interpretation? How can we say that 144,000 is a symbolic number, when 7:5-8 refers specifically to 12,000 from each of 12 tribes in Israel?

Neopostmillennialists also tend to take numbers in Revelation symbolically. For instance Chilton writes that 1,000 years in 20:4-6 means "a large, rounded number . . . standing 'for manyness.'"[11]

Many amillennialists reason that since Revelation is a highly symbolical book, most if not all prophetic literature is to be taken nonliterally, that is, in a "spiritual" sense. Allis seeks to support this approach by saying, "God is a Spirit; the most precious teachings in the Bible are spiritual."[12] True, the Bible deals with many spiritual facts and truths. And yet this is no basis for taking prophetic literature in an allegorical sense, reading into the passages what is not there as understood by normal, grammatical interpretation, with its figurative language. For example there is no basis for taking the daughter of Zion (Zech. 9:9) to refer to the church. The rest of the verse is to be understood literally, with its reference to Christ the King "riding on a donkey." Therefore to be consistent, the reference to the daughter of Zion and the daughter of Jerusalem should also be understood as referring to Jews, not to the church.

Sometimes, however, amillenarians argue that the promises made to Abraham are to be understood as fulfilled in a spiritual sense in the church because believers today are called children of Abraham (Gal. 3:7, 29; cf. Rom. 4:11; Gal. 3:9, 14). These verses teach that all believers since Abraham may be considered his "children" in the sense that they are saved by faith, just as he was (Rom. 4:1-3, 9-13, 16-17). The fact that our salvation is by faith, just as was Abraham's, and that we therefore are related spiritually to him, in no way dissipates the promises made to Abraham about his physical descendants possessing the Promised Land as an eternal possession.

View Prophecy as Focusing Primarily on the Messiah and the Establishing of His Reign

This and the following four guidelines relate to the axiom that the Bible is a divine book. Since the divine Author of the book is God, it is not surprising that prophecy focuses on Christ in His first and second advents. As an angel said to the Apostle John, "The testimony of Jesus is the spirit of prophecy" (Rev. 19:10). The purpose of prophecy is to testify of Jesus Christ and to bring Him glory. His first coming was for the purpose of establishing His reign on the earth, but the nation Israel rejected Him (John 1:11) so He said the kingdom would be taken from them and given to a future generation (Matt. 21:43). As Jesus said to His disciples, "He must suffer many things and be rejected by this generation" (Luke 17:25).

Scripture makes it clear that Jesus will return to establish His reign on the earth. He is reigning now from heaven, but the earthly manifestation of His reign when He comes in person is yet future. The Book of Psalms presents Him as "the King of glory," who will enter the gates of Jerusalem (Ps. 24:7-10). According to Isaiah 9:6-7 He is the Son on whose shoulders will rest the government of the world and He will reign on David's throne and over His kingdom. As a righteous Branch of David He will serve as "a King who will reign wisely and do what is just and right *in the land*" (Jer. 23:5, italics added). Jesus, born in Bethlehem, "will be Ruler over Israel" (Micah 5:2), and "the Lord will rule over them in Mount Zion" (4:7). As Zechariah wrote, the Lord "will stand on the Mount of Olives" and the Lord "will come" and "will be King over the whole earth" (Zech. 14:4-5, 9).

History is going somewhere; it is moving according to God's divine plan, which will culminate in the return of Christ, followed by His 1,000-year reign on the earth, which in turn will be followed by the eternal state in the new heaven and the new earth. Obviously it is incorrect to reduce the kingdom of God to the Lord's reign within an individual's soul or to think of His kingdom as only the individual believer's immortality.

Recognize the Principle of "Foreshortening"

Looking ahead, the prophets often envisioned the two advents of Christ as two mountain peaks, with a valley in between. They could see the peaks but not the valleys. From our perspective, however, as we look back we see the time gap between the First and Second Advents. Often the Old Testament blends the two comings of Christ in one passage. An example is Isaiah 61:1-2. The Lord read from this chapter in the synagogue of Nazareth (Luke 4:16-21), and stopped in the middle of verse 2 with the words "to proclaim the year of the Lord's favor." He did not add the words "and the day of vengeance of our God," obviously a reference to the Lord's return when He will take vengeance on His enemies. Isaiah 9:6-7 is another example. The first part of verse 6 refers to Jesus' birth, but the middle part of verse 6 along with verse 7 point to His second advent by speaking of the government being on His shoulders and His reigning on David's throne.

Seeing events related to the two advents of Christ together, the Old Testament prophets often did not understand how it would all unfold. As Peter wrote, "The prophets, who spoke of the grace that was to come to you, searched intently and with the greatest care, trying to find out the time and circumstances to which the Spirit of Christ in them was pointing when He predicted the sufferings of Christ and the glories that would follow" (1 Peter 1:10-11).

"The prophets were often unaware that in the same series there were a whole host of other parts that had only begun to show up in their vision. As a result of prophetic foreshortening, the prophet may have seen only events A, B, and Z, and have had no idea of what intervened."[13] In Joel's prophecy of the Day of the Lord (Joel 2:28-32) he stated that the Holy Spirit would be poured out on Israelites. When Peter stood up on the Day of Pentecost, he indicated that the coming of the Holy Spirit then was "what was spoken by the Prophet Joel" (Acts 2:16). However, this was only a partial fulfillment, because Joel predicted not only the pouring out of the Holy Spirit but also that people would dream dreams and see visions, and that unusual "wonders in the heavens and on the earth" would occur. Obviously "blood and fire and billows of smoke" and the sun turning "to darkness and the moon to blood" (Joel 2:30-31) did not occur on the Day of Pentecost. Those events are yet to be fulfilled. So we have here a partial fulfillment on Pentecost of some of Joel's prophecies, but the final fulfillment awaits the future. It is better to think of this as a partial-final fulfillment rather than a "double meaning" or multiple fulfillment. One event is the harbinger of the other, greater climactic event.

Look for God's Built-in Interpretations

Sometimes the prophetic Scriptures themselves include interpretations. An angel often gave interpretations of events seen in the prophets' visions recorded as apocalyptic literature. In Daniel 2 the head of gold in Nebuchadnezzar's image represents Nebuchadnezzar (vv. 37-38), the silver arms and chest represent the Medo-Persian kingdom, which followed the Babylonian Empire (v. 39), and the kingdom of bronze represents the next kingdom, namely, Greece (v. 39). The rock cut out of a mountain represents God's kingdom (vv. 44-45).

An angel explained to Daniel that the 10 horns on the fourth beast or fourth kingdom represent 10 kings (7:24). The two-horned ram represents the kings of Media and Persia, the shaggy goat represents the king of Greece, and the horn between the eyes of the shaggy goat represents the first king of Greece (8:20-21). The woman in a basket, seen by Zechariah in a vision, represents the iniquity of the Israelites (Zech. 5:6).

Tenney points out that several symbols in the Book of Revelation are explained. These include the seven stars, which are angels of the churches (1:20); the seven lampstands, which are the seven churches of Asia Minor (v. 20); the seven blazing lamps, which are the seven spirits of God (4:5); the bowls of incense, which are the prayers of the saints (5:8); the great dragon, who is Satan (12:9); the seven heads of the beast, which are seven kings (17:9); the ten horns of the beast, which are ten kings (v. 12); the waters on which the prostitute was sitting, which represent "peoples, multitudes, nations and languages" (v. 15); and the woman who is the great city (v. 18), which is identified in 18:2 as Babylon.[14]

Some symbols in the Book of Revelation are not explained, including the white stone (2:17), the pillar (3:12), the 24 elders (4:4), the two witnesses (11:3), the woman clothed with the sun (12:1-2, 14), and the winepress (14:19-20; 19:15). Some of these symbols are explainable by local custom, however.

> For example, the white stone may well be explained as the ballot used in a voting urn or as a pebble which was handed out as a ticket for free entertainment. It also may have functioned as the pebble cast by a juryman in acquitting a prisoner. Likewise, the pillar has reference to the colonnades which supported the roofs and graced the porches of the Roman temples. Therefore, each believer is being likened to a stately pillar; only here it is in God's house and not in some Roman temple.[15]

Compare Parallel Passages

Since so much (about one fourth) of the Bible was prophetic at the time it was written and since all of it was given under the inspiration of the Holy Spirit, we should not be surprised to see that all the prophecies of Scripture can be put together for a consistent pattern of the future. In all the numerous details of forthcoming events no contradictions exist. Revelation 13 needs to be studied in correlation with Daniel 9, and the closing verses of Joel 2 need to be studied in relation to Revelation 19. The numerous passages on the Millennium in Isaiah 9; 24; Joel 2; Zechariah 14; and Revelation 20:1-10 all need to be studied together. Chafer pointed out that the Old Testament includes seven major prophetic themes: prophecies regarding the Gentiles, the nation Israel, the dispersions and regatherings of Israel, the advent of the Messiah, the Great Tribulation, the Day of the Lord, and the messianic kingdom. He adds that New Testament themes of prophecy pertain to the new Church Age, the new divine purpose, the nation Israel, the Gentiles, the Great Tribulation, Satan and the forces of evil, the second coming of Christ, the messianic kingdom, and the eternal state.[16] All these events are noncontradictory and fit together under divine inspiration in a consistent pattern of the future.

Look for Prophecies That Are Fulfilled and Prophecies That Are Yet to Be Fulfilled

As discussed earlier, it is important to recognize that only a portion of the closing verses of Joel 2 were fulfilled in any sense on the Day of Pentecost. The final fulfillment of Joel 2:18-32 awaits the millennial reign of Christ.

Since the Bible is a divine book, we expect to see consistency in the Bible. This means, for one thing, that since certain predictions have been fulfilled literally, we can expect that unfilled prophecies will be carried out in the same way, literally. "The fact that so many prophecies have already been literally fulfilled lends support for the expectation that prophecies yet to be fulfilled will have the same literal fulfillment."[17]

In summary, the following questions should be asked when studying the prophecies of the Bible.

1. What is conditional and what is unconditional?
2. What is figurative or symbolic, and what is nonfigurative?
3. What is fulfilled, and what, as a "far" fulfillment, remains to be fulfilled?
4. What is interpreted by God in the passage?
5. What is interpreted in parallel passages?

As stated at the beginning of this chapter the study of prophecy, though difficult in some respects, can bring great spiritual blessing. Each believer should love "His appearing" (2 Tim. 4:8), that is, long for His return. As the Apostle John wrote in the next-to-last verse of the Bible, "Come, Lord Jesus" (Rev. 22:20).

CHAPTER ELEVEN

The Use of the Old Testament in the New Testament

The use of the Old Testament in the New Testament is one of the most difficult aspects of Bible interpretation. As you read the New Testament, you are no doubt struck by the numerous times it quotes or alludes to the Old Testament. Examining the quotations closely, you notice they are not always exact word-for-word quotations. Does this overturn all we have said about the principles of normal interpretation? As the New Testament writers exercised freedom in the way they quoted the Old Testament, were they abandoning normal, grammatical, historical interpretation?

How does this relate to the doctrine of verbal inspiration and biblical inerrancy? If there are disparities between the Old Testament and their New Testament quotations, can we still hold to the inerrancy of the Bible?

Were the New Testament writers interpreting the Old Testament by a different standard as they quoted from it? And if so, does that give us liberty today to do the same?

A related problem is this: Were the New Testament writers bringing out meanings in Old Testament passages not seen by the Old Testament writers? Were the New Testament writers then taking undue freedom in their "reinterpretations"? How much did the Old Testament writers intend and know? Did they know all the meanings brought out later in the New Testament? Or did they write more than they knew? Did God have more in mind than the human authors of the Old Testament were aware of? If so, can a verse or passage have more than one meaning? And does that New Testament meaning ever conflict with the meaning of that passage in the Old Testament? How can controls be placed on our understanding of those meanings so that we are not abandoning principles of normal interpretation? Are we at liberty to look for hidden meanings in the Old Testament, meanings that have no basis in the text itself? To what extent, if at all, did the New Testament writers give a "fuller" sense to some Old Testament passages?

We will look first at the extent of the New Testament quotations from the Old. Then we will consider the wording in those quotations and variations in them, also noting how the quotations were introduced and the source from which they quoted (whether from the Hebrew or from the Greek translation of the Old Testament, known as the Septuagint). Following that, we will note various purposes followed in the quotations. Then procedures for interpreting New Testament quotations of the Old will be suggested.

The Extent of New Testament Quotations from and Allusions to the Old Testament

Though scholars differ in the number of Old Testament quotations they see in the New, most agree that the number is somewhere between 250 and 300. Why is it difficult to know the exact number? Since the citations are not always exact in wording, we can't always be sure we have a quotation. Also sometimes quotations are strung together, thus making it difficult to know how many to count as quotations. Other times an Old Testament passage may be summarized and this raises the question of whether to count it as a quotation.

Many evangelicals would probably agree with Nicole's count of 295 separate quotations.[1] Of that number, 224, he observes, are direct citations prefixed by an introductory formula such as, "As it is written." Several others use "and" to connect a second quotation to the one before it. In 19 passages, the writers gave a paraphrase or summary of an Old Testament passage rather than a direct quotation. In 45 quotations the length (e.g., 1 Peter 3:10-12) or the specific nature of the quotation (e.g., Matt. 27:46) are given without being introduced by words that say an Old Testament passage is being quoted.[2]

Nicole also observes that the 295 quotations occupy 352 New Testament verses. According to Bratcher, 23 of the 27 New Testament books cite the Old Testament—all except Philemon and 1, 2, and 3 John.[3] The books with the highest concentrations of Old Testament citations are Matthew, Acts, Romans, and Hebrews, with each book having several dozen.

Of the Old Testament, 278 verses are cited, some several times. The Old Testament verse most frequently quoted in the New is Psalm 110:1, "The Lord says to my Lord: 'Sit at My right hand until I make Your enemies a footstool for Your feet.'" It is cited in Matthew 22:44; Mark 12:36; Luke 20:42-43; Acts 2:34-35; Hebrews 1:13; and 10:13.

Ninety-four of the 278 Old Testament verses cited are from the Pentateuch, 99 from the Prophets, and 85 from the Writings, according to Nicole. These include all the Old Testament books except Ruth, Ezra, Nehemiah, Esther, Ecclesiastes, Song of Songs (and others would add 1 and 2 Chron., Lam., and Obad.).

Allusions are far more numerous. Since these are even more difficult to ascertain, the list varies from 442 to 4,105. All the New Testament books, however, allude to the Old Testament, and probably to all Old Testament books. Allusions include references to Old Testament terminology or phrases, and to Old Testament historical events and people. For example Romans 5:12-14 obviously alludes to but does not quote the fall of Adam and Eve into sin, recorded in Genesis 2 and 3. In 1 Corinthians 10:1-15 Paul made reference to events in Israel's wilderness wanderings, obviously alluding to events recorded in Exodus 32, and in Numbers 11, 14, 21, and 25.

The Book of Revelation alludes to the Old Testament about 331 times, according to Atkinson.[4] And yet the Book of Revelation, with its many allusions has no direct quotations from the Old Testament at all.

"More than 10 percent of the New Testament text is made up of citations or direct allusions to the Old Testament."[5] Such an extensive use of the Old Testament clearly indicates that the two Testaments are organically related. This is to be expected because of the single divine Author. It also indicates that in interpreting the New Testament, Bible students cannot neglect the Old Testament.

By quoting the Old Testament so frequently, the New Testament writers demonstrated their trust in the authority of the Old Testament. Nowhere does a New Testament writer question or repudiate the truth of an Old Testament passage he cited. Fifty-six times the New Testament writers said their Old Testament citations were from God. When the writer to the Hebrews quoted Psalm 95:7-11 in Hebrews 3:11, he began by saying, "So, as the Holy Spirit says" (v. 7). A number of statements made by God in the Old Testament are called Scripture by the New Testament writers, thereby demonstrating that they identified the Old Testament with God's words. In

Romans 9:17, Paul wrote, "For the Scripture says to Pharaoh," and yet the rest of the verse quotes Exodus 9:16, in which the Lord was speaking to Pharaoh. In Galatians 3:8 Paul wrote, "The Scripture . . . announced the Gospel," and the remainder of the verse then quotes Genesis 12:3 in which God is speaking.

Other times the New Testament writers referred to an Old Testament writer by name and also referred to the divine Author, thus demonstrating that the New Testament writers believed in the Bible's dual authorship. A few examples are these: "All this took place to fulfill what the Lord had said through the prophet" (Matt. 1:22). "David himself, speaking by the Holy Spirit, declared" (Mark 12:36). "Brothers, the Scripture had to be fulfilled which the Holy Spirit spoke long ago through the mouth of David" (Acts 1:16). "As He [God] says in Hosea" (Rom. 9:25).

Moses, David, Isaiah, Jeremiah, Daniel, Joel, and Hosea are referred to by name in New Testament quotations.

Ways the Quotations Are Introduced

The New Testament writers introduced their quotations in various ways. The following are some examples.

"It is written"	Mark 7:6; 14:27; Luke 22:37; John 6:45
"Is it not written?"	Mark 11:17; John 10:34
"Haven't you read this Scripture"?	Mark 12:10
"Have you not read in the Book of Moses?"	Mark 12:26
"You have heard that it was said"	Matthew 5:21, 27, 33, 38, 43
"This is what the prophet has written"	Matthew 2:5
"All this took place to fulfill"	Matthew 1:22; 21:4
"And so was fulfilled"	Matthew 2:15
"Then what was said by Jeremiah . . . was fulfilled"	Matthew 27:9
"So was fulfilled"	Matthew 2:23; 13:35
"To fulfill what was said"	Matthew 4:14
"This was to fulfill what was spoken"	Matthew 8:17; 12:17

"If the Law had not said"	Romans 7:7
"It is said"	Ephesians 5:14
"The Scripture says"	1 Timothy 5:18
"The Scripture has said"	John 7:38
"For Moses said"	Mark 7:10
"David himself . . . declared"	Mark 12:36
"He [God] says"	Hebrews 1:6; 2:12 (also note "again" in Heb. 1:5-6; 2:13)
"He says"	Hebrews 1:7-8, 10; 2:12-13
"The Holy Spirit. . . . says"	Hebrews 10:16
"For this is what the Lord has commanded us"	Acts 13:47

Many times Old Testament passages are quoted without introductory phrases or formulas. Examples are Matthew 9:13; 12:7; 18:16; 19:19; 23:39; Mark 9:48; 10:6-8, 19; 12:26, 29, 31; 15:34; Luke 23:30.

Sometimes several quotations are strung together, as in Mark 1:2-3; John 12:38-40; Romans 3:10-18; 9:25-29; 10:18-21; 11:8; 15:9-12; 2 Corinthians 6:16-18; Hebrews 1:5-13; and 1 Peter 2:6-9. If you have a study Bible that indicates the sources of these quotations, it would be an interesting exercise to note the many Old Testament references cited together in each of these passages.

Variations in the Wording of the Quotations

When citing the Old Testament, the New Testament writers often changed the wording or omitted words. They used freedom in changing points of grammar, in paraphrasing, omitting selected portions, giving partial quotations, using synonyms, and recognizing new aspects of truth. We will look at a number of these kinds of changes and then note various purposes the writers had in quoting the Old Testament.

Making Variations in Grammar

1. The New Testament writers sometimes substituted a pronoun for a noun. When Matthew quoted Isaiah 40:3, "make straight in the wilderness a highway for our God," he wrote, "Make straight paths for Him" (Matt. 3:3), substituting "Him" for "our God."

Isaiah wrote, "All your sons will be taught by the Lord" (Isa. 54:13). When Jesus quoted that verse, He said, "They will all be taught by God" (John 6:45). Obviously in His remarks "They" suited His purposes better than "All your sons." In quoting Jeremiah 31:33, "This is the covenant I will make with the house of Israel," the writer to the Hebrews used the words "with them" (Heb. 10:16) rather than "with the house of Israel."

2. Nouns were sometimes used in place of pronouns. "Blessed is the King who comes in the name of the Lord" (Luke 19:38) makes more specific the words of Psalm 118:26, "Blessed is He who comes in the name of the Lord."

3. A plural noun is sometimes used in place of a singular noun. Matthew referred to Jesus speaking in "parables" (Matt. 13:35), but the verse he quoted (Ps. 78:2) has the singular "parable" in the Hebrew. The words "his mouth" (Ps. 10:7) are changed to the plural form "their mouths" when this verse is quoted in Romans 3:14.

4. Sometimes the writers changed a pronoun. Isaiah said, "The virgin . . . will call Him Immanuel" (Isa. 7:14). When Matthew quoted this verse, he said, "They will call Him Immanuel" (Matt. 1:23). Both were obviously true. The virgin named Him Immanuel and others will call Him by the same name. Zechariah 12:10 states, "They will look on Me, the One they have pierced," but when John quoted the verse he wrote, "They will look on the One they have pierced" (John 19:37). Moses told the people that God said, "I will make them envious by those who are not a people" (Deut. 32:21). When Paul quoted this verse, he made it more pointed by changing "them" to "you": "I will make you envious by those who are not a nation" (Rom. 10:19).

5. Occasionally the speaker is identified in the quotation. John the Baptist quoted Isaiah 40:3, but included in it the fact that he was the one Isaiah referred to. Isaiah spoke of "A voice of one calling: 'In the desert prepare the way for the Lord,'" whereas John said in response to a question by the religious leaders about his identity, "I am the voice of one calling in the desert" (John 1:23). Obviously he needed to alter the quotation slightly to answer their question.

6. Sometimes direct discourse is changed to indirect discourse. This is seen in Hosea 2:23, "I will say to those called 'Not My people,' 'You are My people,'" which is quoted in Romans 9:25 as follows: "I will call them 'My people' who are not My people."

7. Other times an indirect discourse is changed to direct discourse. "He" in Isaiah 29:16 ("He did not make me") is changed

to "You" in Romans 9:20 ("Why did You make me like this?"). In addition the affirmative sentence is changed to a question.

8. The verbal form is sometimes altered slightly. The commands beginning with the words "You shall not" in Exodus 20:13-16 are changed to the imperative "Do not" in Mark 10:19. Regarding the Passover lambs the Lord instructed the people, "Do not break any of the bones" (Ex. 12:46). When John applied this to Jesus, he changed the imperative to an indicative statement, "Not one of His bones will be broken" (John 19:36). Isaiah's words in Isaiah 6:9 are in the imperative mood: "Be ever hearing, but never understanding." But when Jesus quoted this verse in Matthew 13:14 He changed it to the future tense, indicative mood: "You will be ever hearing but never understanding."

9. A general reference is occasionally made more specific in the New Testament quotations. Amos 5:26 refers to "the shrine of your king . . . the star of your god." When Stephen quoted this in Acts 7:43, he referred to "the shrine of Moloch and the star of your god Rephan" (Acts 7:43).

10. Sometimes the extent of the reference is changed. Amos 5:27 referred to "exile beyond Damascus," but Stephen extended it to refer to "exile beyond Babylon" (Acts 7:43).

11. The order of the clauses is sometimes rearranged. When Jesus quoted five of the Ten Commandments in Luke 18:20, He gave them in an order that differs slightly from the order in Exodus 20:12-16.

12. Sometimes two quotations are combined and assigned to the more prominent of the two Old Testament authors. This is the case in Mark 1:2-3. Verse 2 quotes Malachi 3:1 and verse 3 quotes Isaiah 40:3, and yet Mark introduced the verses with the words, "It is written in Isaiah the prophet." Isaiah obviously is the more prominent of the two authors, and his book begins the section in the Hebrew Old Testament known as the Prophets, which concludes with Malachi.

13. Sometimes the New Testament writers rendered the sense of an Old Testament passage loosely as a paraphrase. An example is Matthew 13:35, "I will utter things hidden since the Creation of the world," which paraphrases Psalm 78:2, "I will utter things hidden from of old." Isaiah wrote, "In that day the Root of Jesse will stand as a banner for the peoples; the nations will rally to Him" (Isa. 11:10). Paul rendered this loosely when he wrote, "The Root of Jesse will spring up, One who will arise to rule over the nations; the

Gentiles will hope in Him" (Rom. 15:12). Though not a word-for-word quotation, the thought is basically the same. Paul could be faulted if he had claimed to make it an exact word-for-word quotation, but since he did not make that claim, it seems logical to allow him the freedom, under the inspiration of the Holy Spirit, to paraphrase the thought in Isaiah 11:10.

Other examples are these: Jeremiah 31:34, "For I will forgive their wickedness and will remember their sins no more," becomes "Their sins and lawless acts I will remember no more" in Hebrews 10:17. The last two lines of Isaiah 29:13, "Their worship of Me is made up only of rules taught by men" becomes "They worship Me in vain; their teachings are but rules taught by men" in Jesus' words in Matthew 15:9. Amos referred to idols "which you made for yourselves" (Amos 5:26), but Stephen renders it loosely by referring to "the idols you made to worship" (Acts 7:43).

Omitting Certain Portions of Verses

Writers of New Testament books occasionally shortened Old Testament verses they quoted. An example is seen in the last line of Mark 4:12, where Jesus said, "Otherwise they might turn and be forgiven." This is a condensed rendering of the last half of Isaiah 6:10: "Otherwise they might see with their eyes, hear with their ears, understand with their hearts, and turn and be healed." In addition to the condensing, the synonym "forgiven" replaces the word "healed."

Zechariah wrote regarding the Lord's triumphal entry, "Rejoice greatly, O Daughter of Zion! Shout, daughter of Jerusalem!" When John cited this passage he changed the imperative to a negative, "Do not be afraid, O Daughter of Zion" (John 12:15). Also it is interesting to note that Zechariah 9:9 has six lines, but John selected only three to quote. Matthew, however, cited four of the lines (Matt. 21:5).

Matthew 15:8, "These people honor Me with their lips, but their hearts are far from Me," purposefully selects part of Isaiah 29:13: "These people come near to Me with their mouth and honor Me with their lips, but their hearts are far from Me."

Giving Partial Quotations

When Jesus read from Isaiah 61:2, as recorded in Luke 4:18-19, He stopped in the middle of verse 2 of Isaiah 61, not reading the words, "and the day of vengeance of our God." This was because His carrying out the day of vengeance is yet future and was not relevant to

His first advent. The last part of Isaiah 56:7 reads, "For My house will be called a house of prayer for all nations." However, when Jesus quoted that verse He said, "My house will be called a house of prayer" (Matt. 21:13). He omitted the words "for all nations." Why? Because in His earthly ministry the temple was only for the Jews. It was not for all nations then, as it will be during the Millennium.

When Matthew quoted Zechariah 9:9 in Matthew 21:5, he omitted the words "having salvation" (NASB). This is because Jesus was not bringing national salvation or deliverance to the nation at that time, knowing that He was rejected by the nation and would be crucified within a few days.

Using Synonyms

The word "highway" in Isaiah 40:3 is replaced by the word "paths" in Matthew 3:3. Apparently John the Baptist felt this word was more appropriate as he quoted this passage to his audience in the desert of Judea.

A more difficult use of synonyms is seen in Hebrews 10:5, "A body You prepared for Me." This is also the wording in the Septuagint, the Greek translation of the Old Testament, from which many Old Testament writers quoted. However, the Hebrew has, "My ears You have pierced" (Ps. 40:6). When a slave had his ear pierced, he was symbolizing his giving himself over to his master for lifelong service (Ex. 21:6). The idea of having one's ears pierced is closely connected to the fact that Jesus had a body prepared for Him by God the Father. As Westcott wrote, "The 'body' is the instrument for fulfilling the divine command, just as the 'ear' is the instrument for receiving it."[6] The Septuagint obviously gave a free translation of the Hebrew, using the words "body" and "prepared" in place of "ears" and "pierced."

There was nothing wrong in quoting from the Septuagint, for the writers did so under the inspiration of the Holy Spirit. The common translation available to people in Jesus' day and in the days of the early church was, of course, the Septuagint. Therefore it was natural for them to quote from it. On the other hand many of the citations of the Old Testament in the New are from the Hebrew, with which the Septuagint often agrees.

Giving New Aspects of Truth

When Paul quoted Psalm 68:18 in Ephesians 4:8, he changed the words "received gifts from men" to "gave gifts to men." Paul was simply building on the fact that since the ascended Lord received gifts *from* men, He was then able to give gifts *to* men. Also Paul applied the statement in Psalm 68:18 to spiritual gifts, whereas its Old Testament use referred to a victorious general sharing the spoils of warfare with his soldiers.

When Paul quoted Hosea 2:23 in Romans 9:25, he altered the wording slightly so that it referred to the Lord calling Gentiles "My people" (Rom. 9:24), rather than limiting it, as Hosea did, to Jews.

Paul made a meaningful adjustment in the wording of the command in Deuteronomy 5:16. The Old Testament verse reads, "Honor your father and your mother, as the Lord your God has commanded you, so that you may live long and that it may go well with you in the land the Lord your God is giving you." When Paul quoted the verse in Ephesians 6:2-3, he did not say, "that it may go well with you in the land the Lord your God has given you." Instead he wrote, "that you may enjoy long life on the earth." The difference is a dispensational one. The promise in Deuteronomy held true for Israel to whom the Lord was promising life in the land of Israel in return for their obeying this command. However, since Paul was addressing believers in the Church Age he did not refer to the land the Lord was giving; instead he referred to "life on the earth."

All this above material illustrates that the New Testament writers often preserved the thought of the Old Testament passages cited, rather than always giving verbatim quotations (though they often did that as well). We should not conclude that verbal variations we have noted are inaccurate. They do not affect the doctrine of the verbal inspiration of Scripture, because the Holy Spirit, being God, had the freedom to modify the wording of the Old Testament as He desired. The end product is the inspired Word of God whether the quotation is complete and exact or partial and varied.

The Septuagint is the translation of the Hebrew Old Testament into Greek. It was made by Jewish scholars residing in Alexandria, Egypt approximately 200 years before Christ. Obviously this was not inspired by the Holy Spirit. As we have seen, it varies in many places from the Hebrew. If then it is not always accurate, how can the New Testament writers have quoted from it? Actually this is no problem when we realize that even today our quoting from a book does not mean we approve of it in its entirety. Evangelical scholars have pointed up that no New Testament quotation from the Septuagint differs in any *substantive* way from the Hebrew Old Testament.

About 150 years ago Horne classified the New Testament quotations of the Old into these 11 categories: Quotations that agree exactly with the Hebrew; quotations nearly agreeing with the Hebrew; quotations agreeing with the Hebrew in sense but not in words; quotations that give the general sense but that abridge the material or add to it; quotations taken from several passages of Scripture; quotations differing from the Hebrew but agreeing with the Septuagint; quotations agreeing verbatim with the Septuagint or changing the number of persons; quotations taken from the Septuagint but with some variation; quotations agreeing with the Septuagint in sense but not in words; quotations differing from the Septuagint but agreeing exactly or nearly so with the Hebrew; quotations differing from both the Septuagint and the Hebrew which were probably taken from some other translation or paraphrase.[7]

Purposes of Old Testament Quotations

People who write books or magazine articles often quote other writings. They do it to support what they themselves are saying, to give an example or illustration of their viewpoint, to summarize their points, or to make comparisons or parallels between their material and that of someone else. For similar reasons — though in some cases slightly different — the human writers of the New Testament books quoted from the Old Testament. The following are 10 ways the New Testament quotes the Old.

To Point Up the Accomplishment or Realization of an Old Testament Prediction

According to Matthew 1:22-23 Jesus' virgin birth was in fulfillment of the prophecy in Isaiah 7:14. Matthew wrote, "All this took place to fulfill what the Lord had said through the prophet: 'The virgin shall be with Child and will give birth to a Son, and they will call Him Immanuel'—which means, 'God with us.'" Matthew also referred to Jesus' birthplace in Bethlehem as being in fulfillment of the prophecy in Micah 5:2.

Another example is Matthew 8:17 in which Matthew wrote that Jesus' ministry of healing the sick was in fulfillment of words in Isaiah 53:4, "He took up our infirmities and carried our diseases." This makes it clear that Jesus bearing our infirmities was fulfilled in His earthly ministry of healing and is not related, as some suggest, to "healing in the Atonement." Also Matthew 4:14-16 was in fulfillment of the prophecy in Isaiah 9:1-2. According to Matthew 21:4, Jesus' riding on a donkey in His triumphal entry into Jerusalem was in fulfillment of the prophet's words in Zechariah 9:9.

Antitypes, which fulfill the prefigurings or types, also come under this rubric of the New Testament usage of the Old. An example is 1 Corinthians 5:7, "For Christ, our Passover Lamb, has been sacrificed."

To Confirm That a New Testament Incident Is in Agreement with an Old Testament Principle

At the Jerusalem Council, after much discussion, including words by Peter and then by Barnabas and Saul, James spoke up, saying that the salvation of Gentiles does not conflict with the Old Testament. He stated, "The words of the prophets are in agreement with, as it is written" (Acts 15:15), and then in the following three verses he quoted Amos 9:11-12.

Another example of a New Testament truth being in accord with an Old Testament principle is Romans 2:23-24. Paul commented that though the Jews bragged about the Law, they dishonored God by breaking it. This is confirmed, Paul said, by a statement in Isaiah 52:5 that God's name is blasphemed among the Gentiles because of the Jews breaking the Law.

To Explain a Point Given in the Old Testament

On the Day of Pentecost when Peter quoted from Joel 2:28-32 in Acts 2:16-21 he began (v. 17) with the words, "In the last days." However, Joel 2:28 begins, "And afterward." Peter, then, guided by the Holy Spirit, was explaining that the "afterward" referred to the last days.

To Support a Point Being Made in the New Testament

A good number of Old Testament citations are used to give support to the points being made in the New Testament. In Matthew 22:32 Jesus quoted Exodus 3:6, "I am the God of Abraham, the God of Isaac, and the God of Jacob," to support His point that God is the God of the living and that the resurrection will therefore be a reality.

In speaking against divorce Jesus emphasized that a husband and wife "are no longer two, but one" (Mark 10:8). In support of this statement He quoted Genesis 2:24, "For this reason a man will leave his father and mother and be united to his wife, and they will become one flesh."

Paul supported his point that righteousness is by faith (Rom. 1:17) by quoting Habakkuk 2:4, "The righteous will live by faith." And his point that God justifies the wicked (Rom. 4:5) is verified by his quotation of Psalm 32:1-2 in Romans 4:7-8.

God "blesses all who call on Him," Paul wrote (Rom. 10:12), and this is verified by Paul's stating in the next verse (v. 13) the words of Joel 2:32, "Everyone who calls on the name of the Lord will be saved."

That every Christian will "stand before God's judgment seat" (Rom. 14:10) is verified in the next verse by Paul's quotation of Isaiah 45:23.

In addressing the question of whether believers should eat meat sacrificed to idols, Paul advised the Corinthian believers to "eat anything sold in the meat market" (1 Cor. 10:25). Support for this instruction was added in the following verse (v. 26) by his citing Psalm 24:1, "The earth is the Lord's, and everything in it."

The writer to the Hebrews encouraged his readers "to persevere so that when you have done the will of God, you will receive what He has promised" (Heb. 10:36). The writer then quoted from Habakkuk 2:3, to underscore the truth that God's promises would soon be fulfilled. However, in quoting from Habakkuk he altered the wording slightly to adapt it to his purpose. Habakkuk 2:3 indicates that the revelation from the Lord to the prophet would be forthcoming. As Habakkuk wrote, "Though it linger, wait for it; it will certainly come and will not delay." In Hebrews 10:37 the words "it will certainly come" are changed to refer to the Lord, so that the quotation, with its slight adjustment to the purpose of the writer, reads "He who is coming will come and will not delay."

The fact that God "gives us more grace" (James 4:6) is verified by the citation of Proverbs 3:34, "God opposes the proud but gives grace to the humble."

To Illustrate a New Testament Truth

Paul wrote that many Israelites did not accept the good news of the Gospel (Rom. 10:16). This is illustrated by the same situation in Isaiah's day. Isaiah wrote, "Who has believed our message?" (Isa. 53:1)

The truth that "the message of the Cross is foolishness to those who are perishing" (1 Cor. 1:18) is illustrated by the Old Testament verse, Isaiah 29:14, which is cited in 1 Corinthians 1:19: "I will destroy the wisdom of the wise."

To Apply the Old Testament to a
New Testament Incident or Truth

In Romans 9:15 Paul quoted Exodus 33:19: "I will have mercy on whom I have mercy, and I will have compassion on whom I have compassion." In Exodus God spoke these words to Moses to assure him of His presence and blessing (see Ex. 33:14-20). But in Romans 9 Paul applied these words to a different situation, namely, God's election of Jacob rather than Esau (Rom. 9:11-13). Paul was pointing up the fact that those whom God chooses are based not on their efforts but on God's mercy (v. 16).

In 1 Corinthians 9:9 Paul quoted Deuteronomy 25:4, "Do not muzzle an ox while it is treading out the grain." Paul was applying that Old Testament verse, set in the context of kindness and justice to the poor and the needy, to his argument that those who serve the Lord have a right to be supported by those they serve.

Soldiers, vinedressers, and shepherds all benefit from their work (1 Cor. 9:7). A soldier is paid for his service, a vinedresser eats of the grapes from the vine, and a shepherd drinks of the milk of the flock. In verse 10 Paul stated that those who plow and thresh also share in the harvest. So Paul gave his punch line by asking two rhetorical questions in verses 11 and 12: "If we have sown spiritual seed among you, is it too much if we reap a material harvest from you? If others have this right of support from you, shouldn't we have it all the more?" Paul then added an additional illustration to make his point. Temple workers get food from the temple, and priests "share in what is offered on the altar" (v. 13). Again Paul made his point: "In the same way, the Lord has commanded that those who preach the Gospel should receive their living from the Gospel" (v. 14).

In quoting Deuteronomy 25:4, regarding the fact that farmers allow oxen to eat from the grain when they are treading it, Paul was using another of several agricultural illustrations to make his point. However, immediately after quoting verse 4 from Deuteronomy 25, the apostle wrote, "Is it about oxen that God is concerned? Surely He says this for us, doesn't He? Yes, this was written for us" (1 Cor. 9:9-10). This poses a problem because it seems that Paul was misunderstanding Moses. How could he say that God was not talking about oxen in Deuteronomy 25:4?

To get at an answer to this question, it is important to note the context in Deuteronomy 24–25. In dealing with matters of justice and concern for the needy, God discussed exemption from military service for the first year of one's marriage (24:5), the prohibition against taking millstones as a debt security (v. 6), capital punishment for kidnapping a fellow Israelite and selling him (v. 7), following instructions regarding leprosy (vv. 8-9), returning cloaks taken as pledges against loans (vv. 10-13), prompt payment of wages of poor laborers (vv. 14-15), individual responsibility for sin (v. 16), giving justice to aliens, orphans, and widows (vv. 17-18), being gracious to the needy by allowing them to pick up "leftovers" from the harvesting of wheat, picking olives, or gathering grapes (vv. 19-22), and limiting punishment of the guilty to no more than 40 lashes (25:1-3). Then verse 4 gives the command to be kind to oxen when they are treading grain. Not putting a muzzle on them means they would be allowed to eat some of the grain. The chapter then continues with directives about fairness in human relations. Deuteronomy 25:5-10 spells out the levirate regulation, in which the brother of a man who dies without children was required to marry the widow to perpetuate his family name. Verses 11-12 address the punishment of a wife who is unfair and inconsiderate in treating an assailant of her husband, and verses 13-16 address the subject of justice in weights and measures used in buying and selling.

All these regulations in Deuteronomy 24:5–25:16 refer to the rights of human beings, except for the one verse prohibiting the muzzling of an ox. Did Paul misunderstand the verse when he wrote that the verse referred to Christian workers? (1 Cor. 9:9-10) One explanation is that the "ox" refers to "creatures who serve" and that these creatures "could imply oxen, donkeys, or human beings."[8] However, does the word "ox" in Deuteronomy 25:4 suggest other animals, or humans? What other animals would be muzzled? And obviously humans would not be muzzled in grain-treading.

A better explanation is to understand that verse 4 includes a proverb, much like the modern-day maxim, "Don't look a gift horse in the mouth." When we use this proverb we seldom use it to refer to a literal horse, though that was its original meaning. The original thought was that if someone gave you a horse, you ought not examine the condition of its mouth (which would tell something of the horse's health). This came to mean, figuratively, don't carefully examine or question what someone may give you as a gift.

Seen as a proverb, verse 4 expresses the principle of justice and fairness to laborers. They should be given opportunity to benefit materially from the work they perform. Seen in this light, Moses was in fact speaking of people, not animals. Therefore Paul was correct in using the verse to refer to laborers. Paul was applying the Old Testament principle of Israelites being kind to their laborers to New Testament congregations who were to be kind to Christian workers. In each case the kindness was to be expressed by giving of their material possessions.

The paragraphs in Deuteronomy 24:5–25:16 have an interesting pattern, as the following chart shows.

1. Kindness – to newlyweds (24:5)
2. Debts (24:6)
3. Punishment (24:7-9)
   a. Debts (24:10-13)
   b. Kindness – to poor laborers (24:14-15)
   c. Punishment (24:16)
   a' Debts (24:17-18)
   b' Kindness – to gleaners (24:19-22)
   c' Punishment (25:1-3)
1' Kindness – to oxen, proverbially representing laborers (25:4)
2' Debts (obligation to a widowed, childless sister-in-law; 25:5-10)
3' Punishment (for harsh treatment, and for dishonest buying and selling; 25:11-16).

To Summarize an Old Testament Concept

Twice Matthew wrote quotations that are not to be found in the Old Testament. It seems he was summarizing Old Testament concepts rather than quoting specific verses. One occasion is Matthew 2:23, in which he wrote that Jesus' living in Nazareth "fulfilled what was said through the prophets: 'He will be called a Nazarene.'" Since no Old Testament verse says, "He will be called a Nazarene" (the Greek is *Nazoraios),* it may be that Matthew was making a play on words based on Judges 13:5, which refers to a Nazirite and/or, more likely, Isaiah 11:1, which indicates that from the "roots" of Jesse will come a branch (Heb., *nezer*).

To Use Old Testament Terminology

Occasionally individuals in the New Testament quoted Old Testament passages simply to make their point by quoting the words of the Old Testament. Psalm 19:4 reads, "Their voice goes out into all the earth, their words to the ends of the world." This is referring to the declaration the heavens give of "the glory of God" (v. 1), in what we call "natural revelation." Paul used this terminology in Romans 10:18, but he was not referring to the communication of the heavens at all. Instead he was pointing up the fact that the Israelites (v. 16) had heard the message of the Gospel "through the word of Christ" which resulted in faith (v. 17). Paul found it convenient to quote Psalm 19:4, not to apply that verse to the point he was making, and not to discuss natural revelation, as some have suggested, but rather to use Old Testament wording to get across his point that the Israelites had heard the message because it had been spread abroad by believers. Since the Israelites had heard the good news of the Gospel, they should have responded to it in faith, calling on the name of the Lord in order to be saved (Rom. 10:13).

When Simeon took the Baby Jesus in his arms and praised God and blessed Mary and Joseph, Simeon said to Mary, "And a sword will pierce your own soul too" (Luke 2:35). In saying those words, Simeon may have had in mind the words of Psalm 37:15, "But their swords will pierce their own hearts." If he did, then he was saying the psalmist spoke directly of Mary, because the psalmist was referring to retribution on the wicked, and David's words had nothing to do with the birth of Jesus. But Simeon was simply using the words of Psalm 37:15 to express his point.

This may also be the way in which Jesus used the Old Testament when He shouted on the cross, "My God, My God, why have You forsaken Me?" (Matt. 27:46) These words are taken from Psalm 22:1, a psalm that has immediate reference to David, as verses 1-2 make clear. In addition to Jesus' using the words of Psalm 22:1, He was also relating David's situation to Himself. This is discussed further under the tenth way in which the New Testament uses the Old.

To Draw a Parallel with an Old Testament Incident

In speaking of "a remnant chosen by grace" (Rom. 11:5), that is, a remnant of believing Jews, Paul said this was redolent of Elijah's day when a remnant of 7,000 people did not worship Baal (v. 4, quoting 1 Kings 19:18). The situation in Paul's day paralleled the Old Testament incident.

In the same chapter Paul drew a parallel between the hardening in the nation Israel in the present Church Age (Rom. 11:7-8) and a similar hardening in Israel in Isaiah's day, as indicated by Paul's quotation of Isaiah 29:10. Paul then expressed a desire for punishment on sinning Israelites, by quoting a prayer of David for punishment on his enemies (Rom. 11:9-10, quoting Ps. 69:22-23).

In Romans 8:36 Paul again drew a parallel with an Old Testament incident. In speaking of believers being subject to persecution, he quoted Psalm 44:22, "For your sake we face death all day long; we are considered as sheep to be slaughtered." This psalm spoke of Israelites facing defeat before their enemies (vv. 10, 19).

To Relate an Old Testament Situation to Christ

On a number of occasions the New Testament writers referred to statements in the Old Testament and then enlarged or extended those statements beyond their original historical setting to refer to Christ. Though the passages in the two Testaments refer to entirely different historical situations, parallels or analogies were seen by the New Testament writers in reference to Christ. The Old Testament situations were "heightened" in the New Testament to speak of Christ. The New Testament references did not contradict the passages quoted from the Old Testament. Nor were they unrelated. Instead, they were expansions of related truths.

In Matthew 2:15, Matthew quoted Hosea 11:1, "Out of Egypt I called My son," introducing this quotation with the words, "And so was fulfilled what the Lord had spoken through the prophet." A problem arises when we note the context of Hosea 11:1. That verse is clearly speaking of Israel (which is also called God's "son" in Ex. 4:22). Since the "son" in Hosea 11:1 is Israel and the "Son" in Matthew 2:15 is Christ, how can Matthew have said that Jesus' being in Egypt as a Child till the death of Herod was a fulfillment of Hosea 11:1? One answer is to recognize that the word *fulfilled* does not *always* mean the realization of a prediction. This has already been seen in Matthew 2:23. The Greek words translated "that it might be fulfilled" *do* indicate accomplishment of prophecy, as in Matthew 1:22; 4:14; 8:17; 12:17; and 21:4. On the other hand "fulfilled" in 2:15, 17, 23; 13:14, 35; and 27:9 points to an enlarging or a heightening of the Old Testament statements to refer to Christ. In these verses the Old Testament incidents or statements were "fulfilled" not in the sense of prophecies being realized but in the sense that they were "filled with more (a higher) meaning."

When God the Father "called" His Son "out of Egypt," it was analogous to His calling Israel out of Egypt at the time of the Exodus. What was in one sense incomplete is now filled up or brought to a climax.[9] Several analogies are evident between Jesus and Israel: both were in "exile" in Egypt; both, being the objects of God's love, were delivered; both came out of Egypt; both passed through the waters (Ex. 13:17–14:31; Matt. 3:13-17); both were tested in the wilderness (Ex. 15:22–17:15; Matt. 4:1-11); in both cases the multitudes were fed with "manna" from heaven (Ex. 16; Matt. 14:13-21; 15:29-39). From these parallels it is evident that Jesus was seen as the ideal Israel. His experience was an enlargement of the experience of the nation.

Matthew 2:17-18 presents Herod's slaughter of the children of Bethlehem (v. 16) as a fulfillment of Jeremiah 31:15. However, that verse in Jeremiah describes the mothers in Ramah, not Bethlehem, weeping as their children were carried into Assyrian exile in 722 B.C. Obviously, then, Jeremiah 31:15 was not a direct prediction of Herod's act. But a pattern between the two events is clear. The slaughter of the infant boys of Bethlehem corresponded to or was analogous to the Old Testament event, but was not identical to it. Both speak of God's people suffering under a cruel ruler. When Matthew said Herod's oppression "fulfilled" what Jeremiah wrote, he was saying it was analogous to the earlier event. And since Christ was involved, it was a heightening of the earlier event.

The following are other examples of this kind of usage of the Old Testament in the New.

New Testament Passage and Incident	Old Testament Passage Quoted
1. Matthew 13:13-14 — When Jesus spoke in parables, Israel's spiritual blindness kept them from understanding His words.	1. Isaiah 6:9-10 — When Isaiah spoke to Judah, spiritual blindness kept her from understanding His message.
2. Matthew 13:35-36 — Jesus spoke in parables.	2. Psalm 78:2 — Asaph spoke in parables.
3. Matthew 27:9-10 — Jesus was betrayed by Judas in return for 30 pieces of silver, and when the chief priests retrieved the money they bought the potter's field (vv. 5-8).	3. Zechariah 11:12-13 — Zechariah was paid 30 pieces of silver, which he then threw into the house of the Lord to the potter.
4. John 13:18 — Jesus said that Judas' betrayal would "fulfill" the Old Testament verse, "He who shares My bread has lifted up his heel against Me."	4. Psalm 41:9 — In this psalm David referred to "my close friend, whom I trusted." Obviously David had in mind a contemporary, not Judas.

5. John 15:25 — Jesus told His disciples that the hatred of unbelievers for Him "fulfilled what is written in their Law: 'They hated Me without reason.' "

6. John 19:24 — When the soldiers gambled for Jesus' seamless undergarment, this "fulfilled" the words, "They divided My garments among them and cast lots for My clothing."

7. John 19:36 — The soldiers did not break Jesus' legs when He was on the cross (vv. 32-33) "so that the Scripture would be fulfilled: 'not one of His bones will be broken.' "

8. Romans 9:25-26 — Paul stated (v. 24) that Gentiles who were not God's people would become so.

5. Psalm 35:19 — David prayed that "those who hate me" not be allowed by God to continue acting maliciously.

6. Psalm 22:18 — In this psalm David spoke of his enemies, referring figuratively to them as bulls, lions, and dogs (vv. 12-13, 16) and as people who "cast lots for [His] clothing."

7. Psalm 32:20 — David wrote that "a righteous man," though having "many troubles," is delivered by the Lord and his bones are protected and "not one of them will be broken."

8. Hosea 2:23; 1:10 — Hosea wrote that Israel, rejected by God and therefore "not My people," would become God's "people."

It is clear that these eight Old Testament passages were not written as direct predictions of Jesus Christ or related events. The contexts in each case show that the Old Testament verses had no initial reference to Jesus. Yet, as the passages were quoted in the New Testament, we can now see that the Old Testament passages were looked on in the New Testament as being "heightened." They were "fulfilled" in the sense that they were filled with more meaning. Seen from the vantage point of the New Testament, we see that the statements, though having local significance in the Old Testament, were heightened by New Testament writers to refer to Jesus.

This is not to suggest that the New Testament writers saw "hidden" meanings in the Old Testament passages. They were not changing the meanings of the statements in the Old Testament. For example Matthew did not write in 2:17-18 that "Ramah means Bethlehem" or that when Jeremiah referred to Rachel in Jeremiah 31:15 he was using a word that was to be understood as meaning the mothers in Bethlehem. Nor did Matthew, in quoting Zechariah

11:12-13, suggest in any way that he was reinterpreting the passage so that Zechariah did not actually write about himself, but instead was writing only of Judas. When Jesus quoted Psalm 41:9 in John 13:18 He did not deny the literal, historical reference in that psalm to a friend of David's.

When the New Testament authors, writing under the inspiration of the Holy Spirit, quoted the Old Testament, they had legitimate purposes in mind; they were not playing loose with the Scriptures and denying the historical validity of the Old Testament.

For an interesting exercise look up each of the following New Testament verses and see which 1 of the above 10 purposes in quoting the Old Testament is followed in each case.

Matthew 11:10 _____

John 13:18 _____

Acts 4:24 _____

Acts 13:40-41 _____

Romans 10:18 _____

Galatians 5:14 _____

Hebrews 1:13 _____

Did the Old Testament Authors
Understand All They Wrote?

The preceding discussion on the tenth way in which some New Testament passages use the Old raises a problem. Did God intend more in some Old Testament passages than the human authors understood or intended?

Several observations may be made concerning the understanding of the authors.

1. *The human authors of the Bible books apparently did not always fully comprehend all they wrote.* Some things were hidden from their understanding, which suggests that God had in mind some facts not fully revealed to the human authors. For example Daniel wrote, "I heard, but I did not understand. So I asked, 'My lord, what will the outcome of all this be?' He replied, 'Go your way, Daniel, because the words are closed up and sealed until the time of the end'" (Dan. 12:8-9). Even the high priest Caiaphas said, "It is better for you that one man die for the people than that the whole nation perish" (John 11:50). He unknowingly spoke of the substitutionary death of Christ (18:14; cf. 1 Peter 3:18).

Peter wrote that the Old Testament prophets "searched intently and with the greatest care, trying to find out the time and circumstances to which the Spirit of Christ in them was pointing when He predicted the sufferings of Christ and the glories that would follow" (1:10-11). God "revealed to them" that they were writing about future events; they "spoke of the grace that was to come to you" (v. 10), and "they were not serving themselves but you" (v. 12).

Not all agree with this view, however. Kaiser, for example, indicates that the human authors were aware of all the events they prophesied, but that they did not know the time when their prophecies would be finally fulfilled. Kaiser writes, "Theirs was not a search for the *meaning* of what they wrote; it was an inquiry into the *temporal* aspects of the *subject,* which went beyond what they wrote."[10]

Kaiser then holds that whatever God intended in an Old Testament passage, the human authors fully understood. However, did David understand he was writing about Judas (Ps. 41:9), or did Asaph know he was referring to Jesus' teaching in parables when he, Asaph, said he was speaking in parables? (Ps. 78:2) Was Hosea consciously thinking of Jesus Christ when he wrote that God called Israel His son "out of Egypt"? (Hosea 11:1) Other passages also suggest that the writers did not always know what was being revealed to them until God or a messenger of His explained the meaning to them. Examples are Daniel 7:15-16, 19-20; 8:15-16; 10:12-14; Zechariah 4:5.

It seems that the human authors of the Scriptures did not comprehend the full significance of all they wrote. Certainly God had in mind implications that would then be drawn out in the New Testament, ways in which Old Testament passages would be applied to New Testament situations or truths and/or heightened or escalated to refer to Christ.

2. *Progress of revelation must be acknowledged.* As the books of the Bible were written, God progressively revealed more truths about many subjects. This does not mean that what was given earlier was in error; it means it may have been incomplete. What was partial was added to. An example is the serpent in Genesis 3. In that chapter the serpent is not called Satan. Later the serpent is specifically identified as "the devil or Satan" (Rev. 12:9). And yet the serpent was more than a mere animal, as seen in the fact that he spoke to Eve (Gen. 3:1-5) and God spoke to the serpent (vv. 14-15).

Man's condition after death is presented in the Old Testament as a vague kind of existence in which man knows little (Job 14:20-21; Ecc. 9:5-6). In the New Testament more facts are given about life after death (see, e.g., Luke 16:19-31).

Even in Jesus' ministry the apostles did not fully understand all He was doing and teaching. But as they looked back after His resurrection (John 2:22) and ascension (12:16), they understood what the Scriptures taught. There was progress in their understanding.

The progress of revelation certainly suggests that God may have had in mind certain facts that some of the human authors did not fully comprehend, but that others may have known with additional revelation given later. If Moses did not understand that the serpent in Genesis 3 referred to Satan, certainly the Apostle John's statement in Revelation 12 makes that clear to all readers since the apostle's time.

3. *Some passages may not have been recognized as prophetic until they were fulfilled.* "So one must distinguish, then, between what the passage initially declared and what one comes to realize later was ultimately meant by the passage."[11] If readers did not realize certain passages were prophetic until they were fulfilled, the human authors of those passages may not have understood them in that way either. For example many of the prophets wrote of events in the first and second advents of Christ as if those events would occur together. Only now do we, looking back, know that two separate comings of Christ were spoken of. In other words they did not always understand that the Messiah would be the Suffering Servant in His first advent and the reigning King in His second advent.

On the other hand the human authors no doubt understood much of what they predicted. Surely Micah knew that the Messiah, the "Ruler over Israel" would be born in Bethlehem, as he wrote in Micah 5:2. And certainly Isaiah knew that the Messiah, on whose shoulders would rest "the government" of Israel is the one who is the Mighty God, and who will reign on David's throne (Isa. 9:6-7). But did David consciously have in mind Jesus Christ when he wrote about his own enemies dividing his garments and casting lots for his clothing? (Ps. 22:18)

4. *As discussed earlier, the enlarging or heightening of passages in relation to Christ is another factor that suggests that God had in mind more than the authors knew.* This enlarging or heightening is not contradictory to the Old Testament meaning nor is it unrelated; it instead is a related expansion.

Do the Scriptures Have Single Meanings or Multiple Meanings?

This question flows naturally from the previous question on whether God intended more in some passages than the human authors understood. If it is agreed that God intended more, then what limits can be placed on those meanings? And does this suggest that passages have multiple meanings? If so, how does this relate to the emphasis in hermeneutics on the single, grammatical meaning of each text? This obviously is a crucial question in interpreting the Bible.

Four views are held by Bible scholars.

1. One view is that each passage has a single meaning, and only one meaning, and this meaning was understood by the human author. As indicated, this view is held by Kaiser.

2. A second view is that readers may find in any given passage of Scripture a number of meanings that are unrelated. Or one reader may find in a passage one meaning and another reader may find in the same passage an entirely different and unrelated meaning. This view, of course, provides no sense of controls in interpretation. How does one, for example, demonstrate which of two conflicting meanings of a passage is correct? Also if one sentence can mean many things, how can one know if he has ever arrived at the correct meaning? If a Bible passage can mean numerous things, depending on the moods and ideas of the readers, then Bible study becomes an exercise in hunting for the deepest "spiritual" meanings hidden in the text. This disregard for the clear, grammatical statements of Scripture makes it impossible to have any objective approach to the Bible. Looking for multiple, esoteric meanings in the text nullifies the fact that the Bible is God's *revelation* to man, His written Word that communicates His truth to mankind.

3. A third view, a view that needs to be considered in some detail, is called *sensus plenior*. This term was coined by a Roman Catholic writer, Andrea Fernandez, in 1925, and has been more fully developed by other Roman Catholic scholars in recent years, notably by Raymond E. Brown. *Sensus plenior* means "fuller sense." The idea is that some scriptural passages may have a "fuller sense" than intended or understood by the human author, a sense that was, however, intended by God. Brown defines *sensus plenior* as "that additional deeper meaning, intended by God but not clearly intended by the human author, which is seen to exist in the words of the biblical text (or group of texts, or even a whole book) when they

are studied in the light of further revelation or development in the understanding of revelation."[12]

As discussed earlier, I would agree that God may intend more than was clearly intended by the human authors. It is also commendable that Brown speaks of the meaning "which is seen to exist in the words of a biblical text." However, several elements in his understanding of *sensus plenior* pose problems. He writes, "In the long history of exegesis . . . texts of Scripture have been interpreted in a way that goes beyond their literal sense."[13] Also it is unclear what he means by the sentence, "Individual passages of a biblical book have greater meaning when seen in the context of the whole Bible."[14] What deeper meanings is he suggesting?

Another problem with the Roman Catholic view of *sensus plenior* is that authorative interpretation becomes "authorative in the sense that it comes from one of the guides to revelation, e.g., the NT, the Church Fathers, Church pronouncements, etc."[15] This leaves the interpretation of Scripture open to fallible church dogma. This apparently is what Brown means in his definition by "development in the understanding of revelation." However, we cannot accept all the views of the church fathers because many of those statements conflict with Scripture itself and conflict with each other. Church pronouncements also are guilty of reading into Scripture what is not there. In this view the connection between the human author's sense and what God intended becomes blurred if not lost.

4. A fourth view is that each text of Scripture has a single meaning, though some may have related implications or, as Johnson puts it, "related submeanings."[16] In this view Psalm 78:2 has a single meaning (the writer said he "will open [his] mouth in parables") but it has two referents, that is, it refers to two people—Asaph, the author of the psalm, and Jesus, who applied it to Himself in Matthew 13:35. Johnson calls this view *references plenior*.[17] This seems a commendable way to express this view, for Psalm 78:2 and Matthew 13:35 refer to more than one item, while still having a single meaning.

This fourth view seems preferable to the others for these reasons:

(a) Historical, grammatical interpretation requires seeing a single meaning, not multiple meanings in each biblical text. As stated in the *Chicago Statement on Biblical Hermeneutics,* "We affirm that the meaning expressed in each biblical text is single, definite, and fixed. . . . What a passage means is fixed by the author and is not subject to change by readers. This does not imply that further revelation on the subject cannot help one come to a fuller understanding, but simply that the meaning given in a text is not changed because additional truth is revealed subsequently."[18]

(b) The idea that a single meaning may have more than one referent is consistent, as seen earlier, with the way the New Testament uses the Old.

(c) This view is consistent with the progress of revelation. For example Eve's "seed" (NASB; "offspring" in the NIV) in Genesis 3:15 most likely refers initially to her children including Cain and Abel, and then to all other descendants of hers. But ultimately the Seed, who would be in conflict with the serpent, is Jesus Christ, as Paul clearly specified in Galatians 3:16. While "seed" has one single meaning, it refers to several individuals or groups of individuals, but ultimately to Christ.

(d) The related meanings are not bases for approaching the Scriptures allegorically, in which the interpreter looks for hidden meanings. As Packer states, any one of these related submeanings or referents "remains an extrapolation on the grammatico-historical plane, not a new projection on to the plane of allegory."[19] Speaking of instances in which the Old Testament is said to be fulfilled in the New, Caird writes, "In all such cases it is legitimate to transfer an utterance to a fresh referent without violence to the principle that its sense is determined by the intention of the original speaker."[20]

(e) This view seems to be the best way to understand the use of Psalms 8, 16, and 22 in the New Testament. Hebrews 2:6 quotes Psalm 8:4-6, and explains that this refers to Christ (Heb. 2:8-9). Did David have Christ in mind when he wrote Psalm 8:4-6? When David said, "You made him a little lower than the heavenly beings and crowned him with glory and honor," did he not refer to man, beginning with Adam, as indicated in verse 4? When David wrote in verse 6, "You made him ruler over the works of Your hands; You put everything under his feet," was he not again referring to man?

How then can this be used by the writer to the Hebrews to refer to Christ? Was he failing to follow normal, literal interpretation? No, he was seeing Christ as the "last Adam" (1 Cor. 15:45), in contrast to "the first man Adam." Christ then is viewed as the "perfect Man." "The ideal not realized by Adam [is] now embodied in the 'last Adam.' . . . The psalm itself gives no indication that anything other than man in his ideal, created state is in view; but in the light of the New Testament, it can now be seen that none other than Christ fulfills this role of the ideal man."²¹ In appealing to Psalm 8, the writer to the Hebrews did not make "an appeal to a meaning deliberately hidden in the text by God but to the meaning that that text can now be seen to have in the light of the significance of Christ."²² The same thought holds true for Paul's quotation of Psalm 8:6 (He has "put everything under His feet") in 1 Corinthians 15:27.

On the Day of Pentecost, Peter stated that Jesus had risen from the dead, and he supported this affirmation by quoting Psalm 16:8-11 in Acts 2:28. Peter stated that David was referring to Jesus' resurrection. Peter explained that since "the patriarch David died and was buried" (v. 29) "he spoke of the resurrection of the Christ, that He was not abandoned to the grave, nor did His body see decay" (v. 31). Paul affirmed the same truth by quoting Psalm 16:10 in Acts 13:35. Paul said that David's "body decayed," but that "the One whom God raised from the dead did not see decay" (vv. 36-37).

In Psalm 16, David praised the Lord for His counsel and His presence at David's "right hand" so that David therefore sensed security (vv. 7-8). He then added that he felt joyful and secure (v. 9) and confident that God would "not abandon" him to the grave nor let him "see decay" (v. 10). He would continue to enjoy God's presence at the Lord's "right hand" (v. 11; cf. the reference to David's "right hand" in v. 8).

In verse 10 David was stating not that he would be resurrected but that he would be protected from a premature death at the hands of his enemies. The word *decay* may be understood in the sense of "pit," which often refers in the Old Testament to death or the grave (30:3; 88:3-4). It is a good synonym of "grave" in the first line of 16:10. The "Holy One" in the second half of verse 10 may be a reference by David to himself, as indicated in the NIV footnote: "Your faithful one."

Though David had himself in mind, Peter and Paul pointed out that from the New Testament perspective the psalm refers to Christ. Like David, Christ suffered at the hands of His enemies, but He went further and actually faced death – but was resurrected. This seems to be a case of the Old Testament being expanded or heightened to refer to Christ. Psalm 16:10 still retains a single meaning – not being "abandoned to the grave" – but with two referents, namely, David and ultimately, in the fullest sense, Christ. If Psalm 16 is taken to refer only to Christ, then one is still faced with the question of what that psalm meant to David. This does not mean "that Psalm 16 takes on added meaning in the light of further revelation but that further revelation enables us to understand the ultimate significance of David's words."[23]

A similar situation is evident in Psalm 22. David spoke of himself when he wrote, "Many bulls surround me; strong bulls of Bashan encircle me. Roaring lions tearing their prey open their mouths wide against me. I am poured out like water, and all my bones are out of joint. My heart has turned to wax; it has melted away within me. . . . Dogs have surrounded me; a band of evil men has encircled me., they have pierced my hands and my feet" (vv. 12-14, 16). He prayed that the Lord would deliver him "from the sword," "from the power of the dogs," "from the mouth of the lions," and "from the horns of the wild oxen" (vv. 20-21).

A number of verses from Psalm 22 are applied to Christ in the New Testament. Matthew 27:35 and John 19:24, on the dividing of garments and the casting of lots for clothing, relate Psalm 22:18 to Jesus. Matthew 27:46 records Jesus' quotation of Psalm 22:1, "My God, My God, why have You forsaken Me?" and Hebrews 2:12 quotes Psalm 22:22 in connection with Christ's declaring the Father's "name to My brothers." As in Psalms 8 and 16, this psalm too has more than one referent; in its immediate referent the single meaning refers to David, but in its ultimate New Testament sense the referent is Christ. David spoke of evil men who "have pierced my hands and my feet" (22:16). This is likely a figurative reference to their oppression of him, but in the case of Christ, it is understood literally. David figuratively referred to his enemies as bulls, lions, dogs, and oxen (vv. 12-13, 16, 20-21). These statements also figuratively suggest the vicious attacks of Jesus' enemies against Him.

Some writers suggest that some passages of biblical poetry, such as Psalm 23, take on multiple meaning. They see these passages in conflict with the idea that each passage of Scripture has a single meaning. For example Ryken writes, "Psalm 23 is on one level a description of the shepherd's relationship to his sheep, but throughout the poem there is a second, human set of meanings."[24] However, it seems that Psalm 23 has a single meaning — the relationship of the Lord to His people — which is presented in a figurative way, namely, the figure of a shepherd caring for his sheep. The meaning of Psalm 23:3, "He restores my soul," is single. Just as a shepherd restores a sheep, so the Lord restores David (and by application, other believers). Verse 2, "He makes me lie down in green pastures," might seem to have two meanings: (a) a shepherd causing a sheep to rest in good pastureland, and (b) the Lord helping David (and by application other believers) experience spiritual rest. However, the second idea (b) is the single meaning, which is presented in the figurative language of a shepherd and his sheep. Of course, the *ways* in which believers experience that rest, or the ways they experience the Lord's restoring of their souls may be multiple. But these experiences of rest and restoration are in the realm of application, not in the initial interpretation.

What Procedures Should Be Followed in Interpreting New Testament Quotations of the Old Testament?

Based on the discussions above, the following procedures may be suggested in summary.

1. Investigate the New Testament context in which the quotation of or allusion to the Old Testament occurs.

2. Investigate the Old Testament context of the passage to which the quotation or allusion refers. Be sure not to read back into the Old Testament for the original readers what is now known only by New Testament revelation. In other words, note what the passage would have conveyed to the Old Testament readers before the New Testament quoted it, and then note separately how it is understood in the New Testament.

3. Note the differences, if any, between the Old Testament passage and its New Testament quotation or allusion.

4. Determine how the New Testament passage is using the Old Testament passage. Which of the 10 purposes discussed in this chapter seem to be used? Is the New Testament passage citing the Hebrew text or the Septuagint or neither? Is it paraphrasing the passage or using synonyms? Does it include an introductory formula?

5. Relate these conclusions to the interpretation of the New Testament passage.

CHAPTER TWELVE

Applying God's Word Today

Christians tend to make one of two errors in applying the Bible. Either they give too little attention to application or they give too much attention to it.

In the first error some feel interpretation is enough, that Bible study is complete when a passage has been interpreted. In the second error others tend to move toward application before fully and accurately interpreting the passage. However, application without interpretation leaves us open to applying the Bible improperly.

Neglecting to apply the Scriptures reduces Bible study to an academic exercise in which we are concerned only for interpretation with little or no regard for its relevance for and impact on our lives. It is wrong to think of the Scriptures as only a sourcebook of information, as a book to be examined merely for the knowledge we can gain from it.

Of course knowledge of the contents of the Bible and correct interpretation of it are essential. But more is needed. We must have a responsive heart, a willingness to appropriate the truths of the Scriptures into our experience. As James wrote, we are to "not merely listen to the Word"; we are also to do what it says (James 1:22). In verse 25 James said that listening to the Word is like looking at it: "The man who looks intently into the perfect Law that gives freedom" should be "doing it." Merely listening to what the Bible says and looking into its contents without doing what it says, that is, studying the Bible without obeying it, is deceptive (v. 22). We deceive ourselves into thinking we have fulfilled our obligations before God when actually we have not.

Martin Luther wrote that the Bible "is not merely to be

279

repeated or known, but to be lived and felt."[1]

Interestingly one of the classic passages on the inspiration of the Scriptures, which states that "All Scripture is God-breathed" (2 Tim. 3:16), also speaks pointedly to the fact that the Scriptures are to be applied. The Bible "is useful for teaching" (showing us God's ways), for "rebuking" (calling our attention to those times we fail to heed what the Scriptures have taught us), for "correcting" (restoring us back to an obedient path), and for "training in righteousness" (continuing to nurture us in righteous living). As a result of these four ways in which the Word of God works, "the man of God may be thoroughly equipped for every good work" (v. 17). The words "thoroughly equipped" translate two Greek words with similar meanings. They could be rendered "adequate and equipped." The first word, *artios*, means "in fit shape or condition" and the second word, *exertismenos*, means "all together fit."[2]

These two words occur only here in the New Testament. The idea in these words is that God wants each believer to be so influenced by the Scriptures that he is ready to live for and serve the Lord effectively, in a Christ-honoring way.

Many statements in Scripture indicate that the Bible is given to us for more than satisfying our curiosity about what God is like, what He has done in the past, or what He will do in the future. Its intended impact on lives is seen in that the Bible convicts (Heb. 4:12-13), regenerates (2 Tim. 3:15; 1 Peter 1:23), nurtures (2:2), cleanses (Ps. 119:9; John 15:3; 17:17; Eph. 5:25-26), counsels and guides (Ps. 119:24, 105), prevents sin (v. 11), renews (vv. 50, 93, 107, 149, 154, 156), strengthens (v. 28), sustains (vv. 116, 175), gives wisdom (vv. 98, 130, 169), and delivers (v. 170).

The Scriptures are called a fire, to consume false teaching (Jer. 23:29); a hammer, to shatter people's hard hearts (v. 29); food, to sustain one's soul (Ps. 119:103; Jer. 15:16; 1 Cor. 3:2; Heb. 5:13-14; 1 Peter 2:2); a light, to guide our paths (Ps. 119:105); and a sword, for offense against Satan (Eph. 6:17; cf. Luke 4:4, 8, 12). In Psalm 119 the psalmist used many verbs to speak of his response to God's Word: *walk according to, keep, obey, follow, trust in, seek out, delight in, meditate on, consider, rejoice in, see, understand, hope in, teach, speak of, remember, not forget, not forsake, not depart from, not stray from, not turn from, believe in, consider, long for, love, stand in awe of, tremble at, sing of,* and *choose*.

Having been born again by the Word of God (1 Peter 1:23), believers are to grow in the Lord by the same means—God's Word

(2:2). In application, then, we are concerned about relating the Bible to life today. This involves seeing how the Bible, written to initial audiences thousands of years ago, relates to audiences today — and how we should respond to it. Do the Scriptures have relevance for today, and if so how is that relevance determined? What is the significance of the Bible to us? How do we determine how we should respond?

Problems in Bible Application

In chapter 1 we discussed several gaps that exist between Bible times and the present day. One such gap is the historical distance between the original biblical writings and the present day. How do God's words given to Abraham 4,000 years ago relate to us now? Are all the stipulations of the Old Testament Law to be imposed on Christians today?

If not, what relevance, if any, does the Law have for the present age? Another gap that poses problems in applying the Scriptures to the present day is the cultural settings of the Bible, which often differ from those of Bible interpreters today.

Each human writer of the books of the Bible wrote for particular audiences in their times. How then do their words relate to present-day audiences? Do their messages relate to us in the same way they related to those original audiences?

The New Testament makes it clear that the Old Testament does have current relevance. For example Paul wrote that the words, God "credited it to him [Abraham] as righteousness" (Gen. 15:6) "were written not for him alone, but also for us" (Rom. 4:23-24). In the same epistle Paul stated, "For everything that was written in the past was written to teach us, so that through endurance and the encouragement of the Scriptures we might have hope" (15:4). Several events in Israel's wilderness wanderings "occurred as examples, to keep us from setting our hearts on evil things as they did" (1 Cor. 10:6) and "these things happened to them as examples and were written down as warnings for us" (v. 11).

Surely the Bible is relevant, since it is *God's* Word, and "is living and active," penetrating the soul and judging the "thoughts and attitudes of the heart" (Heb. 4:12). Determining how God's Word relates to us and how we ought to *respond* to it is the task of application. Application is a bridge between the biblical meaning and present-day life situations.

Guidelines for Relevance-and-Response Application

The following nine steps are suggested as ways to apply the Bible properly to our lives.

Build Application on Interpretation

Be sure the application stems directly out of proper interpretation. As I have written elsewhere,

> Unfortunately many people go to the Bible for a "blessing" or for guidance for the day, ignoring the interpretive process altogether. In their intense desire to find something devotional or practical, Christians sometimes distort the original meaning of some passages of Scripture. To bypass the purpose and original meaning of the passage, looking for a subjective impression, can lead to a serious misuse of the Bible. Without proper interpretive controls, people can attempt to make the Bible mean almost anything they want it to mean.[3]

Our applications should be based directly on the meaning and relevance of the text to its original audience in light of the purpose of the book. "Sound interpretation is the only adequate basis for relevant application."[4]

If a text is interpreted wrongly, then the application may be faulty as well. Interpretation asks, What does this passage mean? Application asks, What does this passage mean to me? If we have not accurately determined the meaning of the passage for the initial hearers, we may not accurately apply that meaning to today.

For example if we say in our interpretation that *every* reference to oil in the Bible refers to the Holy Spirit, then we end up interpreting the story of the widow's lack of oil in 2 Kings 4:1-7 as meaning that she lacked the Holy Spirit. In turn this wrong interpretation would then lead to a faulty application if we said that believers today are not indwelt by the Holy Spirit.

In God's wrestling with Jacob (Gen. 32:24-30), He was seeking to gain Jacob's submission to His will. It would be a faulty interpretation to say this passage teaches that Jacob wrestled in his prayer life with God until he got God to give him what he desired. That faulty interpretation in turn would lead to an inaccurate application if we said that we, like Jacob, must wrestle with God in our prayer life to free Him to answer our prayers.

Determine What Was Expected of the Original Audience

Since the human authors of the Bible wrote to particular audiences regarding particular situations (see chap. 3), they had certain expectations from their readers. It is important then as a first step in application to ask what application(s) the writers expected from their initial readers.

Sometimes commands are given in the New Testament that are clearly indicated as for all Church-Age believers. In Ephesus the Christians to whom Paul wrote Ephesians were members of the body of Christ, just as are believers today. Therefore much of what Paul wrote in that epistle is directly applicable to present-day Christians. The commands, admonitions, and exhortations for the Ephesians are also directives for all generations of believers since then.

Richard points out that the New Testament includes several forms of discourse: commands and prohibitions, exhortations ("let us"), wishes (e.g., 2 Thes. 3:5; 1 Peter 1:2), permissions (e.g., 1 Cor. 7:15; Matt. 8:32), examples (e.g., 1 Cor. 4:16; 11:1), narratives (Rom. 15:4; 1 Cor. 10:6, 11), parables, and themes.[5] The commands, prohibitions, exhortations, wishes, and permissions give instruction for direct application, whereas the others are more indirect. For example many of the verses in Proverbs tell of the benefits of following certain actions or the undesirable consequences of following other actions. Not direct commands, they nevertheless give commands indirectly or implicitly. The many verses that state the consequences of not controlling one's temper imply the command, "control your temper." These passages then *inform* the reader whereas others basically *direct* the reader.

Usually narratives are teaching by illustration, thus informing the reader, rather than teaching by explicit command or other directives. Fee and Stuart speak of explicit and implicit teachings. "Explicit teaching is that which the inspired narrator actually says, 'God was with Joseph.' Implicit teaching is that which is clearly present in the story, but not stated in so many words. You must see it implied in the story, rather than just being able to read it right off the page."[6] McQuilkin suggests God reveals His will in Scripture by both "explicit declarations" and "generic principles."[7]

Base Applications on Elements Present-day Readers Share with the Original Audience

The commonality between the original audiences and people today is the basis for valid applications. "The relationship between the present and the early church is one of direct theological heritage."[8] Both belong to the universal church, and both depend on apostolic authority for guidance in faith and practice. The command in Colossians 3:2, "set your minds on things above," and the command in verse 9, "do not lie to each other," are as relevant and authoritative for Christians today as for believers in Colosse 2,000 years ago. The two audiences have much in common, though separated by time and geography.

However, God's command to Israel in the wilderness to pick up manna six days each week is obviously a specific historical instance in which Israel and the church have little in common other than the fact that they both are people of God.

Similarly God's instruction to Noah to build an ark is hardly a directive for the twentieth century. Though Christians today, like Noah, trust in the true God, the Lord's directive to Noah to construct an ark was addressed individually without any parallel instruction being given later to other believers. This leads to the fourth guideline.

Recognize How God's Working Varies in Different Ages

Since God's dealings with mankind have differed from one dispensation to another, we need to be aware of those differences as we seek to apply the Bible. Of course some matters never change. For example the command to love one's neighbor is given not only in the Old Testament Law but also in the New Testament. This command was first given in Leviticus 19:18, and is repeated in Matthew 5:43; 19:19; 22:39; Romans 13:9; Galatians 5:14; and James 2:8. In addition nine of the Ten Commandments are repeated in the New Testament, and yet when repeated they are given with higher standards. The Mosaic Law commanded, "You shall not murder" (Ex. 20:13), but the New Testament Church-Age command prohibits not only murder (Matt. 5:21) but even hatred ("Anyone who hates his brother is a murderer," 1 John 3:15).

Of course some regulations in the Old Testament Law have been annulled for believers in the present age. An example is the prohibition against eating certain foods (Lev. 11), which Peter learned is no longer valid (Acts 10:9-16; cf. 1 Tim. 4:4).

Determine What Is Normative for Today

We must be careful not to generalize for today everything that happened in Bible times. This is especially true in narrative passages of the Bible, which report experiences peculiar to individuals in their isolated cases. Because God has done something in the past for an individual does not mean we can expect Him to do the same for us. As Mayhue writes,

> We are not expecting a trip to the third heaven like Paul's (2 Cor. 12:1-10). Nor do we believe that God restocks the food supply of those who feed traveling preachers as He did for the widow of Zarephath in 1 Kings 17:8-16. Leprosy patients do not dip seven times in a river to be cured (2 Kings 5:1-14). Nor do we throw sticks on the ground and expect them to turn into serpents (Ex. 4:2-3).[9]

We must see if the principle in the passage is taught elsewhere. If what happened to someone in Bible times is considered normative for all believers, it must be in harmony with what is taught elsewhere in Scripture. The fact that God used Elijah and Elisha each to raise a young man from death to life (1 Kings 17:17-23; 2 Kings 4:17-37) and used Peter to restore Dorcas to life (Acts 9:36-43) does not mean God intends for believers today to raise others from the dead. This is never indicated in Scripture as normative for all believers. Jesus' command to the Twelve to raise the dead (Matt. 10:8) was given only to the Twelve on their special mission to announce the message of the kingdom to Israel. This command was never given to anyone else. Furthermore if this command were for today, then those who seek to raise the dead should also follow Jesus' instructions in the following verses: "Do not take along any gold or silver or copper in your belts; take no bag for the journey, or extra tunic, or sandals or a staff" (vv. 9-10). One reason we know Matthew 10:9-10 is not telling present-day Christians to travel without money is that later Christ changed that instruction (Luke 22:36).

As McQuilkin has written, "To be authoritative as a model for behavior—a God-given norm for all people of all time—any historic event must be so designated by an authorized spokesman for God. That an event was reported to have truly happened does not necessarily make it a revelation of God's universal will."[10]

A Nazarite in the Old Testament was not to cut his hair; this was to be a sign of his dedication to and holiness before the Lord (Jud. 13:5; 1 Sam. 1:11). This practice has been rescinded because the entire Old Testament Law, as a unit, has been done away with

(Gal. 3:25; Eph. 2:15; Heb. 7:12) and because the regulation is nowhere repeated in the New Testament. In addition Paul indicated that long hair was not normal for men (1 Cor. 11:4).

Abraham, Jacob, David, and others had more than one wife. Does this mean polygamy is acceptable, as some believe? No, this is not an acceptable practice. Even though God did not specifically condemn them individually for such a practice, as far as the scriptural record is concerned, we know polygamy is wrong because God gave Adam one wife and He said, "For this reason a man will leave his father and mother and be united to his wife, and they will become one flesh" (Gen. 2:24) and because numerous passages in the New Testament speak of marital fidelity to one's wife (e.g., Matt. 5:27, 31-32; 1 Cor. 7:2-3; Eph. 5:22-33; Col. 3:18-19; 1 Thes. 4:3-7).

We must look to the Scriptures themselves to determine what God would have us follow today. The Scriptures may give a specific statement limiting the relevance of the situation to that historic incident. Or if it does not make that clear, other passages need to be consulted. McQuilkin's maxim is commendable: "Since the Bible is God's revelation of His will for all mankind, any teaching of Scripture should be taken as normative for contemporary faith and living *unless Scripture itself indicates otherwise.*"[11]

Bestiality is prohibited by Old Testament command (Lev. 18:23), but it is not specified in the New Testament as a sinful act. However, this silence does not mean it is acceptable now. Certainly the many statements about sexual purity in the New Testament would imply that bestiality is considered sinful.

See the Principle Inherent in the Text

Sometimes the Scriptures give specific commands, directives specified for all believers, as discussed earlier. However, other times such declarations are not explicit. Therefore we look for principles inherent within the text.[12] These principles stem directly from the Scriptures; they are not something imposed on the biblical text. "When Jesus said, 'If someone forces you to go one mile, go with him two miles' (Matt. 5:41), He was putting a general principle into concrete terms. The application goes far beyond the particular situation."[13] What if someone were to force us to travel with him *two* miles? Would Jesus' words then no longer apply? No, the point is that when we are forced in this way we ought not retaliate but should do the opposite.

When Jesus said we should not call anyone "Raca," an Aramaic term of contempt (v. 22), the implied principle is that we ought not call others by *any* words of contempt.

The principle "is a generalized statement deduced from the specific original situation then and applicable to different though specific, similar situations now."[14] Principles, to be valid, must be affirmed elsewhere in Scripture. How does God's sending ravens to feed Elijah during a drought (1 Kings 17:6) apply to us today? Obviously this does not mean God desires to feed Christians by means of birds. Instead the principle is that God sometimes meets human needs by unusual means. The application of this principle is that believers can trust the Lord to supply their needs.

We must exercise caution in drawing principles from narratives of Scriptures. It would be wrong to say that the way to obtain a bride is to pray she will appear and do some kind deed for the prospective groom or a friend of the groom, as in the case of Rebekah and Abraham's servant (Gen. 24). Instead one principle that could be drawn from the chapter is that God guides us as we depend on Him. Nor does Genesis 22 teach fathers to sacrifice their sons. Instead the principle is that, like Abraham, believers ought to obey the Lord even when His commands call for personal sacrifice.

The incident in Genesis 24 is an illustration of a truth or principle stated elsewhere in Scripture, as in, for example, Proverbs 3:5-6. The principle in Genesis 22 is also clearly confirmed elsewhere in Scripture. From these examples two points become clear. First, we should derive principles directly from the text. No hint is given in Genesis 22 that the intention of the story is to teach fathers to sacrifice their sons as God commanded Abraham, nor is there any hint at all in Genesis 24 that the chapter is written to inform us how to obtain a bride. Those points simply are not in the biblical text.

Second, we should be sure the principle is consistent with Scripture elsewhere. Abraham's taking Hagar to bear him a son does not suggest that childless married couples today should commit adultery in order to have children. Such a principle flies in the face of all the Bible says about marital purity. In fact the difficulties Abraham experienced with Hagar and Ishmael, and the ensuing conflict between Isaac and Ishmael (and the conflict between their descendants even to today, as seen in the ongoing conflicts between the Jews and the Arabs) suggest just the opposite, namely, that Abraham was disobeying God rather than trusting Him. A principle then that can be derived from this narrative is this: we ought not take things in our own hands as a way of "helping" God fulfill His plans for us.

Think of the Principle as an Implication (or Extrapolation) of the Text, and as a Bridge to Application

Seeing the principle in a text is an essential step in drawing out what is legitimately intended or implied in the Scriptures, and in formulating a bridge by which to relate the Scriptures to present-day contexts or situations.

For example Christians in Antioch took an offering for poor believers in Judea (Acts 11:27-30). What does that situation almost 2,000 years ago have to do with us? A principle that can be seen in this action on the part of the believers in Antioch is this: Christians in one locale should help meet the needs of Christians in other areas. Obviously this thought is not explicitly stated in Acts 11, but it is certainly implied. Therefore the principle serves as a bridge between interpretation and application. The application for today could be stated as follows: I will send money this week to help poor believers in Haiti (or some other needy country or area).

When Elizabeth was pregnant with John the Baptist, Mary went to see her. "When Elizabeth heard Mary's greeting, the baby leaped in her womb" (Luke 1:41). We may extrapolate from this statement the principle or implication that the unborn have life and that therefore abortion is wrong. Again the text does not specifically state that the unborn have life, nor does it say anything about abortion. But these points, though not *explicitly* stated, seem to be there *implicitly*. The application could then be, I will not support abortion. The same can be seen in Jeremiah 1:5.

Take another example. Second Samuel 16:5-14 tells that David did not retaliate when Shimei cursed him and called him names. A principle that may be drawn from this incident is that believers should not retaliate against those who do them harm. This principle may serve as a bridge to the application, I will not seek to get even with [you may supply the name] who has wronged me.

For another example, we read in 1 Thessalonians 4:7, "For God did not call us to be impure, but to live a holy life." A principle that may be drawn from this statement, as well as from Philippians 4:8, is that viewing pornographic literature or films is wrong. Obviously such media is not explicitly condemned in Scripture, but sexual purity in thought and action is a principle clearly seen in these and other passages. A personal application of this principle would be, I will not view pornographic literature or films.

Principles drawn from narrative passages seem to be more in the nature of extrapolations than clear implications. Also narratives do not teach directly as do other portions of Scripture. Narratives illustrate what is taught directly elsewhere. How then do we determine which narratives may have principles for today and which ones do not? As stated earlier, obviously Peter's walking on the water or Timothy's taking a cloak and scrolls to Paul have little relevance to us.

McQuilkin suggests that "a historic event always has some implication. Otherwise, it would not be included in Holy Writ."[15] He adds:

> Scripture leaves many historic events uninterpreted, but of many it renders a judgment: the behavior is either commended or condemned. In some of those instances Scripture goes even further; it gives a reason for the commendation or condemnation. Such interpreted events are the legitimate raw material for refining general principles. For example, if Abraham is held up as an example of faith in the sacrifice of Isaac, then we are safe in considering his act commendatory, although we may not have thought so on our own.[16]

McQuilkin points up that Paul's policy of not preaching the Gospel where it had already been done (Rom. 15:20) does not suggest a principle for missionaries to follow today; it was *Paul's* specific "job description." Then McQuilkin writes,

> But when [Paul] said that the Gentile churches had a duty to help materially the Christians at Jerusalem because they had benefited spiritually those Christians (Rom. 15:26-27), he seemed to imply a general principle. Why? Not only because that teaching is given explicitly elsewhere, but also because Paul gave, in the passage, the reason for the duty. And that reason is given as a basic principle: they should give because they had benefited spiritually.[17]

Write Out Specific Action-Responses

As you study the Scriptures, drawing principles or implications from your interpretation, then you are ready to take the next step of applying the Scriptures to your life. This is the ultimate goal of Bible study.

As you study the Bible, note ways you can apply the truth. Be sensitive to the Holy Spirit's leading as He seeks to show you areas in your life where you may need to improve spiritually. For example as you read Colossians 1:4-5 ask yourself, Do I have some of these needs — to have more faith or trust in Christ; to show more love to other Christians; to have more confidence in the Lord's control over my future?

Hall suggests application can be done by writing answers to five questions, the first letters of which form the acronym "SPECS": Does the passage speak of any *Sin* to be forsaken, *Promise* to be claimed, *Example* to be followed, *Command* to be obeyed, or *Stumbling block* or hindrance to be avoided?[18]

Think of application in terms of relationships: your relationship to God, to Satan, to others (at home, church, work, school), to the world, and to yourself.

Recognize that application can be in the form of improved attitudes as well as in improved actions. Attitudinal responses may take longer to develop.

Make your applications personal. Use the words *I, me, my, mine,* not *we, us, our.* Application statements that remain in the "we" category are too general.

Also be specific. Saying, "I should be more like Jesus," or "I should love my wife more," or "I will try to control my anger better" are inadequate. Rather than saying, "I should love my wife more," be specific, by saying something like this: "I will take my wife out to dinner this Friday evening." Or, "On my way home from work Thursday I will buy my wife some flowers." Or "I will not criticize my wife any time this weekend."

Adding a time element, such as Friday evening, Thursday, or this weekend helps insure that the application is not delayed indefinitely. On the other hand some applications may take longer to carry out. You may have a month-long goal of being more patient with your children, or of avoiding pornography, or of controlling your anger. But even these can be broken down into shorter time segments. For example the goal, "I will seek to control my temper this month," may include the more specific application-goal, "I will not get angry when I am driving each morning in heavy, slow traffic."

Healing a broken relationship may involve the specific action/response of apologizing to a friend. Developing the attitude of goodness may mean helping a friend move his furniture.

It is also important to be selective. "Stockpiling" your applications, that is, writing numerous applications for every Bible passage you study, may give you far more applications than you can possibly implement in a reasonable amount of time. Rather than having numerous activities or attitudes to perform each day, and thus developing a burdensome attitude toward the Christian life, it is better to have fewer and more specific applications. As Henrichsen wrote,

> Sometimes your application will require one specific thing like returning a book you borrowed months before, or apologizing to someone for a wrong you did. At other times your application will require time. It may be a habit God wants you to break, or a series of steps you may have to take like paying installments on a large overdue bill. Then too there will be times when the Holy Spirit will give you a long-range project to work on, such as working on an attitude or a virtue.[19]

Some Bible students record the progress they make on their applications. If your application includes a time limit, as suggested, then record at the end of that period whether you completed that application-response, and if not, what remains to be done.

In writing "I will . . ." application sentences you may want to choose from the following list of 90 action verbs for completing those sentences.

Accept	Count	Help
Admit	Create	Invite
Analyze	Decide	Isolate
Ask	Develop	Keep
Ask myself	Direct	List
Avoid	Discuss	Listen
Be sensitive	Do	Look for
Be willing	Eliminate	Look up
Build	Encourage	Love
Buy	Enjoy	Meet with
Choose	Evaluate	Memorize
Claim	Exemplify	Organize
Collect	Experiment	Plan out
Commit	Find	Pray
Compliment	Follow	Pray about
Comply	Give	Pray to
Confess	Go	Pray with
Control	Guard	Prefer

Pursue	Share	Thank
Read	Show	Think about
Realize	Sing	Value
Record	Spend time	Visit
Rejoice	Stay away	Wait
Repair	Stop	Wake up
Respond	Study	Walk
Sacrifice	Substitute	Watch
Save	Take	Witness
Schedule	Talk with	Work on
Select	Teach	Write down
Send	Telephone	Write to

Rely on the Holy Spirit

Make a firm decision to follow through with the application. Ask the Lord to give you the desire and determination to carry out the application. Ask for the Lord's enabling. Applying the Scriptures should not be attempted in our own strength. The Christian life must be lived in the power of the Holy Spirit.

We must be sure that in the entire process of studying, interpreting, and applying the Bible, we are relying on the Holy Spirit to guide us. We need to ask the Holy Spirit to show us areas in our lives where application is needed, and then to make us sensitive to that need, and to give us the desire to change by appropriating the truth. In applying God's Word we need to ask the Holy Spirit to work in us to bring about changes in our lives that will make us more Christlike. It is not enough to perceive the truth; we must also receive it, by responding as God would have us to do. As Klooster wrote, "Understanding Scripture requires more than an intellectual grasp of the historical setting of the text or the literary structure of the passage. . . . Heart-understanding demands the heart response in the totality of one's being to the living, Triune God."[20]

Application, the crowning step in Bible study, can be exciting as you see the Scriptures working in your own life. As the Word of God penetrates our souls, it enables us to see areas where improvement is needed and enables us also to overcome weaknesses by the Holy Spirit's enabling and to "grow thereby" (1 Peter 2:2, KJV). Knowing the truth of God is essential, but blessing comes from *doing* it. As Johann Bengel wrote in 1742, "Apply yourself wholly to the text and apply the text wholly to yourself."

NOTES

Chapter One

1. John F. MacArthur, *The Charismatics* (Grand Rapids: Zondervan Publishing House, 1970), 57.
2. John Balchin, *Understanding Scripture* (Downers Grove, Ill.: InterVarsity Press, 1981), 8.
3. Milton S. Terry, *Biblical Hermeneutics,* 2d ed. (1883; reprint, Grand Rapids: Zondervan Publishing House, n.d.), 20.
4. F.F. Bruce, "Interpretation of the Bible," in *Evangelical Dictionary of Theology,* ed. Walter A. Elwell (Grand Rapids: Baker Book House, 1986), 505.
5. Also see Roy B. Zuck, *The Holy Spirit in Your Teaching,* rev. ed. (Wheaton, Ill.: Victor Books, 1984), 62–63.
6. H.C.G. Moule, *Veni Creator: Thoughts on the Person and Work of the Holy Spirit* (London: Hodder & Stoughton, 1890), 63.
7. For more discussion of the role of the Holy Spirit in biblical interpretation, see *The Holy Spirit in Your Teaching,* 58–66, 136–46.
8. Bernard Ramm, *Protestant Biblical Interpretation,* 3d rev. ed. (Grand Rapids: Baker Book House, 1979), 14.
9. On the puzzling words, "You do not need anyone to teach you" (1 John 2:27), see *The Holy Spirit in Your Teaching,* 55–57.
10. For more on this subject see Moisés Silva, *Has the Church Misread the Bible?* (Grand Rapids: Zondervan Publishing House, 1987), 77–97.

Chapter Two

1. A. Berkeley Mickelsen, *Interpreting the Bible* (Grand Rapids: Wm. B. Eerdmans Publishing Co., 1963), 20.
2. Milton S. Terry, *Biblical Hermeneutics* (reprint, Grand Rapids: Zondervan Publishing House, n.d.), 609, n. 1.
3. Frederic W. Farrar, *History of Interpretation* (1886; reprint, Grand Rapids: Baker Book House, 1961), 73.
4. Ibid., 73–74.
5. James D. Wood, *The Interpretation of the Bible* (London: Gerald Duckworth and Co., 1958), 14.

6. Bernard Ramm, *Protestant Biblical Interpretation*, 3d rev. ed. (Grand Rapids: Baker Book House, 1970), 25.

7. Jeff Sharp, "Philo's Method of Allegorical Interpretations," *East Asia Journal of Theology* 2 (April 1984): 98.

8. Charles Theodore Fritsch, *The Anti-Anthropomorphisms of the Greek Pentateuch* (1943), 918, cited in Jeff Sharp, "Philo's Method of Allegorical Interpretation," 97.

9. Farrar, *History of Interpretation*, 150.

10. Terry, *Biblical Hermeneutics*, 634.

11. Robert M. Grant with David Tracy, *A Short History of the Interpretation of the Bible*, 2d ed. (Philadelphia: Fortress Press, 1984), 49.

12. Ibid., 50.

13. R.P.C. Hanson, "Notes on Tertullian's Interpretation of Scripture," *Journal of Theological Studies* 12 (1961): 276.

14. Farrar, *History of Interpretation*, 178.

15. Ernest F. Kevan, "The Principles of Interpretation," in *Revelation and the Bible*, ed. Carl F.H. Henry (Grand Rapids: Baker Book House, 1958), 291.

16. G.H. Gilbert, *The Interpretation of the Bible: A Short History*, cited by Ramm, *Protestant Biblical Interpretation*, 50.

17. Terry, *Biblical Hermeneutics*, 649.

18. Ibid., 650.

19. Ramm, *Protestant Biblical Interpretation*, 36.

20. Ibid.

21. Mickelsen, *Interpreting the Bible*, 35.

22. Grant and Tracy, *A Short History of the Interpretation of the Bible*, 70.

23. Mickelsen, *Interpreting the Bible*, 35.

24. Ibid.

25. Grant with Tracy, *A Short History on the Interpretation of the Bible*, 83.

26. Eugene H. Merrill, "Rashi, Nicholas de Lyra, and Christian Exegesis," *Westminster Theological Journal* 38 (1975): 69.

27. Ibid.

28. Ramm, *Protestant Biblical Interpretation*, 52.

29. Terry, *Biblical Hermeneutics*, 671.

30. Quoted by Farrar, *History of Interpretation*, 328.

31. Ramm, *Protestant Biblical Interpretation*, 30.

32. Terry, *Biblical Hermeneutics*, 674.

33. James D. Wood, *The Interpretation of the Bible: A Historical Introduction* (London: Gerald Duckworth and Co., 1958), 91.

34. Terry, *Biblical Hermeneutics*, 707.

35. Ramm, *Protestant Biblical Interpretation*, 60.

36. Ibid., 61.

37. Mickelsen, *Interpreting the Bible*, 43.

38. Ibid., 47.

39. Ramm, *Protestant Biblical Interpretation*, 64.

40. Hans-Georg Gadamer, *Truth and Method* (London: Sheed and Ward, 1975), 273.

41. Clark H. Pinnock, *Biblical Revelation – The Foundation of Christian Theology* (Chicago: Moody Press, 1971), 223. Also see Hendrick Krabbendam, "The New Hermeneutic," in *Hermeneutics, Inerrancy, and the Bible*, ed. Earl D. Radmacher and Robert D. Preus (Grand Rapids: Zondervan Publishing House, 1984), 535–58; cf. 559–84.

42. For an evaluation of Structuralism, see Craig L. Blomberg, *Interpreting the Parables* (Downers Grove, Ill.: InterVarsity Press, 1990), 144–52.

43. Donald K. McKim, "Hermeneutics Today," *Reformed Journal* (March 1987), 10–15.

Chapter Three

1. Moses Stuart, "Are the Same Principles of Interpretation to Be Applied to the Scriptures as to Other Books?" *American Biblical Repository* (January 1832): 124–26; also cited in Milton S. Terry, *Biblical Hermeneutics* (reprint, Grand Rapids: Zondervan Publishing House, n.d.), 173–74.

2. Robert L. Cate, *How to Interpret the Bible* (Nashville: Broadman Press, 1983), 161.

3. Walter Henrichsen, *A Layman's Guide to Interpreting the Bible* (Grand Rapids: Zondervan Publishing House, 1985), 49–50.

4. Bernard Ramm, *Protestant Biblical Interpretation,* 3d rev. ed. (Grand Rapids: Baker Book House, 1970), 123.

5. New Haven, Conn.: Yale University Press, 1967.

6. *Myles Coverdale's Rules for Reading the Bible,* 1535, cited in F.J. Miles, *Understandest Thou? Principles of Biblical Interpretation* (London: Marshall, Morgan, & Scott, 1946), xi.

7. Roy B. Zuck, *The Holy Spirit in Your Teaching,* rev. ed. (Wheaton, Ill.: Victor Books, 1984), 49.

8. Ibid., 48.

9. John Knox, *The History of Reformation of the Church of Scotland,* Book 4, 1587.

10. Charles Ogers, *The Construction of Deeds and Statutes,* 4th ed. (Boulder, Colo.: Sweet and Maxwell, 1956), 27, cited in John R.W. Stott, *Understanding the Bible* (Glendale, Calif.: G/L Publications, 1972), 230–31.

11. Charles C. Ryrie, *Basic Theology* (Wheaton, Ill.: Victor Books, 1986), 114.

Chapter Four

1. Lewis Carroll, *Through the Looking-Glass* (1872; reprint, New York: Macmillan Co., n.d.), 88.

2. John F. Johnson, "Analogei Fidei as Hermeneutical Principle," *Springfielder* 36 (1973): 249.

3. For details on this covenantal vassal treaty form and its relationship to the structure of Deuteronomy, see *The Bible Knowledge Commentary,* Old Testament, ed. John F. Walvoord and Roy B. Zuck (Wheaton, Ill.: Victor Books, 1985), 137, 260.

4. R.C. Sproul, *Knowing Scripture* (Downers Grove, Ill.: InterVarsity Press, 1979), 102.

5. Alan Johnson, "History and Culture in New Testament Interpretation," in *Interpreting the Word of God,* ed. Samuel J. Schultz and Morris A. Inch (Chicago: Moody Press, 1976), 131.

6. Bernard Ramm, *Protestant Biblical Interpretation,* 3d rev. ed. (Grand Rapids: Baker Book House, 1970), 157.

7. Philo, *De Virtute* 143, cited in Jacob Milgrom, "You Shall Not Boil a Kid in Its Mother's Milk," *Bible Review* 1 (October 1985): 54.

8. Avinoam Danin, "Do You Know When the Ibexes Give Birth?" *Biblical Archaeology Review* 5 (November/December 1979): 50-51.

9. For an interesting sketch of how the Jericho walls with houses between them may have looked see Bryant G. Wood, "Did the Israelites Conquer Jericho?" *Biblical Archaeology Review* (March/April 1990): 47.

10. This material is used by permission from *Wherever* (Spring 1982), published by The Evangelical Alliance Mission. The exercise is adopted from material by Mont Smith, a former missionary to Ethiopia.

11. J. Robertson McQuilkin, *Understanding and Applying the Bible* (Chicago: Moody Press, 1983), 245.

12. J. Robertson McQuilkin, "Limits of Cultural Interpretation," *Journal of the Evangelical Theological Society* 23 (June 1980): 119.

13. Henry A. Virkler, *Hermeneutics: Principles and Processes of Biblical Interpretation* (Grand Rapids: Baker Book House, 1981), 224.

Chapter Five

1. Johann August Ernesti, *Elements of Interpretation,* 3d ed., ed. and trans. Moses Stuart (Andover: N.p., 1837), 50.

2. Stephen Ullmann, *Semantics: An Introduction to the Science of Meaning* (Oxford: Blackwell, 1964), 97.

3. Peter Cotterell and Max Turner, *Linguistics and Biblical Interpretation* (Downers Grove, Ill.: InterVarsity Press, 1989), 131.

4. James Barr, *The Semantics of Biblical Language* (Oxford: Oxford University Press, 1961), 109. Also see Darrell L. Bock, "New Testament Word Analysis," in *Introducing New Testament Interpretation,* ed. Scot I. McKnight (Grand Rapids: Baker Book House, 1989), 97–113.

5. D.A. Carson, *Exegetical Fallacies* (Grand Rapids: Baker Book House, 1984), 33.

6. Ibid.

7. Milton S. Terry, *Biblical Hermeneutics,* 2d. ed. (1883; reprint, Grand Rapids: Zondervan Publishing House, n.d.), 123.

8. Ibid., 191.

9. *Encyclopedia Judaica,* 7:1318.

10. A. Berkeley Mickelsen, *Interpreting the Bible* (Grand Rapids: Wm. B. Eerdmans Publishing Co., 1963), 100.

11. Cotterell and Turner, *Linguistics and Biblical Interpretation,* 176–78.

12. Moisés Silva, *Biblical Words and Their Meaning* (Grand Rapids: Zondervan Publishing House, 1983), 149–50.

13. For a thorough discussion of the many ways *of* is used (in genitive constructions) in the New Testament see John Beekman and John Callow, *Translating the Word of God* (Grand Rapids: Zondervan Publishing House, 1974), 249–66.

14. For more on this verse see Stanley D. Toussaint, "Acts" in *The Bible Knowledge Commentary,* New Testament, ed. John F. Walvoord and Roy B. Zuck (Wheaton, Ill.: Victor Books, 1983), 359.

Chapter Six

1. Leland Ryken, *The Literature of the Bible* (Grand Rapids: Zondervan Publishing House, 1974), 13.

2. Ryken, "Literary Criticism of the Bible: Some Fallacies," in *Literary Interpretations of Biblical Narratives,* ed. Kenneth R.R. Gros Louis with James Ackerman, and Thayer S. Warshaw (Nashville: Abingdon Press, 1974), 29.

3. Martin Dibelius, *A Fresh Approach to the New Testament and Early Christian Literature* (London: Nicholson & Weston, 1937), 17.

4. Ryken, "Literary Criticism of the Bible: Some Fallacies," 40.

5. Ryken, *The Literature of the Bible,* 14.

6. Ibid., 24.

7. R.C. Sproul, *Knowing Scripture* (Downers Grove, Ill.: InterVarsity Press, 1979), 49.

8. I. Howard Marshall, "How Do We Interpret the Bible for Today?" *Themelius* 5 (1980): 7.

9. The Chicago Statement on Biblical Hermeneutics was formulated at a conference in Chicago sponsored by the International Council on Biblical Inerrancy. The statement is available from ICBI, P.O. Box 13261, Oakland, CA 94661. It was also published in the *Journal of the Evangelical Theological Society* 24 (December 1982): 397–401.

10. Jay Adams, *Pulpit Speech* (Philadelphia: Presbyterian and Reformed Publishing Co., 1973), 24.

11. Peter Cotterell and Max Turner, *Linguistics and Biblical Interpretation* (Downers Grove, Ill.: InterVarsity Press, 1989), 245.

12. The examples listed are from Gordon D. Fee and Douglas Stuart, *How to Read the Bible for All It's Worth* (Grand Rapids: Zondervan Publishing House, 1981), 175–77.

13. Ibid., 184.

14. Ryken, *The Literature of the Bible*, 275.

15. Kenneth E. Bailey calls this "step parallelism" (*Poet & Peasant* [Grand Rapids: Wm. B. Eerdmans Publishing Co., 1976], 48).

16. S. Bar-efrat, "Some Observations on the Analysis of Structure in Biblical Narrative," *Vetus Testamentum* 30 (April 1980): 168.

17. Adapted from William H. Shea, "The Structure of the Genesis Flood Narrative and Its Implications," *Origins* 6 (1979): 22–23.

18. For examples of inversions and other structural patterns in some of the parables in the Gospel of Luke, see Bailey, *Poet & Peasant*, 95, 112–15, 120, 128, 135, 144–45, 156, 159–60, 191.

19. Bar-efrat, "Some Observations on the Analysis of Structure in Biblical Narrative," 162.

20. Ibid., 169.

21. This is pointed out by Fee and Stuart, *How to Read the Bible for All It's Worth*, 116. It is interesting to see in the Book of Acts the several statements about the numerical growth and geographical expansion of the church (see Acts 6:7; 9:31; 12:24; 13:49; 16:4; and 19:20).

Chapter Seven

1. Cited by George S. Hendry, "Biblical Metaphors and Theological Constructions," *Princeton Seminary Bulletin*, n.s., 2 (1979): 258.

2. *Figures of Speech Used in the Bible: Explained and Illustrated* (London: Eyre and Spottiswoode, 1898; reprint, Grand Rapids: Baker Book House, 1968), xix–xlvi.

3. Ibid., xv.

4. T. Norton Sterrett, *How to Understand Your Bible*, rev. ed. (Downers Grove, Ill.: InterVarsity Press, 1974), 93.

5. G.B. Caird, *The Language and Imagery of the Bible* (Philadelphia: Westminster Press, 1980), 188.

6. Earl D. Radmacher, "The Current Status of Dispensationalism and Its Eschatology," in *Perspectives on Evangelical Theology*, ed. Kenneth S. Kantzer and Stanley M. Gundry (Grand Rapids: Baker Book House, 1979), 167.

7. Robert Mounce, "How to Interpret the Bible," *Eternity* (May 1963), 21.

8. Radmacher speaks of "plain-literal" and "figurative-literal" ("The Current Status

of Dispensationalism and Its Eschatology," 167).

9. Bernard Ramm, *Protestant Biblical Interpretation,* 3d rev. ed. (Grand Rapids: Baker Book House, 1970), 124.

10. Paul Lee Tan, *Literal Interpretation of the Bible* (Rockwille, Md.: Assurance Publishers, 1978), 15.

11. "In a metaphor there exists some feature common to both parts of the metaphor, but a feature which is not normally identified as common" (Peter Cotterell and Max Turner, *Linguistics and Biblical Interpretation* [Downers Grove, Ill.: InterVarsity Press, 1988]), 301.

12. Ibid., 134.

13. For more on this subject see Edwin M. Good, *Irony in the Old Testament* (Philadelphia: Westminster Press, 1965), R. Alan Culpepper, *Anatomy of the Fourth Gospel* (Philadelphia: Fortress Press, 1983), and Paul D. Duke, *Irony in the Fourth Gospel* (Atlanta: John Knox Press, 1985).

14. Mildred L. Larson, *Meaning Based Translation: A Guide to Cross Language Equivalents* (New York: University Press of America, 1984), 20.

15. Ibid., 115.

Chapter Eight

1. Richard M. Davidson, *Typology in Scripture* (Berrien Springs, Mich.: Andrews University Press, 1981), 184.

2. A. Berkeley Mickelsen, *Interpreting the Bible* (Grand Rapids: Wm. B. Eerdmans Publishing Co., 1963), 246.

3. Walter L. Wilson, *Wilson's Dictionary of Bible Types* (Grand Rapids: Wm. B. Eerdmans Publishing Co., 1957), 9.

4. Ada R. Habershon, *The Study of the Types* (Grand Rapids: Kregel Publications, 1957).

5. Herbert Marsh, *Lectures on the Criticism and Interpretation of the Bible* (London: J.G. & Rivington, 1838), 373.

6. Ernest F. Kevan, "The Principles of Interpretation," in *Revelation and the Bible,* ed. Carl F.H. Henry (Grand Rapids: Baker Book House, 1958), 288.

7. Benjamin Keach, *Preaching from the Types and Metaphors of the Bible* (reprint, Grand Rapids: Kregel Publications, 1972), 977.

8. Sylvester Burnham, *The Elements of Biblical Hermeneutics* (Hamilton, N.Y.: Publican Press, 1916), 49.

9. Thomas E. Fountain, *Keys to Understanding and Teaching Your Bible* (Nashville: Thomas Nelson Publishers, 1983), 128.

Chapter Nine

1. William Barclay, *And Jesus Said: Handbook on the Parables of Jesus* (Philadelphia: Westminster Press, 1970), 13.

2. Geraint V. Jones, *The Art and Truth of the Parables* (London: S.P.C.K., 1964), 114.

3. For more on the cultural and literary aspects of the parables see Kenneth E. Bailey, *Poet & Peasant* (Grand Rapids: Wm. B. Eerdmans Publishing Co., 1976) and Kenneth E. Bailey, *Through Peasant Eyes* (Grand Rapids: Wm. B. Eerdmans Publishing Co., 1980).

4. Leland Ryken, *How to Read the Bible as Literature* (Grand Rapids: Zondervan Publishing House, 1984), 141–44.

5. G.B. Caird, *The Language and Imagery of the Bible* (Philadelphia: Westminster Press, 1980), 164.

6. For more on these features in the parables see Norman A. Huffman, "Atypical Features in the Parables of Jesus," *Journal of Biblical Literature* 97 (1978): 207–20.

7. Ryken, *How to Read the Bible as Literature,* 142.

8. For more on the doctrine of the kingdom in the parables see J. Dwight Pentecost, *The Parables of Jesus* (Grand Rapids: Zondervan Publishing House, 1982), 161–80.

9. Augustine *Quaestiones Evangeliorum* 2. 19.

10. Louis A. Barbieri, Jr., "Matthew," in *The Bible Knowledge Commentary*, New Testament, ed. John F. Walvoord and Roy B. Zuck (Wheaton, Ill.: Victor Books, 1983), 51.

11. For more on the parables see Craig L. Blomberg, *Interpreting the Parables* (Downers Grove, Ill.: InterVarsity Press, 1990); R.C. McQuilkin, *Our Lord's Parables* (1929; reprint, Grand Rapids: Zondervan Publishing House, 1980); Bernard Brandon Scott, *Hear Then the Parable* (Minneapolis: Fortress Press, 1989); David Wenham, *The Parables of Jesus* (Downers Grove, Ill.: InterVarsity Press, 1989); and Warren W. Wiersbe, *Meet Yourself in the Parables* (Wheaton, Ill.: Victor Books, 1979).

12. Blomberg, however, suggests that each principal character in a parable points to a major point of comparison *(Interpreting the Parables,* 68–69). He suggests that 18 of Jesus' parables are three-point parables—parables that have three main characters each and thus teach three major truths (ibid., 171–253). Sixteen others, Blomberg says, are two-point or one-point parables (ibid., 255–88).

Chapter Ten

1. Anthony A. Hoekema, "Amillennialism," in *The Meaning of the Millennium,* ed. Robert G. Clouse (Downers Grove, Ill.: InterVarsity Press, 1977), 181.

2. Oswald T. Allis, *Prophecy in the Church* (Philadelphia: Presbyterian and Reformed Publishing Co., 1945), 3.

3. Lorraine Boettner, *The Millennium* (Philadelphia: Presbyterian and Reformed Publishing Co., 1957), 90.

4. Allis, *Prophecy in the Church,* 17–18.

5. Charles C. Ryrie, *The Basis of the Premillennial Faith* (New York: Loizeaux Bros., 1953), 48–49.

6. Earl D. Radmacher, "The Current State of Dispensationalism and Its Eschatology," in *Perspectives on Evangelical Theology,* ed. Kenneth S. Kantzer and Stanley M. Gundry (Grand Rapids: Baker Book House, 1979), 171.

7. Charles C. Ryrie, *Dispensationalism Today* (Chicago: Moody Press, 1965), 21.

8. Hoekema, "Amillennialism," 178.

9. Elliott E. Johnson, "Apocalyptic Genre in Literal Interpretation," in *Essays in Honor of J. Dwight Pentecost,* ed. Stanley D. Toussaint and Charles H. Dyer (Chicago: Moody Press, 1986), 202.

10. Robert Mounce, "Why Do the Experts Disagree?" *Eternity,* September 1975, 59–60. As Hoekema wrote, a thousand years stands for "a complete period, a very long period of indeterminate length" ("Amillennialism," 161).

11. David Chilton, *Days of Vengeance* (Fort Worth: Dominion Press, 1987), 506.

12. Allis, *Prophecy in the Church,* 17.

13. Walter C. Kaiser, Jr., *Back toward the Future* (Grand Rapids: Baker Book House, 1989), 122.

14. Merrill C. Tenney, *Interpreting Revelation* (Grand Rapids: Wm. B. Eerdmans Publishing Co., 1975), 187.

15. Kaiser, *Back toward the Future*, 46.
16. Lewis Sperry Chafer, *Systematic Theology, Abridged Edition*, ed. John F. Walvoord, 2 vols. (Wheaton, Ill.: Victor Books, 1988), 2: 383–95.
17. John F. Walvoord, *The Prophecy Knowledge Handbook* (Wheaton, Ill.: Victor Books, 1990), 17. In two lengthy appendixes Walvoord lists the scores of Bible prophecies with their now-past or yet-future fulfillments (pp. 647–769).

Chapter Eleven

1. Roger Nicole, "The Old Testament in the New Testament," in *The Expositor's Bible Commentary*, ed. Frank E. Gaebelein (Grand Rapids: Zondervan Publishing House, 1979), 1: 617.
2. Ibid.
3. Robert G. Bratcher, ed., *Old Testament Quotations in the New Testament*, 3d rev. ed. (New York: United Bible Societies, 1987), v.
4. B.F.C. Atkinson, "The Textual Background of the Use of the Old Testament by the New," *Journal of the Transactions of the Victoria Institute* 79 (1947): 49.
5. Roger Nicole, "New Testament Use of the Old Testament," in *Revelation in the Bible*, ed. Carl F.H. Henry (Grand Rapids: Baker Book House, 1958), 142.
6. B.F. Westcott, *The Epistle to the Hebrews: The Greek Text with Notes and Essays*, 3d ed. (1889; reprint, Grand Rapids: Wm. B. Eerdmans Publishing Co., 1980), 308.
7. Thomas H. Horne, *An Introduction to the Critical Study and Knowledge of the Holy Scriptures* (Philadelphia: J. Whetham & Son, 1841), 311–13.
8. Elliott E. Johnson, *Expository Hermeneutics: An Introduction* (Grand Rapids: Zondervan Publishing House, 1989), 109.
9. Douglas J. Moo, "The Problem of Sensus Plenior," in *Hermeneutics, Authority, and Canon*, ed. D.A. Carson and John D. Woodbridge (Grand Rapids: Zondervan Publishing House, 1986), 191, 205.
10. Walter C. Kaiser, Jr., "The Single Intent of Scripture," in *Evangelical Roots*, ed. Kenneth Kantzer (Nashville: Thomas Nelson, 1978), 126. In his excellent book on the relationship of the two Testaments, Kaiser sees five ways the New Testament uses the Old: apologetic, prophetic, typological, theological, and practical (*The Uses of the Old Testament in the New* [Chicago: Moody Press, 1985], chaps. 2–11).
11. Darrell L. Bock, "Evangelicals and the Use of the Old Testament in the New," Part 2, *Bibliotheca Sacra* 142 (October–December 1985): 311.
12. Raymond E. Brown, *The "Sensus Plenior" of Sacred Scripture* (Baltimore: St. Mary's University, 1955), 92.
13. Raymond E. Brown, "Hermeneutics," in *The Jerome Biblical Commentary*, 2 vols. (Englewood Cliffs, N.J.: Prentice-Hall, 1968), 2: 616.
14. Ibid.
15. Ibid., 617.
16. Johnson, *Expository Hermeneutics: An Introduction*, 34.
17. Elliott E. Johnson, "Author's Intention and Biblical Interpretation," in *Hermeneutics, Inerrancy, and the Bible*, ed. Earl D. Radmacher and Robert D. Preus (Grand Rapids: Zondervan Publishing House, 1984), 416.
18. Earl D. Radmacher and Robert D. Preus, eds., *Hermeneutics, Inerrancy, and the Bible* (Grand Rapids: Zondervan Publishing House, 1984), 893.
19. J.I. Packer, "The Biblical Authority, Hermeneutics, and Inerrancy," in *Jerusalem and Athens: Critical Discussion on the Theology and Apologetics of Cornelius Van Til*, ed. E.R. Geehan (Nutley, N.J.: Presbyterian and Reformed Publishing Co., 1971), 148.
20. G.B. Caird, *The Language and Imagery of the Bible* (Philadelphia: Westminster Press, 1980), 58.

21. Moo, "The Problem of Sensus Plenior," 207.
22. Ibid.
23. Ibid., 209.
24. Leland Ryken, *The Literature of the Bible* (Grand Rapids: Zondervan Publishing House, 1974), 135.

Chapter Twelve

1. Cited by A. Skevington Wood, *The Principles of Biblical Interpretation* (Grand Rapids: Zondervan Publishing House, 1967), 80.
2. R.C.H. Lenski, *The Interpretation of St. Paul's Epistles to the Colossians, to the Thessalonians, to Timothy, to Titus, and to Philemon* (Minneapolis: Augsburg Publishing House, 1961), 847.
3. Roy B. Zuck, *Applying God's Word in Your Life* (Dallas, Texas: Dallas Theological Seminary, n.d.), 5.
4. Ibid.
5. Ramesh P. Richard, "Application Theory in Relation to the New Testament," *Bibliotheca Sacra* 143 (July–September 1986): 215–16.
6. Gordon D. Fee and Douglas Stuart, *How to Read the Bible for All It's Worth* (Grand Rapids: Zondervan Publishing House, 1981), 80–81.
7. J. Robertson McQuilkin, *Understanding and Applying the Bible* (Chicago: Moody Press, 1983), 256, 258.
8. Richard, "Application Theory in Relation to the New Testament," 208.
9. Richard Mayhue, *How to Interpret the Bible for Yourself* (Chicago: Moody Press, 1986), 148–49.
10. McQuilkin, *Understanding and Applying the Bible*, 240.
11. Ibid., 254 (italics added).
12. Fred L. Fisher, *How to Interpret the New Testament* (Philadelphia: Westminster Press, 1966), 167–68. Generally principles should not be drawn from minor points in a passage. Instead, they should be drawn from the passage by noting the outstanding or main subject, the outstanding or main action, and/or the outstanding reason, motive, or result.
13. Zuck, "Application in Biblical Hermeneutics and Exposition," in *Walvoord: A Tribute*, ed. Donald K. Campbell (Chicago: Moody Press, 1982), 27.
14. John Kuhatschek has given helpful suggestions on how to apply biblical commands, examples, and promises by seeing principles that are indicated explicitly or implicitly in the Scriptures (*Taking the Guesswork out of Applying the Bible* [Downers Grove, Ill.: InterVarsity Press, 1990], chaps. 7–9). Also see James Braga, "Principles," *Moody Monthly* (November 1980), 59–62, 64.
15. McQuilkin, *Understanding and Applying the Bible*, 259.
16. Ibid.
17. Ibid., 261.
18. Terry Hall, *7 Ways to Get More from Your Bible* (Chicago: Moody Press, 1987), 50–51.
19. Walter A. Henrichsen, *A Layman's Guide to Interpreting the Bible* (Colorado Springs, Colo.: NavPress, 1978), 218.
20. Fred H. Klooster, "The Role of the Holy Spirit in the Hermeneutic Process," paper presented at the Chicago Summit Conference II (Oakland, Calif.: International Council on Biblical Inerrancy, 1982), 16.

ANSWERS TO EXERCISES

Chapter 5, pages 107–8

a. John 3:16
e (or f). 1 John 2:15-16
g. 1 Peter 3:3
a. John 17:5
f. 1 Corinthians 7:31
d. 1 Timothy 6:7

a. Exodus 14:13
c. Luke 17:1
b. Luke 18:42
d. John 3:17
d. Acts 15:11
d. Acts 16:30

a. Acts 27:20
e. Romans 5:9
e. Romans 13:11
a. Philippians 1:19
b. James 5:15

Chapter 5, pages 119–20
1. Compound
2. Complex
3. Simple
4. Compound
5. Simple
6. Compound
7. Complex

1. Causal
2. Conditional
3. Causal or Temporal
4. Purpose
5. Temporal
6. Result
7. Purpose

Chapter 7, pages 149-50
Isaiah 53:6   Simile

Chapter 7, pages 149–50 (Continued)

Psalm 84:11	Metaphor
2 Peter 2:17	Metaphor
John 2:19	Hypocatastasis
Isaiah 57:20	Simile
Psalm 23:1	Metaphor
Psalm 1:3	Simile

Chapter 7, page 167

1. c
2. a
3. d
4. e
5. b

1. b
2. c
3. a
4. e
5. d

1. b
2. e
3. a
4. c
5. d

Chapter 7, page 168

Psalm 114:3	Personification
John 21:25	Hyperbole
Jeremiah 17:6a	Simile
Matthew 23:33a	Hypocatastasis
Isaiah 49:13	Apostrophe
2 Thessalonians 3:2b	Litotes
Psalm 105:4b	Anthropomorphism
Micah 5:2a	Apostrophe
Matthew 26:26	Metaphor
Ruth 2:12b	Zoomorphism
2 Corinthians 6:9-10	Paradox
Genesis 42:38b	Synecdoche
Exodus 34:14	Anthropopathism

Chapter 7, page 168 (Continued)

Mark 15:32	Irony
Genesis 4:1a	Euphemism
Amos 3:3-4	Rhetorical questions

Chapter 8, pages 183–84

1. I	14. I	26. A
2. A	15. A	27. A
3. A	16. T	28. I
4. I	17. A	29. I
5. I	18. A	30. I
6. I	19. A	31. I
7. I	20. A	32. A
8. I or T	21. A	33. I
9. A	22. A	34. A
10. A	23. A	35. A
11. A	24. T	36. T
12. I	25. I	37. A
13. A		

Chapter 11, page 270

Matthew 11:10	To point up the accomplishment or realization of an Old Testament prediction
John 13:18	To relate an Old Testament situation to Christ
Acts 4:24	To use Old Testament terminology or expression
Acts 13:40-41	To apply the Old Testament to a New Testament incident or truth
Romans 10:18	To apply the Old Testament to a New Testament incident or truth
Galatians 5:14	To summarize an Old Testament concept
Hebrews 1:13	To point up the accomplishment or realization of an Old Testament prediction

INDEX OF PERSONS

SCRIPTURE INDEX

310

311

SUBJECT INDEX